Library of Shakespearean Biography and Criticism

Series II, Part A

SHAKESPEARE IN MUSIC

Shakespeare in Music

A Collation of the Chief Musical Allusions in the Plays of Shakespeare, with an Attempt at Their Explanation and Derivation, Together with Much of the Original Music

By
LOUIS C. ELSON

BOOKS FOR LIBRARIES PRESS
FREEPORT, NEW YORK

First Published 1900
Reprinted 1970

STANDARD BOOK NUMBER:
8369-5257-X

MS

LIBRARY OF CONGRESS CATALOG CARD NUMBER:
78-113646

PRINTED IN THE UNITED STATES OF AMERICA

TO

𝕻𝖗𝖔𝖋. 𝕵𝖆𝖒𝖊𝖘 𝕲𝖊𝖎𝖐𝖎𝖊, 𝕷𝕷.𝕯., 𝕯.𝕮.𝕷., 𝕱.𝕽.𝕾., 𝖊𝖙𝖈.

(of Edinburgh University)

WITH CORDIAL REMEMBRANCE OF MANY PLEASANT CONFERENCES
ON THIS AND KINDRED TOPICS THIS VOLUME IS
AFFECTIONATELY DEDICATED BY
THE AUTHOR

PREFACE.

In preparing this volume on the music of Shakespeare, the author has been animated by a desire to show how closely the great poet allied himself to the Divine Art. Few of the readers of Shakespeare are aware of how much of his musical material can be traced home; many are unable to follow some of the poet's most subtile metaphors because they are unfamiliar with the musical works to which he refers, or with the song or melody which enriches the scene. It is hoped that this effort may in some degree give light upon a few of the dark places in the text. The classification has been difficult, for, in many of the scenes, different branches of music are simultaneously touched upon. In such cases, in order to preserve the beauty of the text, the author has deemed it best to cite the entire passage, rather than give it piecemeal, and refer back to it as often as necessary; he hopes that the repetition made imperative by such a course will find its apology in the poetic gain of reading a complete thought, or sequence of thoughts. As far as possible, musical technicalities have been avoided, for Shakespeare's musical allusions were intended, not for musicians only, but for all the world.

Louis C. Elson.

CONTENTS.

———•———

CHAPTER I.

LIST OF ILLUSTRATIONS.

LIST OF MUSIC.

xiii

SHAKESPEARE IN MUSIC.

CHAPTER I.

The Musical Side of the Poet — His Versatility — The Orchestra in
the Time of Shakespeare — Drayton's Description of English
Instruments — Bacon's Summary of Music in Elizabethan Days
— A Comparison of Bacon and Shakespeare in Their Musical
Allusions — A Contribution to the Baconian Controversy — Con-
certed Music at the End of the Sixteenth Century.

THREE centuries ago there existed upon the earth
a man with a mind so wonderful and versatile that
hundreds of commentators and thousands of commen-
taries have not exhausted the many topics which he
has presented to posterity.[1] It is our purpose, in
this volume, to examine but one phase of that mind,
— its musical side only, — yet even when confined to
this single field the investigator is confronted with
an amount of material and a wealth of suggestions
that makes the task far larger than would at first
sight be imagined.

[1] In the Boston Public Library there are more than 3,250 different works connected with this topic.

In order to comprehend many of the Shakespearian allusions, it is necessary to begin by examining the orchestra of his time, for, while voices remain practically the same in all ages, the instruments of music undergo changes that cause the music of one epoch to be very dissimilar from that of another. Such a combination of instruments as a modern would call an "orchestra" scarcely existed at the end of the sixteenth century.

During the poet's life, the opera was invented in Italy (1594–1600) and new combinations of instruments began. But the influence of the new school was not felt in England during the lifetime of Shakespeare. Nevertheless, England had been accustomed to combinations of musical instruments from a very early epoch. Chaucer mentions

> " Cornemuse and Shalmyes
> And many other maner pipe,"

which were undoubtedly instruments with which he was acquainted, and also speaks of concerted playing, " Bothe yn Dowced and yn Rede." [1]

---

[1] Prof. T. R. Lounsbury invited the author, in 1894, to join in the search of the solution of the mystic words, " Bothe yn Dowced and yn Rede," which end this citation. But beyond the fact that Grassineau, in 1740, defines it as " Douced, a musical instrument with strings of wire, commonly called a Dulcimer," no reference to " Dowsed " was found in any of the old musical dictionaries to which reference was had. Murray's new Oxford dictionary, however, defines it as " a wind-instrument resembling a flute."

A detailed account of English instruments of the Elizabethan epoch is given by Michael Drayton (1563–1631), contemporary and friend of Shakespeare, in his great work entitled "Poly-Olbion," the first part of which was published in 1613. The following extract is found in the fourth song, and illustrates a trial or contention between the Welsh and the English; the Welsh have displayed their instruments in detail and the English answer them :

"The English that repined to be delayed so long,
All quickly at the hint, as with one free consent,
Strook up at once and sung each to the instrument;
(Of sundry sorts there were, as the musician likes)
On which the practiced hand with perfect'st fingering strikes,
Whereby their right of skill might liveliest be expressed.
The trembling lute some touch, some strain the violl best,
In setts [1] which there were seene, the Musick wondrous choice,
Some likewise there affect the Gamba with the voice,
To shew that England could varietie afforde.
Some that delight to touch the sterner wyerie chord,
The Cithron, the Pandore, and the Theorbo strike;
The Gittern and the Kit the wandering fidlers like.
So there were some againe, in this their learned strife,
Loud instruments that loved, the Cornet and the Phife,
The Hoboy, Sagbut deepe, Recorder and the Flute,
Even from the shrillest Shawm unto the Cornemute,
Some blow the Bagpipe up, that plaies the country 'round,
The Tabor and the Pipe some take delight to sound."

Most of these instruments will be defined in the ensuing chapters ; it is interesting to find them thus

---

[1] Of "sets of viols" more hereafter.

grouped together in a poem which Shakespeare must have been familiar with.

There can be little doubt as to the reliability of Drayton in his list of instruments. The elder Disraeli, in his " Amenities of Literature," sums up the " Poly-Olbion " thus :

" This remarkable poem remains without a parallel in the poetical annals of any people. . . . It is a chorographical description of England and Wales; an amalgamation of antiquarianism, of topography, and of history. . . . This poem has the accuracy of a road-book ! "

But we can complete our survey of the musical combinations of the Shakespearian epoch by studying a more prosaic writer than Michael Drayton. Francis Bacon, Lord Verulam, has left to the world a very precise description of Elizabethan music in the second and third centuries, or chapters, of his " Sylva Sylvarum."

As a passing eccentricity of the time is occupying itself with endeavouring to prove that Bacon was really the author of Shakespeare's works, it may be of double interest to compare the stolid cataloguing of the one with the poetic musical fervour of the other, and in a later chapter, devoted to the dances of Shakespeare, we shall find the poet enthusiastic, the philosopher disdainful, when commenting upon a similar subject.

Bacon says :

" Music, in the practice, hath been well pursued, and in good variety; but in the theory, and especially in the yielding of the causes of the practique, very weakly; being reduced into certain mystical subtilties, of no use and not much truth. We shall therefore, after our manner, join the contemplative and active part together. . . .

" The diapason or eighth in music is the sweetest concord; insomuch as it is in effect a unison; as we see in lutes that are strung in the base strings with two strings, one an eighth above another; which make but as one sound. And every eighth note in ascent (as from eight to fifteen, from fifteen to twenty-two, and so on *ad infinitum*) are but scales of diapason. The cause is dark and hath not been rendered by any; and therefore would be better contemplated."

After which Lord Verulam goes on to show that the air is forced "to recur into one and the same figure, only differing in greatness and smallness" in making these consonances. We cannot resist stating that Shakespeare makes not a single metaphor upon these points which Bacon so strongly emphasises.

Of the emotions of music Bacon speaks at considerable length :

" Tones are not so apt altogether to procure sleep as some other sounds; as the wind, the purling of water, the humming of bees, a sweet voice of one that readeth, etc.; the cause whereof is for that tones, because they are equal and slide not, do more strike and erect the sense than the other. And overmuch attention hindereth sleep."

Yet Shakespeare causes the boy in Brutus's tent — "Julius Cæsar," Act iv. Sc. 4 — to fall asleep to music.

Bacon, however, fully understood the effects of consonance and dissonance, as witness the following :

"There be in music certain figures or tropes; almost agreeing with the figures of rhetoric, and with the affections of the mind, and other senses. First, the division and quavering, which please so much in music, have an agreement with the glittering of light; as the moonbeams playing upon a wave. Again, the falling of a discord to a concord, which maketh great sweetness in music, hath an agreement with the affections, which are reintegrated to the better after some dislikes; it agreeth also with the taste, which is soon glutted after that which is sweet alone. The sliding from the close or cadence hath an agreement with the figure in rhetoric which they call *præter expectatum;* for there is a pleasure even in being deceived. . . . It hath been anciently held and observed, that the sense of hearing and the kinds of music have most operation upon manners; as to encourage men and make them warlike; to make them soft and effeminate; to make them grave; to make them light; to make them gentle and inclined to pity, etc. The cause is for that the sense of hearing striketh the spirits more immediately than the other senses, and more incorporeally than the smelling. For the sight, taste, and feeling have their organs not of so present and immediate access to the spirits as the hearing hath. And as for the smelling (which indeed worketh also immediately upon the spirits, and is forcible while the object remaineth), it is with a communication of the breath or vapour of the object odorate; but harmony, entering easily, and mingling not at all, and coming with a manifest motion, doth by custom of often affecting the spirits and putting them in one kind of posture, alter not a little the nature of the spirits, even when the object is removed. And, therefore, we see that tunes and airs, even in their own nature, have in themselves some affinity with the affections: as there be merry tunes, doleful tunes, solemn tunes; tunes inclining men's minds to pity; warlike tunes, etc. So as it is no marvel if they alter the spirits, considering the tunes have a predisposition to the motion of the spirits themselves. But yet it hath been noted, that though this variety of tunes doth dispose the spirits to variety of passions conform unto them, yet generally music feedeth that disposition of the spirits which it findeth. We see also that several airs and tunes do please several nations and persons, according to the sympathy they have with their spirits."

Shakespeare has stated similar facts, but very much more fluently. Bacon continues:

" All instruments that have either returns, as trumpets; or flexions, as cornets; or are drawn up and put from, as Sackbuts, have a purling sound: but the recorder or flute, that have none of these inequalities, give a clear sound. Nevertheless, the recorder itself, or pipe, moistened a little on the inside, soundeth more solemnly, and with a little purling or hissing. Again, a wreathed string, such as are in the base strings of bandoras, giveth also a purling sound. But a lute-string, if it be merely unequal in his [1] parts, giveth a harsh and untuneable sound; which strings we call *false*, being bigger in one place than in another, and therefore wire strings are never false."

The above sentence speaks of many instruments that we shall examine in the next two chapters; at present we need merely state that the "cornet" was

wind
Mstr.

---

[1] The use of "his" instead of "its" was a characteristic of this and earlier times; Shakespeare sometimes used the one, sometimes the other, the change taking place in Elizabethan times.

a serpentine, or curved, instrument of wood or of brass, utterly unlike the instrument of the present, having finger-holes along its surface, in the style of a flute; the name was also applied to an instrument like the oboe, of wood, but with a mouthpiece like a trumpet (see Chapter XIII.). The "sackbut" that is "drawn up and put from," is simply a slide trombone. The "recorder" was a straight flute with a flageolet mouthpiece. The "wreathed string" means a string wound around with wire, as the G string of a violin.

Regarding the union of such instruments, or "scoring," Bacon says, very properly:

"The sweetest and best harmony is, when every part or instrument is not heard by itself, but a conflation of them all, which requireth to stand some distance off. Even as it is in the mixture of perfumes, or the taking of the smells of several flowers in the air."

Farther on, still speaking of the same subject, the union of different instruments, our author says:

"All concords and discords are (no doubt) sympathies and antipathies of sounds. And so, likewise, in that music which we call broken music,[1] or consort music, some consorts of instruments are sweeter than others (a thing not sufficiently yet observed): as the Irish harp and base viol agree well, etc.; but the virginals and the lute, or the Welsh harp and the Irish harp, or the voice and pipes alone, agree not so well. But for the melioration of music there is yet much left (in this point of exquisite consorts) to try and inquire."

[1] Of "broken music" and "consorts" we shall speak later on.

We have quoted thus much from the " Sylva Sylvarum" because the work gives as clear and exact
a statement of many of the instruments of the Shakespearian epoch as any volume of its time, and also
because it may afford the reader an opportunity to
compare the Baconian and Shakespearian estimates
of music. Bacon approaches the art with all the
exactness of a scientist, Shakespeare with the ardour
of a music lover ; Bacon is most precise and careful
in every statement, while Shakespeare occasionally
makes an error, proving the lack of the investigating
mind. Once having touched upon the Baconian controversy, we may be permitted to leave a subject
foreign to the object of this volume, with the statement that, until recently, Shakespeare's knowledge
of law was held to be a stumbling-block in the path of
those who chose to believe that Shakespeare really
wrote his own works ; his amount of legal lore was
held to be too great for a humble actor to possess,
and even those who laughed cryptograms and Baconian ciphers to scorn felt moved to explain this matter by suggesting that the poet was for a time in
an attorney's office on his advent in London. Even
this hypothesis seems unnecessary. The Hon. Charles
Allen, ex-justice of the Supreme Judicial Court of
Massachusetts, has recently let in a flood of light
upon the subject, and proves that Shakespeare was
by no means phenomenal in this matter. In his book,

entitled "Notes on the Bacon-Shakespeare Question," he shows that when Shakespeare uses a legal word, technically, other litterateurs of his day have done as he, and oftener than he.   Dekker, Wilkins, Middleton, Spenser, Donne, Beaumont and Fletcher, Field, Chapman, Massinger, Marston, Nash, Heywood, Ford, Shirley, Greene, Peele, Lyly, Webster, Rowley, Cook are cited for their "law," many of them repeatedly.   As for Ben Jonson, his love of this "branch of learning" was violent, and scores of passages are quoted from his works.   Chapman also has a paragraph in his "All Fools," which contains a hundred technical terms of law, so that, as Judge Allen says, "If Hamlet's collection of legal terms goes to show that the play was written by Bacon, the play of 'All Fools' must have been written by Coke himself."

In a remarkably keen and analytical review of this book,[1] and incidentally of the entire controversy, Henry Austin Clapp, Esq., gives a charming glance at the poetic side of the question.   He says:

"Judge Allen has a capitally good chapter on Bacon's acknowledged verses.   And, after quoting Sir Francis's translation of the 1st Psalm and portions of his version of the 90th and 104th, says, 'Of course a good poet may write bad verses occasionally,' but the peculiarity of Bacon's case is that never by an accident did he stumble on a good line.   The proposition of the Baconians involves the conclusion that the

[1] *Boston Daily Advertiser*, April 21, 1900.

writer of " The Merchant of Venice," " The Tempest," and " A Midsummer Night's Dream " had degenerated into writing such clumsy verse as these translations, and that he deemed the latter worthy of preservation and publication with his name. And Judge Allen might go a very little farther and add that Bacon's careful conserving of his lyrics is nearly proof positive that he was void of poetical taste and discrimination as well as of poetical genius. A man possessed with a scrap of judgment in this kind could not have suffered such lyrics to be handed down as the sole authentic examples of his poetic ability. It will not be amiss to reprint here said translation of the 1st Psalm:

> " ' Who never gave to wicked reed
>   A yielding and attentive ear;
> Who never sinner's paths did tread,
>   Nor sat him down in scorner's chair;
> But maketh it his whole delight
>   On law of God to meditate,
> And therein spendeth day and night;
>   That man is in a happy state.

> " ' He shall be like the fruitful tree,
>   Planted along a running spring,
> Which, in due season, constantly
>   A goodly yield of fruit doth bring;
> Whose leaves continue always green,
>   And are no prey to winter's power;
> So shall that man not once be seen
>   Surprised with an evil hour.

> " ' With wicked men it is not so,
>   Their lot is of another kind:
> All as the chaff, which to and fro
>   Is tossed at mercy of the wind.

And when he shall in judgment plead,
A casting sentence bide he must;
So shall he not lift up his head
In the assembly of the just.

" ' For why? the Lord hath special eye
To be the godly's stay at call;
And hath given over, righteously,
The wicked man to take his fall.' "

Since we now leave Lord Verulam and his incon-
testible greatness, we add a final excerpt from another
of his works, the " Essayes." In the course of a few
chapters the reader will be made acquainted with
Shakespeare's love of dancing and revelry; the following is Bacon's essay on one of the principal phases of
the revelry of that epoch, the masques and triumphs
which preceded the introduction of opera into England. As the essay is short, we quote it entire:

"OF MASQUES AND TRIUMPHS.

" These things are but Toyes, to come amongst such Serious
Observations. But yet, since Princes will have such Things,
it is better that they should be Graced with Elegancy, than
daubed with Cost. *Dancing to Song* is a Thing of great
State, and Pleasure. I understand it, that the Song be in
Quire, placed aloft, and accompanied with some broken
Musicke; And the Ditty fitted to the Device.

" *Acting in Song*, especially in *Dialogues*, hath an extreme
Good Grace; I say *Acting*, not *Dancing*, (For that is a Meane
and Vulgar Thing;) And the *Voices* of the *Dialogue* would be
Strong and Manly (A Base and a Tenour; No Treble;) And

the *Ditty*, High and Tragicall; Not Nice or Dainty. *Severall Quires*, placed one over against another, and taking the Voice by Catches, *Antheme*-wise, give great Pleasure. *Turning Dances*, into *Figure*, is a childish Curiosity. And generally, let it be noted, that those Things, which I here set downe, are such as doe naturally take the Sense, and not respect Petty Wonderments.

"It is true, the *Alterations of Scenes*, so it be quietly, and without Noise, are Things of great Beauty and Pleasure: for they feed and relieve the Eye, before it be full of the same Object. Let the *Scenes* abound with *Light*, specially *Coloured* and *Varied :* And let the Masquers, or any other, that are to come down from the *Scene*, have some Motions, upon the *Scene* itselfe, before their comming down: For it draws the Eye strangely, and makes it with great pleasure, to desire to see that, it cannot perfectly discerne. Let the *Songs* be *Loud* and *Cheerefull*, and not *Chirpings* or *Pulings*. Let the *Musicke* likewise, be *Sharpe*, and *Loud*, and *Well Placed*. The *Colours* that shew best by Candlelight are: White, Carnation, and a Kinde of Sea-Water-Greene ; and *Oes* and *Spangles*, as they are of no great Cost, so they are of most Glory. As for *Rich Embroidery*, it is lost and not Discerned. Let the *Sutes* of the *Masquers*, be Gracefull, and such as become the Person when the Vizars are off; Not after Examples of Knowne Attires; Turkes, Soldiers, Mariners, and the Like. Let *Antimasques* not be long; They have been commonly of Fooles, Satyres, Baboones, Wilde-Men, Antiques, Beasts, Sprites, Witches, Ethiopes, Pigmies, Turquets, Nimphs, Rusticks, Cupids, Statua's Moving, and the like. As for *Angels* it is not Comicall enough, to put them in *Anti-Masques ;* And any Thing that is hideous, as Devils, Giants, is on the other side as unfit. But chiefly, let the *Musicke* of them, be Recreative, and with some strange Changes. Some *Sweet Odours*, suddenly coming forth, without any drops falling, are, in such a Company, as there is Steame and Heate, Things of Great Pleasure & Refreshment. *Double-Masques*, one of Men, another of Ladies, addeth State and Variety. But All is Nothing, except the *Roome* be kept Cleare, and Neat.

"For *Justs* and *Tourneys*, and *Barriers;* The Glories of them, are chiefly in the Chariots, wherein the Challengers make their Entry; Especially if they be drawne with Strange Beasts; As Lions, Beares, Cammels, and the like; Or in the Devices of their Entrance; Or in the Bravery of their Liveries; Or in the Goodly Furniture of their Horses, and Armour. But enough of these Toyes."

CHAPTER II.

THE preceding chapter has shown that, although
England had not, as yet, the Italian development of
orchestra,[1] it possessed a fair knowledge of concerted
music, and used combinations of instruments. These
combinations were called "consorts." Shakespeare
alludes to them in "Romeo and Juliet," when Tybalt
and Mercutio meet (Act iii. Sc. 1).

"*Tybalt.* Mercutio, thou consort'st with Romeo.
Mercutio. Consort![2] what, dost thou make us minstrels? an
thou make minstrels of us, look to hear nothing but discords:
here's my fiddlestick; here's that shall make you dance.
Zounds, consort!"

One finds here the usual Shakespearian pun, and
also a subtle reference to the low caste of the musician in this epoch (whereof more hereafter), for

[1] "L' Anima e nel Corpo," the first oratorio (Rome, 1600), had a
double lyre, a harpsichord, a large guitar, and two flutes, as orchestra. "Euridice," the oldest opera extant (1600), had a combination of harpsichord, large guitar, viol, large lute, flute, and a
triple flute.

[2] "Consorts" were often mentioned by Milton.

Mercutio is mightily indignant at the minstrel impu-
tation — or pretends to be.

At the outset we must accustom ourselves to the
fact that Shakespeare makes but few attempts to
picture the country in which his scene is laid. Musicians were not despised in Verona, where Romeo
and Juliet reside, but the poet is picturing London
instead, and he presents the contemporary English
life, whether the scene be laid in Bohemia, Denmark,
Italy, or elsewhere.

The "consorts" of Shakespeare's time were not
only concerted music, but generally composed of such
instruments as belonged to one family. If, for
example, only viols were employed, the consort was
called "whole," but if virginal, lute, or flute, came
into the combination, the result was a "broken consort," or "broken music," which Shakespeare alludes
to more than once, and which will be described in
connection with Shakespeare's technical terms.

Viols were most employed in these "consorts,"
and were generally sold to music-lovers in "sets," so
that a "chest of viols" usually consisted of six
pieces : two trebles, two tenor viols, and two basses.
The violin was not among these, nor the contrabass.
The golden epoch of violin-making began nearly fifty
years after Shakespeare's death ; Stradivarius, Amati,
Guarnerius, the kings of violin-making, all came
later, and in the first half of the seventeenth century

ARTIST PLAYING VIOL DA GAMBA.

the violin was looked upon in England as rather a vulgar instrument. Even in the eighteenth century Stradivarius had an invoice of violins, which he had sent to England, returned to him with the information that London was not accustomed to paying as much as five pounds for a violin!

The viols alluded to above had generally six strings each, and were fretted, like a guitar. We present herewith a picture (taken from a contemporaneous print) of the viol da gamba of Shakespeare's time, and need only add that the treble viol was just half the size, while the tenor stood between the two in size and compass.

The contrabass existed in England at this time, but was called the "violone;" the word "violoncello" is a derivative of this, meaning the "little violone." One of the curious musical conceits of the Elizabethan days was to cut a door in the back of the violone and introduce a small boy into the instrument; at the concert the contrabass player would render the bass part on his instrument, would sing the "mean," or middle part, and the invisible boy would add a treble, — a trio with but one performer in sight.

Many are the allusions to the viols in Shakespeare's works. In "Twelfth Night" (Act i. Sc. 3), Maria calls Sir Andrew Aguecheek "a fool and a prodigal," whereupon Sir Toby Belch defends him with:

" Fye, that you'll say so ! he plays o' the viol-de-gamboys, and speaks three or four languages word for word without book, and hath all the good gifts of nature."

It was therefore part of a liberal education to play upon the viols ; in fact, many a wealthy gentleman kept his chest of viols at hand for guests to divert themselves with music.

Pericles (Act i. Sc. 1), addressing the daughter of Antiochus, says :

> " You're a fair viol, and your sense the strings;
> Who, finger'd to make man his lawful music,
> Would draw heaven down, and all the gods to hearken ;
> But, being play'd upon before your time,
> Hell only danceth at so harsh a chime :
> Good sooth, I care not for you,"

comparing unruly passions to disordered viol music.

The Duke of Norfolk (in " Richard II.," Act i. Sc. 3), upon hearing his sentence of banishment, bursts forth :

> " A heavy sentence, my most sovereign liege,
> And one unlook'd for from your highness' mouth :
> A dearer merit, not so deep a maim
> As to be cast forth in the common air,
> Have I deserved at your highness' hand.
> The language I have learned these forty years,
> My native English, now I must forego :
> And now my tongue's use is to me no more,
> Than an unstringèd viol or a harp ;
> Or like a cunning instrument cased up,
> Or, being open, put into his hands,
> That knows no touch to tune the harmony."

While England devoted itself to the viols, the violins had made some headway in France. This fact is alluded to somewhat scornfully by our poet in "Henry VIII." (Act i. Sc. 3), where Lovell says: "A French song and a fiddle has no fellow," and Sands replies, "The devil fiddle them!"

In "Coriolanus" (Act v. Sc. 4), at the entrance of the messenger, we find a varied list of instruments:

> "Why, hark you
> [*Trumpets and hautboys sounded, and drums*
> *beaten, all together. Shouting also within.*]
> The trumpets, sackbuts, psalteries, and fifes,
> Tabors, and cymbals, and the shouting Romans,
> Make the sun dance. Hark you!
> [*Shouting again.*]"

It is almost needless to say that the ancient Romans did not indulge in sackbuts (slide trombones) nor psalteries. Regarding the latter instrument, we find the following definition in Grassineau's Dictionary (1740):

> "That now in use is a flat instrument in form of a trapezium, or triangle truncated atop. It is strung with thirteen wire chords set to unison and octave, and mounted on two bridges on the two sides. It is struck with a plectrum, or little iron rod, or sometimes with a little crooked stick, whence 'tis usually ranked among the instruments of percussion. Its chest, or body, resembles that of a spinet."

It was therefore a species of dulcimer, or what the Germans call a *Schlag-Zither*.

The fife is mentioned more than once in the Shakespearian dramas. In "The Merchant of Venice" (Act ii. Sc. 5), Shylock cries out to Jessica:

> "What! are there masques?　Hear you me, Jessica:
> Lock up my doors: and when you hear the drum,
> And the vile squeaking of the wry-neck'd fife,
> Clamber not you up to the casement, then,
> Nor thrust your head into the public street,
> To gaze on Christian fools with varnish'd faces;
> But stop mine house's ears, — I mean, my casements:
> Let not the sound of shallow foppery enter
> My sober house."

The "wry-necked fife" has been the occasion of considerable critical comment. Edward W. Naylor, in his excellent "Shakespeare and Music" (p. 161), suggests that —

> "The adjective 'wry-necked' refers, not to the instrument itself, which was straight, but to the player, whose head has to be slightly twisted around to get at the mouth-piece. Mersennus (b. 1588) says the fife is the same as the tibia Helvetica, which was simply a small edition of the flauto traverso, or German flute. That is, the fife of those days was much the same as the modern fife of the cheaper kind, with the usual six holes, and a big hole near the stopped end, where the breath was applied. The instrument was therefore held across (traverso) the face of the player, whose head would be turned sideways, and hence comes Shylock's description of it as the 'wry-necked' fife."

Some editions have "squeaking," changed to "squealing," which, as Richard Grant White points out, is a more appropriate word in this connection. The very word "wry-necked" was used by another writer in the time of Shakespeare. A pertinent passage from Barnaby Rich's "Aphorisms" (1618), quoted by Boswell, runs : "The Fife is a wry-necked musician, for he looks away from his instrument." But the old fife itself had a sufficiently crooked mouthpiece to be described as "wry-necked." Both Knight and R. G. White think that the instrument itself was meant, and Knight suggests that it may be an imitation of the lines of Horace, —

> "Prima nocte domum claude; neque in vias,
> Sub cantu querulæ despice Tibia," —

which certainly refers to the instrument and not to the musician. We think, since the adjective can be applied both to the instrument and its player, that the more evident meaning may be adhered to.

In "Much Ado About Nothing" (Act ii. Sc. 3) Benedick speaks of the fife as less refined than the pipe. In reading the passage one thinks unconsciously upon Othello's rougher delight in "the spirit-stirring drum and ear-piercing fife." Benedick's soliloquy runs :

"I do much wonder, that one man, seeing how much another man is a fool when he dedicates his behaviours to love, will, after he hath laughed at such shallow follies in others, become the argument of his own scorn, by falling in love: And such a man is Claudio. I have known, when there was

no music with him but the drum and fife; and now had he
rather hear the tabor and the pipe."

Somewhat akin to the fife, but a more developed
instrument, was the recorder. This was a straight
flute, with a mouthpiece very like that of the flageolet (see illustration). Bacon's description of it, in
the preceding chapter, presents rather a primitive
instrument; yet it was preferred in England to the
German flute, our modern instrument.

Shakespeare draws one of his finest metaphors
from this instrument. In "Hamlet" (Act iii. Sc. 2),
when Guildenstern and Rosencrantz are spying upon
the prince, Hamlet suddenly turns upon them with
a musical sarcasm.

"*Enter the* Players, *with Recorders.*

Hamlet. O, the recorders: — let me see one. — To with-
draw with you. — Why do you go about to recover the wind of
me, as if you would drive me into a toil?

Guildenstern. O, my lord, if my duty be too bold, my love
is too unmannerly.

Hamlet. I do not well understand that. Will you play
upon this pipe?

Guildenstern. My lord, I cannot.

Hamlet. I pray you.

Guildenstern. Believe me, I cannot.

Hamlet. I do beseech you.

Guildenstern. I know no touch of it, my lord.

Hamlet. 'Tis as easy as lying: govern these ventages with
your fingers and thumb, give it breath with your mouth, and
it will discourse most eloquent music. Look you, these are
the stops.

GENTLEMAN PLAYING RECORDER.

Guildenstern. But these cannot I command to any utterance of harmony; I have not the skill.

Hamlet. Why, look you now, how unworthy a thing you make of me. You would play upon me; you would seem to know my stops; you would pluck out the heart of my mystery; you would sound me from my lowest note to the top of my compass: and there is much music, excellent voice in this little organ; yet cannot you make it speak. S'blood, do you think, I am easier to be played on than a pipe? Call me what instrument you will, though you can fret me, you cannot play upon me."

It is possible, in Benedick's allusion to "tabor and pipe," above given, that the recorder was meant, for the word "pipe" was used in as general a sense, in Shakespeare's time, as "tibia" among the ancient Romans, — many instruments were embraced in the term. The technical points in the scene in "Hamlet" are quite correct; the thumb was used, as the poet indicates; the change of metaphor from the recorder to "what instrument you will" is evidently done to allow the obvious pun on the word "fret," for, of course, frets would only be found on stringed instruments.

A more legitimate pun upon the recorder is found in "Midsummer Night's Dream" (Act v. Sc. 1), after the Prologue of "Pyramus and Thisbe" has muddled all his punctuation:

" *Theseus.* This fellow does not stand upon points.

Lysander. He hath rid his prologue like a rough colt; he knows not the stop.

Hippolyta.   Indeed he hath played on this prologue like a child on a recorder, a sound, but not in government."

There is genuine humour in each of the three speeches, and the suggestion of the sound being right and the sense wrong, like a child playing an instrument, is charmingly dainty and feminine.

The bagpipe was too characteristic an instrument for Shakespeare to pass by, and we find several allusions to it in the plays.   Musicians may affect disdain of this instrument as much as they please, yet no musical instrument is so interwoven with history as the bagpipe.   Every European nation seems to have used it in ancient times, and the fact that in Italy there is a bagpipe called "zumpogna," an evident derivation from the Greek *sumphonia*, would indicate that the Hellenic music, which is so ecstatically praised by the ancient writers, may have possessed the bagpipe drone occasionally.

Shakespeare alludes to a local bagpipe in the first part of "Henry IV." (Act i. Sc. 2).

"*Falstaff.*   S'blood! I am as melancholy as a gib cat, or a lugged bear.
    Prince Henry.   Or an old lion; or a lover's lute.
    Falstaff.   Yea, or the drone of a Lincolnshire bagpipe."

Steevens thought that "a Lincolnshire bagpipe" was only a jesting allusion to frogs croaking in the marshes, but Malone set this error right by quoting the following from "A Nest of Ninnies," by Robert Armin (1608) :

> " At a Christmas-time, when great logs furnish the hall fire : when brawne is in season, and indeed all revelling is regarded ; this gallant knight kept open house for all commers, were beefe, beere and bread was no niggard. Amongst all the pleasures provided, a noyse of minstrells and a Lincolnshire bagpipe was prepared ; the minstrells for the great chamber, the bag-pipe for the hall ; the minstrells to serve up the knights' meate, and the bagpipe for the common dauncing."

Richard Grant White scoffingly says : " It is impossible to believe that the drone of any one bagpipe could be more melancholy than that of any other." Nevertheless, there must have been some peculiar quality about this instrument to make two authors specify it by name.

Another allusion to the bagpipe, by Shakespeare, has also puzzled many commentators. Shylock (" Merchant of Venice," Act iv. Sc. 1) twice alludes to the instrument (an allusion quite out of place in Venice), the second time speaking of a " woollen bag-pipe." Naylor passes this by with the question, " What is a ' woollen bagpipe ' ? " Steevens thought that " swollen bagpipe " was meant ; Collier's folio of 1632 gives it as " bollen bagpipe ; " White thinks that the adjective refers to the baize covering, which is as likely a solution as any.

The bagpipe is mentioned by English poets before

the Elizabethan time. Even Chaucer says of his miller :

"A baggepipe coude wel he blowe and soune."

The Canterbury pilgrims are mentioned in the same poem as performing their journey to the tones of the same instrument.

Cornet and serpent have already been described in the preceding chapter. The former is called for in some of the stage directions of Shakespeare, to which we shall devote an especial page.

CHAPTER III.

ONE of the most used musical instruments of the Elizabethan epoch was the virginals, a tiny and primitive piano on which the strings were plucked by little pieces of quill, set in "jacks." The tone of the virginals was faint and more like a mandolin than any other instrument. Shading was impossible upon it; the player produced a constant, and rather irritating, pizzicato, which must have been a deadly foe to anything like expression. Yet the instrument was very popular. Every barber's shop of that time had its lute or its virginals (for the instrument was always spoken of in the plural) for the customers to play upon while awaiting their turn to be shaved.[1] As late as 1666, Pepys, speaking of the great fire in London, says:

"River full of lighters and boats taking in goods, and good goods swimming in the water, and only I observed that hardly

[1] In this connection it may be added that the striped pole which indicates the American barber's shop is derived from the bleeding arm in a white bandage which the old English barber-surgeons displayed at their doors.

37

one lighter or boat in three, that had the goods of a house in, but there was a *Pair of Virginalls* in it."

It is singular that Shakespeare only alludes to this instrument once in his plays, although here the metaphor is a fine one. It occurs in "Winter's Tale" (Act i. Sc. 2), when the jealous Leontes watches his queen, Hermione, with Polixenes, and sees her take the Bohemian's hand, while he angrily mutters, "Still virginalling upon his palm."

The action of the virginal player was not very different from that of the pianist, as will readily be seen from the accompanying print of the title-page of the first collection of virginal music.

Perhaps the lack of allusions to the instrument in Shakespeare may be explained by a peculiar error that occurs in one of his sonnets, and which may show that he had not a very perfect knowledge of the instrument. It is a poem written to the "dark lady," [1] the 128th sonnet, and here, for once, the writer speaks at some length of the musical instrument :

> " How oft, when thou, my music, music play'st,
>   Upon that blessed wood whose motion sounds
> With thy sweet fingers, when thou gently sway'st,
>   The wiry concord that mine ear confounds,

---

[1] Possibly Mrs. Fytton, who was Lord Pembroke's mistress. The Earl of Pembroke was William Herbert (" W. H."), who succeeded to the title in 1601.

TITLE-PAGE OF "PARTHENIA."

Do I envy those jacks, that nimble leap
   To kiss the tender inward of thy hand,
Whilst my poor lips, which should that harvest reap,
   At the wood's boldness by thee blushing stand!
To be so tickled, they would change their state
   And situation with those dancing chips,
O'er whom thy fingers walk with gentle gait,
   Making dead wood more bless'd than living lips.
Since saucy jacks so happy are in this,
Give them thy fingers, me thy lips to kiss."

The fifth line is here a puzzle and possibly an error. It is not the odd accent on the third word, for "envy" was sometimes pronounced "en*vy*" in Shakespeare's time, but the "jacks" of the instrument could by no means leap to kiss the lady's hand, any more than the hammers of the piano of the present could touch the fingers of a Paderewski. The same error, it will be noted, occurs in the final lines of the sonnet.

Shakespeare is not the only poet of the time who used the virginal jacks for a metaphor, but none of his contemporaries speak of the hand and the jack coming near each other.

Lord Oxford satirically wrote (or said), referring to Raleigh's favour at court and the execution of Essex: "When 'Jacks' start up, heads go down!" Middleton, in his "Father Hubbard's Tales," describes the frozen Charity with:

" Her teeth chattered in her head and leaped up and down
   Like virginal jacks."

Dekker, in "Satiro-Mastix, or the Untrussing of the Humourous Poet" (published in 1602), says:

"Lord ha' mercy upon us! we women fall and fall still; and when we have husbands, we play upon them like virginal jacks, they must rise and fall to our humours, or else they'll never get any good strains of music out of us."

Yet we may acknowledge that the word "jack" may have been substituted for "key," in the sonnet, either by poetic license or by carelessness.

We shall find one or two other musical slips in our poet, in the course of these chapters, but they cannot detract from the tremendous amount of musical knowledge displayed, nor from the glorious enthusiasm with which the poet has gilded our art. We may recall, in this connection, that another most musical poet, Browning, in his "Toccata of Martini Galuppi," speaks of —

"Sixths, diminished, sigh on sigh."

There happen to be two horns to this last dilemma. While Richter and some other harmonists do not recognise the diminished sixth, Albrechtsberger (the teacher of Beethoven), in the eighteenth division of his great theoretical book, both recognises the chord of the diminished sixth and gives an example. But he speaks of it as very rare, nor do we discover such intervals "sigh on sigh" in Galuppi's works, and, as the diminished sixth is an enharmonic change of the perfect fifth, a succession of them would produce something very like consecutive fifths, which Galuppi would have held a crime, although Bach is not altogether innocent of them.

Tennyson has given us a combination (in "Maud") of "flute, violin, bassoon," that would not please the teacher of orchestration, and a fairly long list of the musical errors of poets and of novelists might be made out; but it will be readily perceived that the Shakespeare and the Browning errors (if they are such) can be readily defended.

But the sparse allusions that Shakespeare has made to the virginals are the more to be wondered at when it is recalled that his patroness and frequent auditor, Queen Elizabeth, loved the instrument and was very proud of her skill upon it.[1] Her pride in this matter once led Sir James Melvil, the ambassador from the Scottish queen, into rather an awkward position. He thus speaks of the incident in his "Memoirs:"

"The same day after dinner, my Lord of Hunsden drew me up to a quiet gallery that I might hear some music (but he said he durst not avow it), where I might hear the queen play upon the virginals. After I had hearkened awhile I took by the tapestry that hung by the door of the chamber, and seeing her back was toward the door, I entered within the chamber, and

[1] Spite of Elizabeth's parade of her love of music, it must be stated that she was extremely parsimonious to her band of musicians.

stood a pretty space, hearing her play excellently well; but she left off immediately so soon as she turned her about and saw me. She appeared to be surprised to see me, and came forward, seeming to strike me with her hand, alleging she was not used to play before men, but when she was solitary, to shun melancholy. She asked how I came there? I answered, as I was walking with my Lord Hunsden, as we passed by the chamber door, I heard such a melody as ravished me, whereby I was drawn in ere I knew how; excusing my fault of homeliness as being brought up in the court of France where such freedom was allowed; declaring myself willing to endure what kind of punishment her Majesty should be pleased to inflict upon me for so great offence. Then she sate down low upon a cushion, and I upon my knees by her; but with her own hand she gave me a cushion to lay under my knee; which at first I refused, but she compelled me to take it. She inquired whether my queen or she played best. In that I found myself obliged to give her the praise."

Melvil was ambassador from Mary Stuart in 1564, and there is every reason to suppose that the neat little comedy described above had been quietly arranged by Queen Elizabeth herself, for our diplomat informs us that, before the stolen musical interview, she had asked him many questions about his queen: How she dressed? what was the colour of her hair? whether that, or hers, was best? which of the two was fairest? which was higher in stature? Melvil describes the first interview thus:

"Then she asked what kind of exercises she used? I answered that when I received my despatch the queen was lately come from the Highland hunting: that when her more serious affairs permitted, she was taken up with the reading of histories: that sometimes she recreated herself in playing upon the lute and virginals. She asked if she played well? I said, reasonably for a queen."

It would be interesting to know just what Queen Elizabeth played for the bold ambassador. There is a piece of virginal music extant which was an especial favourite with the queen, and was, in fact, arranged for her, from an old English melody, by her own music-teacher, Doctor Byrd. It was called "Sellinger's Round," and is probably one of the oldest English country dances extant. The name was probably "St. Leger's Round" originally, and it was also called "The Beginning of the World" in its early days. We append a copy of this as Queen Elizabeth played it on the virginals.

SELLINGER'S ROUND.

As played by Queen Elizabeth.   Harmonies by Dr. Byrd.

Rivalling the virginals in popular favour, and far superior to it in musical effect, was the lute. The lute came into Europe in the middle ages from Spain, where the Moors used the instrument, applying to it the Arabic name "Al ud." Many were the modifications of this instrument. We give a reproduction of an old print of a lute-player with his instrument, but there were many other kinds used at the same

GENTLEMAN PLAYING LUTE.

epoch ; one sort possessed a number of open, harp-like strings, in addition to the fretted, or guitar-like ones, and this instrument was particularly difficult to set in tune and required retuning at each change of key.

If Shakespeare neglected the virginals, he made up for it by many allusions to, and metaphors founded upon, its rival, the lute.

" The Taming of the Shrew " is classed by some commentators as among the " doubtful plays," but few refuse to recognise the hand of Shakespeare in some of its subtle touches, and nowhere are these more evident than in the musical scenes.   In the first of these (Act ii. Sc. 1), we find Katharine venting her furious temper upon her music-teacher, — the disguised lover of Bianca, — Hortensio :

" *Re-enter* HORTENSIO, *with his head broken.*

Baptista.   How now, my friend ? why dost thou look so pale ?

Hortensio.   For fear, I promise you, if I look pale.

Baptista.   What, will my daughter prove a good musician ?

Hortensio.   I think she'll sooner prove a soldier ;
Iron may hold her, but never lutes.

Baptista.   Why, then thou canst not break her to the lute ?

Hortensio.   Why, no ; for she hath broke the lute to me.
I did but tell her she mistook her frets,
And bow'd her hand to teach her fingering ;
When, with a most impatient devilish spirit,
' Frets call you these ? ' quoth she, ' I'll fume with them : '
And, with that word, she struck me on the head,

And through the instrument my pate made way;
And there I stood amazed for a while,
As on a pillory, looking through the lute:
While she did call me, — rascal fiddler,
And — twangling Jack, with twenty such vile terms,
As she had studied to misuse me so.

   Petruchio.   Now, by the world, it is a lusty wench;
I love her ten times more than ere I did:
O, how I long to have some chat with her!

   Baptista.   Well, go with me, and be not so discomfited:
Proceed in practice with my younger daughter;
She's apt to learn, and thankful for good turns, —
Signior Petruchio, will you go with us;
Or shall I send my daughter Kate to you?

   Petruchio.   I pray you do, I will attend her here, —
       [*Exeunt Baptista, Gremio, Tranio, and Hortensio.*
And woo her with some spirit when she comes.
Say, that she rail, — why, then I'll tell her plain,
She sings as sweetly as a nightingale;
Say, that she frown, — I'll say, she looks as clear
As morning roses newly wash'd with dew;
Say, she be mute, and will not speak a word, —
Then, I'll commend her volubility,
And say — she uttered piercing eloquence;
If she do bid me pack, I'll give her thanks,
As though she bid me stay by her a week:
If she deny to wed, I'll crave the day
When I shall ask the banns, and when be married. —
But here she comes; and now, Petruchio, speak."

We have quoted the last sentence of this scene for a purpose aside from the immediate examination of the lute. Shakespeare has induced myriads of musical settings (some of which we shall examine in their proper place), but seldom have the poet's words undergone such a startling transformation as the phrases of Petruchio, altered to fit a female singer, and made into a dainty soprano song by Sir Henry Bishop. Here is the modern version:

> " Should he upbraid, I'll own that he prevail,
>   And sing as sweetly as the nightingale.
>   Say that he frown, I'll say his looks I view,
>   As morning roses newly tipped with dew.
>   Say he be mute, I'll answer with a smile,
>   And dance and play, and wrinkled Care beguile."

And the above rhymes are ticketed as being "by Shakespeare!"

To return to the lute: the difficulty of tuning the instrument, and the time consumed in its constant retuning at changes of key, can scarcely be exaggerated. Mattheson (about 1720) wrote of the instrument: "If a lute-player have lived eighty years, he has probably spent about sixty years tuning his instrument!" This defect in the instrument is excellently delineated in the scene where Hortensio, disguised as a music-teacher, seeks to drive away Lucentio (disguised as a Latin teacher) from the side of Bianca, that he may give his lesson (" Taming of the Shrew," Act iii. Sc. 1).

> " *Enter* LUCENTIO, HORTENSIO, *and* BIANCA.
>
> *Lucentio.* Fiddler, forbear; you grow too forward, sir;
> Have you so soon forgot the entertainment
> Her sister Katharine welcomed you withal?

Hortensio.   But, wrangling pedant, this is
The patroness of heavenly harmony :
Then give me leave to have prerogative ;
And when in music we have spent an hour,
Your lecture shall have leisure for as much.

Lucentio.   Preposterous ass ! that never read so far
To know the cause why music was ordain'd !
Was it not, to refresh the mind of man,
After his studies, or his usual pain ?
Then give me leave to read philosophy.
And, while I pause, serve in your harmony.

Hortensio.   Sirrah, I will not bear these braves of thine.

Bianca.   Why, gentlemen, you do me double wrong,
To strive for that which resteth in my choice :
I am no breeching scholar in the schools ;
I'll not be tied to hours, nor 'pointed times,
But learn my lessons as I please myself,
And, to cut off all strife, here sit we down ;
Take you your instrument, play you the whiles ;
His lecture will be done, ere you have tuned.

Hortensio.   You'll leave his lecture when I am in tune ?

[*To Bianca ; Hortensio retires.*

Lucentio.   That will be never : — tune your instrument."

Lucentio now makes his declaration of love in
the guise of a Latin lesson, construing " Hac ibat
Simois " from Ovid in the following totally novel
fashion :

" *Bianca.*   Where left we last ?

Lucentio.   Here, madam : —
' Hac ibat Simois ; hic est Sigeia tellus ;
Hic steterat Priami regia celsa senis.'

Bianca.   Construe them.

Lucentio.   ' Hac ibat,' as I told you before, — ' Simois,'

I am Lucentio, — 'hic est,' son unto Vincentio of Pisa, — 'Sigeia tellus,' disguised thus to get your love, — 'Hic steterat,' and that Lucentio that comes a wooing, — 'Priami,' is my man Tranio, — 'regia,' bearing my port, — 'celsa senis,' that we might beguile the old Pantaloon.

    Hortensio. Madam, my instrument's in tune. [*Returning.*
    Bianca. Let's hear :   [*Hortensio plays.*
O fy ! the treble jars.
    Lucentio. Spit in the hole, man, and tune again.[1]
    Bianca. Now let me see if I can construe it : 'Hac ibat Simois,' I know you not ; — 'Hic est Sigeia tellus,' I trust you not ; — 'Hic steterat Priami,' take heed he hear us not ; — 'regia,' presume not ; — 'celsa senis,' despair not.
    Hortensio. Madam, 'tis now in tune.
    Lucentio. All but the bass.
    Hortensio. The bass is right ; 'tis the base knave that jars."

A little later Hortensio is permitted to begin his music lesson, which he does somewhat angrily, saying to Lucentio :

" You may go walk, and give me leave awhile,
My lessons make no music in three parts.
    Lucentio. Are you so formal, sir ? well, I must wait,
And watch withal ; for, but I be deceived,
Our fine musician groweth amorous.   [*Aside.*
    Hortensio. Madam, before you touch the instrument,
To learn the order of my fingering,
I must begin with rudiments of art :
To teach you gamut in a briefer sort,
More pleasant, pithy and effectual,
Than hath been taught by any of my trade,
And there it is in writing, fairly drawn.

    [1] The "peg-hole" of the instrument is here spoken of ; a technical point connected with tuning.

Bianca.　　Why I am past my gamut long ago.
Hortensio.　　Yet read the gamut of Hortensio.
Bianca.　　[*Reads*]
Gamut,[1] ' I am the ground of all accord,'
　　A re, ' to plead Hortensio's passion ; '
B mi, ' Bianca, take him for thy lord,'
　　C fa ut, ' that loves with all affection : '
D sol re, ' one clef two notes have I ; '
　　E la mi, ' shew pity or I die.'
Call you this — gamut ? tut ! I like it not :
Old fashions please me best ; I am not so nice
To change true rules for odd inventions."

At present we are concerned but with the introduction of the lute, and the delicate allusions to its
tuning difficulties, but the introduction of the gamut
is a vocal point which will be touched upon in connection with the songs in later chapters, and the
" lessons in three parts " are also connected more
closely with the vocal than with the instrumental
side of the subject.

It was not unnatural for Shakespeare to use vocal
figures in the lute lesson, for the lute was almost
always used as the accompaniment of song in the
sixteenth and seventeenth centuries ; but the sol-
faing and the vocal gamut had nothing to do with
the instrument itself ; in fact the lute had a notation
of its own, different from that of other instruments,
a notation which has become utterly obsolete to-day.

[1] See Chapter VI. for explanation of the vocal terms here used.

In "Henry VI." (Part I. Act i. Sc. 4) Shakespeare uses the lute as a simile which deserves attention ; he causes Talbot to soothe the dying Salisbury with —

"Salisbury, cheer thy spirit with this comfort;
Thou shalt not die, whiles —
He beckons with his hand and smiles on me ;
As who would say, ' When I am dead and gone,
Remember to avenge me on the French.' —
Plantagenet, I will ; and Nero-like,
Play on the lute, beholding the towns burn :
Wretched shall France be only in my name."

This is truer to history than the well-known saying, "Nero fiddled while Rome was burning," for the Romans possessed no instrument resembling the fiddle, but they had some instruments akin to the lute. In "Much Ado About Nothing" (Act iii. Sc. 2) Claudio jests at Benedick and speaks of his dwindling spirits : "Nay, but his jesting spirit ; which is now crept into a lute-string, and now governed by stops." These are not all of Shakespeare's allusions to the instrument, but they are the most important. Occasionally, as above, he speaks intelligently of the strings of the instrument, apart from the rest, as, for example, Cloten's rough allusion in "Cymbeline" (Act ii. Sc. 3), or in the tent scene in "Julius Cæsar" (Act iv. Sc. 3). The lute-strings were apt to be present in Shakespeare's mind as separate from the instru-

ment, for it was a dainty custom of the Elizabethan
court to make especial gifts of these. On New
Year's Day, many an Elizabethan gallant would do
up a packet of lute-strings with pretty ribbons, con-
ceal a poem among them, and send it as a species
of valentine to his lady-love. The queen herself
greatly regarded these presents, as they became a
double tribute to her personal attractions and her
musical abilities.

A very different use of the lute-string was made by
the barbers in the Elizabethan days. As they were
often dentists, they would hang a lute-string fes-
tooned with the teeth they had drawn, in their shop-
windows. This lute-string was usually one that had
been broken, by some impatient customer, while
playing the instrument that always stood in their
shop for the use of the public. Ben Jonson alludes
to this custom, when, in "The Silent Woman" (Act
iii. Sc. 2), Truewit joins with Morose in cursing the
barber, and wishes that he may "draw his own teeth
and add them to the lute-string!" But Shakespeare
does not allude to this side of lute-string utility.

One of the neatest allusions to the strings of
instruments in Shakespeare is found in the First
Part of "King Henry IV." (Act ii. Sc. 4), where
Prince Henry says, regarding his companionship with
the drawers (tapsters), "I have sounded the very
base-string of humility." This is not so very unlike

the playful complaint that Chopin once made regarding his own delicate nature among coarse surroundings. He said: "I am a violin E string on a contrabass!"

With allusions to one other instrument (since it is unnecessary to make a mere catalogue of instrumental references, which can be found in any Concordance) we leave this subject. In "The Tempest" (Act iv. Sc. 1) Alonzo says:

> "The thunder,
> That deep and dreadful organ pipe, pronounced
> The name of Prosper; it did bass my trespass."

This simple sentence contains more than might appear at first sight. It shows how all things transmuted themselves into poetry in that most receptive and assimilative mind. In 1605, Thomas Dallam set up, in King's College, Cambridge, the first complete two-manual organ of England. In it were some tremendous pedal pipes, still used (we believe) in the deepest register of the instrument. All England, or at least the musical part of it, was interested in this great instrument. According to Furnivall, "The Tempest" was written very soon thereafter, and consequently we find the "deep and dreadful organ pipe" preserved to posterity in a still more imperishable play.

In "King John" there is a less important allusion

to the organ.   Prince Henry, on being informed that the dying king had attempted to sing, says (Act v. Sc. 7) :

> " 'Tis strange, that death should sing. —
> I am the cygnet to this pale faint swan,
> Who chants a doleful hymn to his own death ;
> And, from the organ-pipe of frailty, sings
> His soul and body to their lasting rest," —

the voice of the king here being the " organ pipe of frailty."

In the Induction to "Henry IV.," Part II., Shakespeare alludes to "a pipe" without specifying its kind ; here, however, an instrument is evidently meant.

Rumour speaks :

> " Rumour is a pipe
> Blown by surmises, jealousies, conjectures ;
> And of so easy and so plain a stop,
> That the blunt monster with uncounted heads,
> The still-discordant wavering multitude,
> Can play upon it."

Even the *cases* of musical instruments are sometimes spoken of by Shakespeare, as, for example, when the boy in "Henry V." (Act iii. Sc. 2) speaks of the propensity of Falstaff's followers to steal, even at a loss, from the mere habit :

> " They will steal anything, and call it purchase.   Bardolph stole a lute-case, bore it three leagues and sold it for three half-pence."

Or Falstaff's description of Shallow ("Henry IV.," Part I. Act iii. Sc. 2), when he says:

"The case of a treble hautboy was a mansion for him, a court."

In "Much Ado About Nothing" (Act ii. Sc. 1) Hero says to the masked Don Pedro: "God defend that the lute should be like the case." In fact, no part of any musical instrument of the poet's time seems to have been too humble for him to draw some metaphor from.

CHAPTER IV.

So much has been said and written about the literary activity of Shakespeare's time that the "Elizabethan poets" have become a standard subject with
which every schoolboy is acquainted, and the epoch
is accepted as one in which essays, poems, dramas,
etc., flourished as never before. Without impugning
the justice of this estimate, one may regret that it is
too often allowed to overshadow the great musical
advance which took place in the Elizabethan and Jacobean times. The names of Spenser, Massinger,
Beaumont, Bacon, Sidney, Fletcher, Marlowe, Jonson
(not to speak of the greatest of them all), are on
every tongue, but those of Farrant, Weelkes, Morley,
Byrd, Orlando Gibbons, Dowland, Bull, Ravenscroft,
Tye, Tallis, Wilbye, Forde, and others, form a musical roll of honour that ought not to be thrown into
the background by the list of *literati;* in fact, if the
great name of Shakespeare be eliminated, the musical

list may balance the poetic one. It was the era of England's greatest contrapuntal activity, the epoch of the madrigal in its best state, the age of noble religious composition; for a short time England seemed to wrest the sceptre of musical supremacy from Italy itself. But the literary list was crowned with the greatest poet of all time, while England's chief musical genius, Henry Purcell, came a couple of generations later.[1]

In tracing the musical life of this time, however, one must carefully discriminate between the creator and the mere performer of music; the composers seem to have been held in considerable esteem, particularly as Henry VIII., Edward VI., Queen Mary, and Queen Elizabeth were all practical musicians and lovers of the art of music.[2] The average performer was not prized so highly. It is a significant fact that almost all of Shakespeare's musicians are pictured either as Bohemians or vagabonds. We have already alluded to Mercutio's indignation at being classed with "minstrels." More than once does our poet sneer at his musicians and set their songs in a frame of satirical comment. Note, for example, the exquisite sarcasm of the following scene ("Much Ado About Nothing," Act ii. Sc. 3):

---

[1] The influence of Shakespeare upon Purcell was nevertheless a marked one.

[2] James I. was, however, not a musical monarch.

"*Enter* BALTHAZAR *with Music.*[1]

Don Pedro. Come, Balthazar, we'll hear that song again.

Balthazar. O good my lord, tax not so bad a voice
To slander music any more than once.

Don Pedro. It is the witness still of excellency
To put a strange face on his own perfection: —
I pray thee, sing, and let me woo no more.

Balthazar. Because you talk of wooing, I will sing:
Since many a wooer doth commence his suit
To her he thinks not worthy; yet he woos;
Yet will he swear, he loves.

Don Pedro. Nay, pray thee, come:
Or, if thou wilt hold longer argument,
Do it in notes.

Balthazar. Note this before my notes, —
There's not a note of mine, that's worth the noting.[2]

Don Pedro. Why these are very crotchets[3] that he speaks:
Note, notes, forsooth, and noting!   [*Music.*

Benedick. Now, 'Divine air!' now is his soul ravished!

---

[1] The Folio has it "Enter Prince, Leonato, Claudio, and *Jacke Wilson,*" which has led to considerable inquiry as to who Jacke Wilson might have been. It has been suggested that he may have been the celebrated Dr. John Wilson, of Oxford. The very name "Balthazar," however, is thought to be derived from an actual person, Baltazarini (de Beaujoyeux), a prominent composer at the court of Henry III. of France. (See Furness, Variorium Edition, Vol. XII., page 109, for a collation of authorities about "Jack Wilson.")

[2] The ways of the "Shakespearian commentator" are strange and wonderful. It has been suggested, because of this passage, that the title of the play may have originally been, "Much Ado About *Noting!*" The pronunciation of "nothing" in Shakespeare's time was given with the long O, — "no thing."

[3] "Crotchets," a musical pun. The "crotchet" is the English term for the quarter-note.

— Is it not strange, that sheep's guts should hale souls out of men's bodies? — Well, a horn for my money, when all's done.[1]

BALTHAZAR *Sings.*

I.

Balthazar.   Sigh no more ladies, sigh no more,
      Men were deceivers ever;
One foot in sea, and one on shore,
      To one thing constant never:
            Then sigh not so,
            But let them go,
      And be you blythe and bonny;
Converting all your sounds of woe
Into hey nonny, nonny.

II.

Sing no more ditties, sing no mo
      Of dumps so dull and heavy;
The fraud of men was ever so,
      Since summer first was leavy.
            Then sigh not so, etc."

After his song Balthazar again seeks to pump out as many compliments for his performance as possible, by exhibiting the "pride that apes humility;" a better example of the musician "fishing for compliments" than the foregoing and the following can scarcely be imagined:

[1] The horn was not admitted to "consort" in this epoch. It was held to be a vulgar instrument, fit only for hunting and field sports. Even in Handel's time this prejudice against the finest of brass instruments still existed.

"*Don Pedro.*   By my troth, a good song.

Balthazar.   And an ill singer, my lord.

Don Pedro.   Ha? no; no, faith; thou singest well enough for a shift.

Benedick.   [*Aside*]   An he had been a dog, that should have howled thus, they would have hanged him; and I pray God, his bad voice bode no mischief!   I had as lief have heard the night-raven, come what plague could have come after it."

In the second act of "As You Like It" (Scene 5, in the forest of Arden) there is a framework of musical comment around a song that is less derogatory to the vocalist.

"*Enter* AMIENS, JAQUES, *and others.*

SONG.[1]

Amiens.   Under the greenwood tree
          Who loves to lie with me,
          And tunes his merry note
          Unto the sweet bird's throat,
     Come hither, come hither, come hither;
               Here shall he see
               No enemy,
          But winter and rough weather.

Jaques.   More, more, I pr'ythee, more.

Amiens.   It will make you melancholy, Monsieur Jaques.

Jaques.   I thank it.   More, I pr'ythee, more.   I can suck

---

[1] This has received many settings by post-Shakespearian composers.   The oldest music attached to the verses, very popular in the seventeenth century, is here printed, and was very probably used by Shakespeare. (See Chappell's "Collection of National English Airs," page 62.)

melancholy out of a song, as a weasel sucks eggs: More, I prythee, more.,

Amiens. My voice is ragged; I know, I cannot please you.

Jaques. I do not desire you to please me, I do desire you to sing: Come, more; another stanza: Call you them stanzas?

Amiens. What you will, Monsieur Jaques.

Jaques. Nay, I care not for their names; they owe me nothing: Will you sing?

Amiens. More at your request, than to please myself.

Jaques. Well, then, if ever I thank any man, I'll thank you: but that they call compliment, is like the encounter of two dog-apes; and when a man thanks me heartily, methinks I have given him a penny, and he renders me the beggarly thanks. Come, sing; and you that will not, hold your tongues.

Amiens. Well, I'll end the song. — Sirs, cover the while, the duke will drink under this tree : — he hath been all this day to look you.

Jaques. And I have been all this day to avoid him. He is too disputable for my company: I think of as many matters as he: but I give Heaven thanks, and make no boast of them. Come, warble, come.

SONG.

Who doth ambition shun,   [*All together here.*
And loves to live i' the sun,
Seeking the food he eats,
And pleased with what he gets,
Come hither, come hither, come hither;
Here shall he see
No enemy,
But winter and rough weather.

Jaques. I'll give you a verse to this note, that I made yesterday, in despite of my invention.

Amiens.   And I'll sing it.
Jaques.   Thus it goes:

> If it do come to pass
> That any man turn ass,
> Leaving his wealth and ease,
> A stubborn will to please,
> Ducdame, ducdame, ducdame;
> Here shall he see
> Gross fools as he,
> An if he will come to me.

Amiens.   What's that ducdame?
Jaques.   'Tis a Greek invocation to call fools into a circle. I'll go sleep if I can; if I cannot, I'll rail against all the first-born of Egypt.

Amiens.   And I'll go seek the duke; his banquet is prepared.   [*Exeunt severally.*"

In the refrain, " Ducdame," we have Shakespeare jesting at the meaningless character of many burdens. Hanmer, who has given some dainty touches to Shakespearian readings (as we shall see in connection with Cloten's serenade, in "Cymbeline"), suggests that "ducdame" is merely a misprint for "duc ad me" ("bring to me"), and he is very probably correct. That Jaques endeavours to pass off his Latin for Greek is only a furtherance of the jest.

But Hanmer's suggestion is by no means unanimously accepted. The amount of debate regarding "ducdame" is out of all proportion to the subject. If the reader cares to examine the Variorum Edition

UNDER THE GREENWOOD TREE.*

Smoothly and Rather Slow.

Under the Greenwood Tree Who loves to lie with me . . . And

tune his mer - ry note Un - to the sweet bird's throat.

Come hither, come hither, come hith - er, Here he shall see No

en - e-my, No en - e - my, But win-ter and rough weather.

*The oldest setting of these words. The melody very popular in the 17th century.

(Furness), Vol. VIII., pages 97, 98, and 99, he will
be astounded at the amount of learned commentary
upon this single word; and Mr. Furness has condensed his material in a surprising and commendable
degree. A few of the theories may be cited here:

Capell says it is a free Latinisation of "come
hither," and that it should have read "hucdame;"
Farmer suggests that it is a word coined for the
occasion, and suggests an extra rhyme with —

> " Ducdamé, ducdamé, ducdamé,
> Here he shall see
> Gross fools as he,
> An if he will come to *Ami!* " —

the last mysterious word meaning *Amiens*.

Steevens quotes an irrelevant old ballad with —

> " Duck, duck, duck,
> Dame, what makes your chicks to cry, —"

sounding the final "e" in dame, as all agree that
"ducdame" was used by Jaques as a trisyllable.
Knight believes the word to be a duck-call rather
than Latin. Collier thinks it the burden of some old,
undiscovered song. Halliwell adds a very slight bit
of evidence in the same direction by discovering a
similar refrain, "Dusadam-me-me," in a version of
"Piers Ploughman," in the Bodleian Library. Staunton believes it a coined word. "A. A." in "Notes
and Queries," October 8, 1859 (quoted by Furness),

believes it to be "Duc da me," meaning "Lead him from me," the "da" being Italian, and the sentence showing Jaques to be just the opposite of Amiens, with his "Come hither." Another commentator thinks that the word may be merely an imitation of the twang of a guitar. A patriotic Welshman puts in a plea for "Dewch da mi," which, it appears, means "Come with (or "to") me" in Welsh; a challenge similar to "Come, if you dare." Another suggests that the end of the word, "ame," is French, and should be "Ami," and should make a pun on "Amiens" and "friend!"

We have strayed a moment from our musical topic, but the illustration of the fearfully wide scope of Shakespearian comment is too odd to be passed over. Nor are the possibilities exhausted, for nobody has yet suggested that it might mean "Duke d'Ami," and that Jaques is proposing to Amiens to usurp the dukedom; or that it might be "Deuce damme," and that Jaques is swearing at the host of commentators who are to analyse his song in every new edition of Shakespeare!

In this same comedy of "As You Like It," we can find a satirical allusion to the vocalist, as severe, and unfortunately as true to nature, as the excerpt from "Much Ado About Nothing." It is in Act v. Sc. 3, and is a very effective bit of sarcasm directed against those singers (there are a few still extant) who make many apologies before beginning, and require urging to their task, for the First Page says :

"Shall we clap into 't roundly without hawking or spitting, or saying 'we are hoarse,' which are the only prologues to a bad voice?"

Perhaps the most forcible sarcasm against the musician is found in "Romeo and Juliet," and this time it is directed against both instrumentalist and singer.   It is where the wedding festivities of Juliet with Paris are suddenly interrupted by the supposed death of the bride.   The musicians show a most callous disposition in the matter ; they have been sent for to play at a wedding, they will probably be called upon to perform at the funeral, and it seems to matter very little to them.   It may be added that Peter seems as unconcerned as they, and Shakespeare has been criticised for allowing so light a touch to follow such heavy events ; it has, however, been urged in palliation, that the audience know that Juliet is but in a trance, and the dramatic unities are not disturbed by the following passages of wit (Act iv. Sc. 5) :

"*First Musician.*   'Faith, we may put up our pipes, and be gone.
   Nurse.   Honest good fellows, ah, put up, put up,
For, well you know, this is a pitiful case.   [*Exit.*
   Second Musician.   Ay, by my troth, the case may be amended.[1]

[1] Possibly a feeble pun on his instrument-case.

Enter PETER.

Peter. Musicians, O musicians, ' Heart's ease, heart's ease : ' O, an you will have me live, play ' Heart's ease.'

First Musician. Why ' Heart's ease ? '

Peter. O musicians, because my heart itself plays — ' My heart is full of wo : ' O, play me some merry dump, to comfort me.

Second Musician. Not a dump we ; 'tis no time to play now.

Peter. You will not then ?

Musician. No.

Peter. I will then give it you soundly.

First Musician. What will you give us ?

Peter. No money, on my faith : but the gleek ; I will give you the minstrel.

First Musician. Then will I give you the serving-creature.

Peter. Then will I lay the serving-creature's dagger on your pate. I will carry no crotchets : I ll ' re ' you, I'll ' fa ' you : Do you note me ?

First Musician. An you ' re ' us, and ' fa ' us, you note us.

Second Musician. Pray you, put up your dagger, and put out your wit.

Peter. Then have at you with my wit ; I will dry-beat you with an iron wit, and put up my iron dagger : — Answer me like men :

> ' When griping grief the heart doth wound,
>   And doleful dumps the mind oppress,
>   Then music with her silver sound : '

Why, ' silver sound ? ' why, ' music with her silver sound ? ' What say you, Simon Catling ?

First Musician. Marry, sir, because silver hath a sweet sound.

Peter. Pretty ! What say you, Hugh Rebeck ?

Second Musician. I say, ' silver sound,' because musicians sound for silver.

Peter. Pretty too ! What say you, James Soundpost ?

Third Musician. Faith, I know not what to say.

Peter. O, I cry you mercy! you are the singer; I will say for you. It is — 'music with her silver sound,' because such fellows as you have seldom gold for sounding: —

> 'Then music, with her silver sound,
>   With speedy help doth send redress.'
>
> [*Exit singing.*

First Musician. What a pestilent knave is this same?

Second Musician. Hang him, Jack! Come, we'll in here; tarry for the mourners, and stay dinner. [*Exeunt.*"

THE OLD MELODY OF "HEART'S-EASE."

(Probably composed about 1570.)

Singe care away with sport and playe Pastime is all our

pleasure. Yf well we fare, For naught we care, In mearth consists our

treas-ure. Let lur-ges lurke and druges worke, We

do de-fie their slave-rye: He is but a foole that goes to schole, All we de-light in brave-erye.

This entire scene was possibly a sort of *entr'acte* such as is explained in Chapter XIII. Will Kempe (alluded to in the chapter on dances) was the original Peter, and this badinage was probably intended to display him at his best. It is by no means certain that the exact text was adhered to, for Will Kempe would add all possible "gags" and interpolations.

There are many other points of explanation necessary to the above scene. "Heart's-ease" was a favourite tune of the time, the melody of which we append. "My heart is full of woe" was the burden, or refrain, of another song of the day, "The Two Lovers." [1] A dump was a melancholy movement

[1] The first stanza ran:

"Complaine, my Lute, complain on him, that stayes so long away:
He promised to be here ere this, but still unkind doth stay;

(see chapter on dances), and a merry dump would have been as paradoxical as a frolicsome hymn. The poem, "When Griping Grief" (which was probably sung as well as declaimed in this scene), and its musical setting, is the work of Richard Edwards, Master of the Children of the Royal Chapel, in Queen Elizabeth's reign. We give the poem in full, and also its music. The satire of the scene is not directed against the music, but rather against those "intention-finders" who seek for more in a poetic line than the writer ever dreamed of. Some Shakespearian commentators might learn a lesson from this scene, if they chose to study it in this light. The original poem runs :

> " Where gripinge grefes the hart would wounde,
>   And dolefulle dumps the mynde oppresse,
>   There musicke with her silver sound
>   With spede is wont to send redresse :
>   Of troubled mynds, in every sore,
>   Swete musicke hath a salve in store.
>
> " In joye yt maks our mirthe abounde,
>   In woe yt cheres our hevy sprites ;
>   Be-strawghted heads relyef hath founde,
>   By musickes pleasaunt swete delightes :
>   Our senses all, what shall I say more ?
>   Are subjecte unto musicks lore.

But now the proverbe true I finde, once out of sight, then out of mind.
Hey ho ! My heart is full of woe."

" The Gods by musicke have theire prayse ;
   The lyfe, the soul therein doth joye ;
For, as the Romayne poet sayes,
   In seas, whom pyrats would destroy,
A dolphin saved from death most sharpe
Arion playing on his harpe.

" O heavenly gyft, that rules the mynd,
   Even as the sterne dothe rule the shippe !
O musicke, whom the Gods assinde
   To comforte manne, whom cares would nippe !
Since thow both man and beste doest move,
What beste ys he, wyll the disprove ? "

A SONG TO THE LUTE IN MUSICKE.

RICHARD EDWARDES.

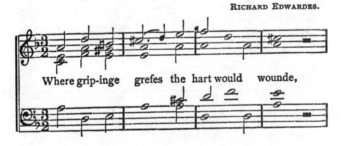

Where grip-inge   grefes the hart would   wounde,

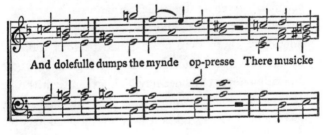

And dolefulle dumps the mynde op-presse There musicke

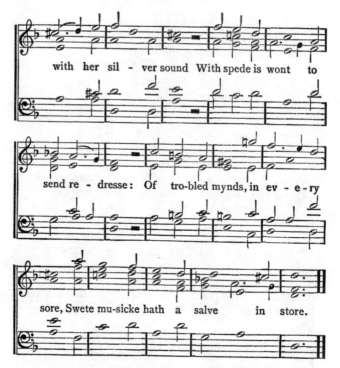

with her sil - ver sound With spede is wont to send re - dresse: Of tro-bled mynds, in ev - e - ry sore, Swete mu-sicke hath a salve in store.

In Peter's condescending reply to James Sound-post, we find another Shakespearian fling at the vocalist. Even in the Elizabethan epoch, although the education of the singer was more rigid than it is nowadays, there were often found persons endowed by nature with a beautiful voice (or a high one), whose education never extended any higher than their throat. It is against such ignorant ones that the shaft seems to be aimed; Peter takes it as a matter of course that the *singer* is duller than the other musicians. In taking this direct view of the meaning of the remark, we are obliged to differ from the ingenious solution offered by Richard Grant White (Houghton, Mifflin & Company's edition), which is that the phrase — "You are the singer" — shows that Shakespeare understood the violin; that the soundpost stands under the highest string of the instrument; that the E string of the violin was called the *Cantore*, that is, the "Singer!" After all this explanation, one is tempted to ask, — ".What of it?" Never was a little jest pursued so far afield. Even to-day there exist plenty of singers who could stand as "terrible examples" of Shakespeare's meaning.

It may be recalled, in connection with the status of the Shakespearian musicians, that Prince Hal broke Falstaff's head for comparing his father to "a singing-man of Windsor" (Second Part, "Henry IV.," Act ii. Sc. 1).

Regarding the low degree of the itinerant musician, Naylor ("Shakespeare and Music," p. 96) quotes the following passage from Brandt's "Ship of Fools," the famous satirical poem written in 1494, which (since the English paraphrase was written several years later) shows the estimation in which musicians were held at the beginning of the sixteenth century :

"The Furies fearful, sprong of the floudes of hell,
  Bereft these vagabonds in their mindes so

> That by no meane can they abide ne dwell
> Within their houses, but out they nede must go ;
>   More wildly wandering thon either bucke or doe.
> Some with their harpes, another with their lute,
> Another with his bagpipe, or a foolishe flute."

This, to be sure, treats of serenaders, but regular musicians were among them.

One can find traces of mediæval contempt for the wandering musicians in the many laws fulminated against them in the thirteenth and fourteenth centuries.   The gleemen and wandering minstrels (such as Autolycus, in " Winter's Tale "), in old England, had scarcely any rights whatever; they might be abused, robbed, or even killed, and no redress could be obtained.   In York, Chester, Canterbury, and Beverly, the minstrels established guilds to protect themselves.   For a graphic picture of the helpless state of the minstrel in England, in early times, we must refer the reader to Rowbotham's " Troubadours and Courts of Love ; "[1] we cite the case here only to show that there was good cause for the humble status of the musician in the Elizabethan era ; it was an inheritance from bygone times. Singular to relate, some of the English laws against wandering musicians, having fallen into desuetude, have never been repealed ; it is barely possible that

---

[1] See also Chappell's " National English Airs," Percy's " Reliques," and Ritson's " Collection of English Songs."

they might be resuscitated, at some inopportune moment, as was the case with another statute, in 1819, when a convicted murderer escaped punishment by demanding the right of trial by combat, and challenging his accuser (in this case the counsel for the prosecution) to a battle to the death.

But, as there was a decided difference in station between the ordinary musician and the composer, so there was also distinction made between the musician and the amateur. Every gentleman dabbled in music to some degree, and, in addition to the viol-playing described in Chapter II., it was held to be necessary for every cultured person to be able to descant, or add a part to any melody that was sung. Nor was this singing confined to the upper classes; in the old English plays we find tinkers and tailors, millers and soldiers, in short, all classes, high and low, recreating themselves with vocal music. The especial catch of the tinkers, for example, ran :

> " Now God be with old Simeon,
>   For he made cans for many a one,
>   And a good old man was he :
>   And Jinkin was his journey-man,
>   And he could tipple of every can,
>   And thus he said to me :
>   To whom drink you ?
>   Sir Knave, to you.
>   Then, hey ho ! jolly Jinkin,
>   I spy a knave in drinking.
>   Come trole the bowl to me."

That servants were occasionally expected to be able to take part in the music of their masters is clearly proved, also.   Pepys seems often to have caused his wife and her maid to join with him in song.

The "musicians" introduced by Shakespeare into his plays are generally of the lower and less esteemed sort, and he often seems to allude to their humble station either directly or by innuendo, as illustrated above.

Carmen were especially musical.   Falstaff (Second Part of "Henry IV.," Act iii. Sc. 2) speaks of Shallow hearing "the carmen whistle," and there exists an old English folk-song, which the early contrapuntists did not disdain to make "divisions" upon, called "The Carman's Whistle," which we present herewith.

THE CARMAN'S WHISTLE.

The words to this melody were rather broad, and do not require reprinting, since Shakespeare alludes only to the *music* of the Carman.

Nor were carmen, tailors, and tinkers, the only practical musicians among the trades. A very pretty custom was borrowed from Germany, where, in mediæval times, every 'prentice lad was obliged to learn the melodies which custom had assigned to his trade, and chant the rhymes reciting the names of his tools. Doloony, in his "History of the Gentle Craft," thus portrays a meeting of shoemakers (1598):

"And coming in this sort to Gilford, they were both taken for shoemakers, and verie hartilie welcomed by the jorneymen of that place, especially Harry, because they never saw him before: and at their meeting they askt him if he could sing, or sound the trumpet, or play upon the flute, or recon up his tooles in rime, or manfully handle the pike-staff, or fight with sword and buckler? 'Beleeve me,' quoth Harrie, 'I can neither sound the trumpet nor play on the flute; and beshroe his nose that made me a shoomaker, for he never tought me to recon up my tooles in rime nor in prose.'"

Whereupon Harrie was adjudged an impostor.

Fitz-Stephen describes the joyous music of the London 'prentices and their sweethearts, as early as 1174. Decidedly, the English were a musical people in ancient times; more so than at present.

CHAPTER V.

Shakespeare's Technical Knowledge of Music — "Broken Music" — John Skelton's Diatribe — Time Keeping — Harmony Prized Above Mere Melody — The Eighth Sonnet — Similar Views of Browning — The Proper Wedding of Poetry and Music — "The Passionate Pilgrim" — Wagner and Herbert Spencer on the Union of the Two Arts.

WE now approach certain passages written by Shakespeare, which indicate that the poet not only appreciated the art, but actually had become acquainted with some of its technicalities. In the thirty-seven plays (in this numeration we include "Titus Andronicus") only five are barren of musical allusions, while the sonnets and "Tarquin and Lucrece," as well as the "Passionate Pilgrim," possess some very subtle passages relative to the art. In studying many of the passages, the conviction is borne in upon us that Shakespeare was himself a singer. The vocal allusions are more detailed, and exhibit a surer hand than those connected with instrumental work.

We have already given (in Chapter I.) a tolerably complete list of the instruments of Shakespeare's time, as recited by Michael Drayton. In that cita-

tion, little was said of the vocal side of music.
Naylor, in his " Shakespeare and Music " (pp. 66 and
67), quotes a very interesting set of rhymes from John
Skelton, which allude to the vocal as well as the
instrumental side of the musical life of the time of
Henry VIII. John Skelton was one of the coarsest
of the poets of a very coarse epoch (we shall read of
him again in connection with the bacchanalian music
of the time), yet, as he was tutor to Henry VIII., was
allowed unchallenged to assume the titles of " Poeta
Laureatus " and "Orator Regius," and was praised
by the great Erasmus as a literary light of England,
his lucubrations may not be slightingly rated. He
lived a most litigious life, a veritable Dean Swift of
his time ; and it is because of this that the subjoined
poem (?) exists. A fashionable music teacher had
sneered at Skelton's mode of life (he was *persona non
grata* to many), and Skelton replied in his usual invective, sneering at the musician :

> " With hey troly loly, lo whip here Jak,
>   Alumbek, sodyldym syllorym ben,[1]
>   Curiously he can both counter and knak,
>   Of Martin Swart, and all his merry men ;
>   Lord, how Perkyn is proud of his Pohen,

---

[1] " Hey Troly Loly " is the old refrain which afterward became
" tol de rol " in drinking songs. It is an old Scottish exclamation
similar to " alack-a-day." Possibly the second line is also a refrain.
" Rumbill-down, tumbill-down " may admit of a similar explanation.

> But ask wher he findeth among his monachords
> An holy-water-clark a ruler of lordes.

> " He cannot fynd it in rule nor in space,
> He solfyth too haute, hys trybyll is too high,
> He braggyth of his byrth that borne was full base,
> Hys musyk withoute mesure, too sharp, is his 'my,'
> He trymmeth in his tenor to counter pardy,
> His descant is besy, it is without a mene,
> Too fat is his fantsy, his wyt is too lene.

> " He tumbryth on a lewde lewte, Rotybulle Joyse,
> Rumbill downe, tumbill downe, hey go, now now,
> He fumblyth in his fyngering an ugly rude noise,
> It seemyth the sobbyng of an old sow:
> He wolde be made moch of, and he wyst how;
> Well sped in spindels and tuning of travellys
> A bungler, a brawler, a picker of quarrels.

> " Comely he clappyth a payre of clavicordys
> He whystelyth so swetely he maketh me to swet,
> His discant is dashed full of discordes,
> A red angry man, but easy to intrete," etc.

Further on he adds :

> " For lordes and ladyes lerne at his scole,
> He techyth them so wysely to solf and to fayne,
> That neither they sing wel prike-song nor plain."

We shall find the meaning of almost all of the vocal expressions of this poem in the subsequent Shakespearian citations ; the instruments have already been spoken of in Chapter I., with two exceptions ; the clavichord was an instrument like the virginals, with the important exception that the tone

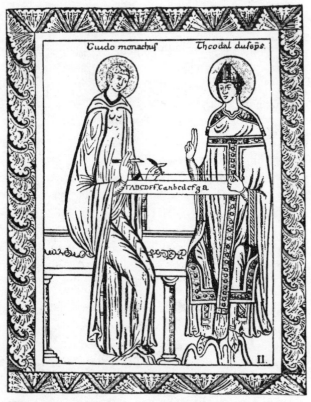

Guido monachus   Theodal dux eps.

ΓABCDFf.Ganbcdefg a

GUIDO OF AREZZO AND HIS PROTECTOR, BISHOP THEODAL,
WITH THE MONOCHORD.

was produced by push of a sharp-edged tangent against the string, instead of the pluck of a quill; the "monochord" (Skelton spells it "monachord" to aid his pun, "monachi" or monks) was the progenitor of clavichords, spinets, virginals, in short, of all instruments of the piano family. It consisted of a single wire (sometimes of two), under which a movable bridge was placed, and the string thus made longer or shorter, the tone higher or lower, as the performer desired. It was plucked with a quill or plectrum, as the mandoline is nowadays. We give a very ancient picture of Guido of Arezzo and his patron, Bishop Theodal, with a monochord. We need only to add that "Rotybulle Joyse" is the title of an old song of the time.

The employment of the instruments, either in accompanying vocal music, or in purely instrumental forms, had one peculiar restriction, in the sixteenth and seventeenth centuries. It was the habit of keeping each family of instruments by itself in a "consort." Thus there could be "a consort of viols," a "consort of hautboys," but if one kind of instrument entered into a "consort" of other instruments than those of its own family the result was called "broken music." [1]

[1] See Chapter I.; also "Proceedings of the Musical Association" (London), 12th session, 1885–86, p. 41, Sir G. A. Macfarren on this subject.

More than once does Shakespeare allude to "broken music." In "Troilus and Cressida" (Act iii. Sc. 1), we find the following:

"*Pandarus.* Fair be to you, my lord, and to all this fair company! fair desires, in all fair measure, fairly guide them! especially to you, fair queen! fair thoughts be your fair pillow!

Helen. Dear lord, you are full of fair words.

Pandarus. You speak your fair pleasure, sweet queen. Fair prince, here is good broken music.

Paris. You have broke it, cousin; and, by my life, you shall make it whole again; you shall piece it out with a piece of your performance: — Nell, he is full of harmony.

Pandarus. Truly, lady, no."

Richard Grant White considers Shakespeare occasionally to have meant *part-music* when speaking of broken music, and imagines it so applied in this case, but the weight of evidence is in favour of the explanation given above.

It is natural enough that the great punster should not have omitted the chance to make his play upon words whenever he uses this metaphor. King Henry V., in his wooing of Queen Katharine, speaks thus (Act v. Sc. 2):

"Come, your answer in broken music; for thy voice is music, and thy English broken; therefore, queen of all, Katharine, break thy mind to me in broken English. Wilt thou have me?"

In "As You Like It," Act i. Sc. 2, Rosalind pun-
ningly speaks of the wrestling, in which the duke's
wrestler has broken the ribs of three opponents:

" But is there any else longs to see this broken music in his
sides?"

Naturally enough the poet draws many metaphors
from the tuning of instruments. The tuning of
heart-strings is spoken of in "Lucrece," in a passage
that is so embroidered with musical metaphor that
we give it entire:

" 'You mocking birds,' quoth she, 'your tunes entomb
　　Within your hollow swelling feather'd breast,
　And in my hearing be you mute and dumb!
　　(My restless discord loves no stops nor rests;
　　A woful hostess brooks not merry guests:)
　Relish your nimble notes to pleasing ears;
　Distress likes dumps when time is kept with tears.

" 'Come, Philomel, that sing'st of ravishment,
　　Make thy sad grove in my dishevel'd hair.
　As the dank earth weeps at thy languishment,
　　So I at each sad strain will strain a tear,
　　And with deep groans the diapason bear:
　For burthen-wise I'll hum on Tarquin still,
　While thou on Tereus descant'st better skill.

" 'And whiles against a thorn thou bear'st thy part,
　　To keep thy sharp woes waking, wretched I,
　To imitate thee well, against my heart
　　Will fix a sharp knife, to affright mine eye:
　　Who, if it wink, shall thereon fall and die.

These means, as frets upon an instrument,
Shall tune our heart-strings to true languishment.

" ' And for, poor bird, thou sing'st not in the day,
　　As shaming any eye should thee behold,
Some dark deep desert, seated from the way,
　　That knows not parching heat nor freezing cold,
　　Will we find out; and there we will unfold
To creatures stern, sad tunes, to change their kinds;
Since men prove beasts, let beasts bear gentle minds.' "

" Discord," " stops," " dumps," " rests," " diapason "
(the fundamental bass in this case), " burthen-wise "
(containing a burden), " descant," " bearing a part,"
" frets," and " tuning ! "　Rarely can one find a
poem where music is so heavily drawn upon for
similes.

A fitting complement to this tuning with heart-
strings is found in the stringing of Orpheus's lute
with poets' sinews. [1]　The simile is found in " Two
Gentlemen of Verona " (Act iii. Sc. 2) where Proteus
hypocritically gives advice to Thurio as to the best
mode of wooing Sylvia.　It will be noticed that concerted music is again alluded to, and again we meet
with that slow dance or song, called the " dump "

---

[1] In this connection the description of John of Gaunt's death in
" Richard II.," Act ii. Sc. 5, may be mentioned:

" *Northumberland.*　My liege, old Gaunt commends him to your
　　majesty.
　King Richard.　What says he now?
　Northumberland.　Nay, nothing; all is said:
His tongue is now a stringless instrument."

(see preceding chapter, and also the chapter on dances).

" *Proteus.*   Say, that upon the altar of her beauty
You sacrifice your tears, your sighs, your heart;
Write till your ink be dry; and with your tears
Moist it again; and frame some feeling line,
That may discover such integrity:
For Orpheus' lute was strung with poets' sinews;
Whose golden touch could soften steel and stones,
Make tigers tame, and huge leviathans
Forsake unsounded deeps to dance on sands.
After your dire lamenting elegies,
Visit by night your lady's chamber window
With some sweet concert: to their instruments
Tune a deploring dump; the night's dead silence
Will well become such sweet complaining grievance.
This, or else nothing, will inherit her.
   Duke.   This discipline shews thou hast been in love.
   Thurio.   And thy advice this night I'll put in practice:
Therefore, sweet Proteus, my direction-giver,
Let us into the city presently,
To sort some gentlemen well skill'd in music:
I have a sonnet that will serve the turn,
To give the onset to thy good advice."

When the serenade takes place (Act iv. Sc. 2), the musical terms and the punning grow thicker.

     " *Enter* THURIO *and* Musicians.

   Thurio.   How, now, Sir Proteus! are you crept before us?
   Proteus.   Ay, gentle Thurio; for you know that love
Will creep in service where it cannot go.
   Thurio.   Ay; but I hope, sir, that you love not here.
   Proteus.   Sir, but I do; or else I would be hence.

Thurio.   Who? Silvia?

Proteus.   Ay, Silvia, for your sake.

Thurio.   I thank you for your own.   Now, gentlemen,
Let's tune, and to it lustily awhile.

Enter Host *and* JULIA *behind;* JULIA *in boy's clothes.*

Host.   Now, my young guest, methinks you're allycholly:
I pray you, why is it?

Julia.   Marry, mine host, because I cannot be merry.

Host.   Come, we'll have you merry.   I'll bring you where
you shall hear music and see the gentleman that you asked
for.

Julia.   But shall I hear him speak?

Host.   Ay, that you shall.

Julia.   That will be music.   [*Music plays.*

Host.   Hark! hark!

Julia.   Is he among these?

Host.   Ay; but peace! let's hear 'em.

SONG.[1]

Who is Silvia? what is she,
　　That all our swains commend her?
Holy, fair and wise is she;
　　The heaven such grace did lend her,
That she might admired be.

Is she kind as she is fair?
　　For beauty lives with kindness:
Love doth to her eyes repair,
　　To help him of his blindness;
And, being help'd, inhabits there.

[1] This song has been gloriously set to music by Schubert.   The
Shakespearian music is lost.

> Then to Silvia let us sing,
>   That Silvia is excelling;
> She excels each mortal thing
>   Upon the dull earth dwelling;
> To her let us garlands bring.

Host. How now! are you sadder than you were before? How do you, man? the music likes you not.

Julia. You mistake; the musician likes me not.

Host. Why, my pretty youth?

Julia. He plays false, father.

Host. How? out of tune on the strings?

Julia. Not so; but yet so false that he grieves my very heart-strings.

Host. You have a quick ear.

Julia. Ay, I would I were deaf; it makes me have a slow heart.

Host. I perceive you delight not in music.

Julia. Not a whit, when it jars so.

Host. Hark! what fine change is in the music.

Julia. Ay, that change is the spite.

Host. You would have them always play but one thing?

Julia. I would always have one play but one thing."

Probably the finest metaphor taken from the tuning and untuning of musical instruments is found in "Othello" (Act ii. Sc. 1).

> "*Othello.* I cannot speak enough of this content,
> It stops me here: it is too much of joy:
> And this, and this, the greatest discords be,
>
>   [*Kissing Desdemona.*
> That e'er our hearts shall make!
>   *Iago.* O, you are well tuned now!
> But I'll set down the pegs that make this music,
> As honest as I am.   [*Aside.*"

The making of discord out of sweet music, by tampering with the tuning-pins, is one that every musician will recognise as the perfection of aptness. Ulysses's metaphor ("Troilus and Cressida," Act i. Sc. 3) is in the same line, if less intense.   He speaks of degrees and rank :

> " Take but degree away, untune that string,
>   And hark, what discord follows ! "

Next to the matter of tune the musician is concerned about time-keeping, and we find our musical poet as ready to draw his similes from the one topic as the other.   The finest passage relative to time in music is found in " Richard II." (Act v. Sc. 5), just before the king meets his death :

> " *K. Richard.*   Music do I hear ?   [*Music.*
> Ha, ha ! keep time : — How sour sweet music is,
> When time is broke, and no proportion kept !
> So is it in the music of men's lives.
> And here have I the daintiness of ear,
> To check time broke in a disorder'd string;
> But, for the concord of my state and time,
> Had not an ear to hear my true time broke.
> I wasted time, and now doth time waste me."

One of the subtlest of musical touches connected with time-keeping is found in " Romeo and Juliet " (Act i. Sc. 4), where Mercutio describes Tybalt to Benvolio :

> " *Benvolio.*   Why, what is Tybalt?
>   *Mercutio.*   More than prince of cats, I can tell you.   O, he

is the most courageous captain of compliments. He fights as
you sing prick-song, keeps time, distance, and proportion;
rests me his minim rest, one, two, and the third in your bosom;
the very butcher of a silk button, a duellist, a duellist; a gentleman of the very first house, — of the first and second cause:
Ah, the immortal passado! the punto reverso! the hay!"

The above passage has not been completely eluci-
dated in any of the comments with which the author
is familiar. The allusions to "Tybert, the cat,"
taken from the old tale of Reineke Fuchs, the ancient
German beast-epic, and the picture of the extreme
politeness of the professional duellist, may be dismissed as foreign to our subject, but not so the
allusions to the time and to the prick-song.

In the Elizabethan day it was held to be part of a
liberal education to be able to sing a second part to
any melody that one might hear. This free addition
to the actual tune was called "Descant," from *Dis
Cantus* (with, or from, the song), and had, of course,
considerable license. On the other hand, often the
composer desired a more intricate and more exact
supporting voice, and therefore wrote his descant
himself; as this was now printed, or "pricked down,"
such a strict counterpoint was called the "prick-
song." [1]   It was counted by tapping the foot in time

[1] Strype's account of the funeral of Henry VIII. says: " Wednesday, 16 February, 1547, the Bishop of Ely begun the *mass* of
the Trinity; his dean and subdeacon were two bishops, mitred,
which was solemnly sung in *prick-song discant*, and organ-playing to
the offertory."

with the music, or, more frequently and more artis-
tically, by waving the hand as the conductor of orchestra or chorus to-day waves his baton. To prove
this mode of motion, we give a quotation from Playford's " Introduction to the Skill of Musick " (1664) :

" OF THE KEEPING OF TIME BY THE MEASURE OF THE
SEMIBREVE OR MASTERNOTE. — Observe that to the measure
of the semibreve all notes are proportioned, and its measure,
when whole, is expressed (naturally by the voice, or artificially
by an instrument) by moving the hand or foot up and down.
In notes of augmentation, the sound is continued to more than
one *Semibreve ;* but in notes of diminution, the sound is vari-
ously broken into *Minims*, *Crotchets*, and *Quavers*, or the
like : so that in keeping time your hand goes down at one half,
which is a *Minim*, and up at the next."

In short, we have here a description of motions
similar to those made by a conductor in leading his
orchestra.   Had the present mode of conducting been
in vogue at that time, we would have found Shakespeare taking his simile from it.   As it is, he uses
the motion of the hand of the singer when counting
his prick-song to picture the motions of the expert
fencer, — " one, two, and the third " (a thrust) " in
your bosom."

One of the surest proofs of Shakespeare's musical
nature is his appreciation of harmony above mere
melody.   This comprehension of musical combinations is one of the best tests of musicianship ; almost
all the world loves a good tune, but it is given only

to the elect to enjoy the intricacies of harmony or counterpoint. In Shakespeare's day the homophonic structures, which we build according to the laws of harmony, did not exist. Combined music was contrapuntal and more complex than that of to-day. Hauptmann has summed this up in a sentence, "Of old music was horizontal, now it has become vertical," and it may be added that the horizontal music, the support of melody by melody, the twining together of various parts like the strands of a rope, was a much more subtle process than the support of a single tune by a chord-mass, as one supports a bridge by occasional pillars. In the eighth sonnet Shakespeare shows, very plainly, his preference for combinations of counterpoint to mere tunes. It is one of the set in which he advises his friend, Mr. "W. H." (probably William Herbert, afterward — 1601 — Earl of Pembroke), to marry:

> " Music to hear, why hear'st thou music sadly?
> Sweets with sweets war not, joy delights in joy.
> Why lov'st thou that which thou receiv'st not gladly,
> Or else receiv'st with pleasure thine annoy?
> If the true concord of well-tunéd sounds,
> By unions married, do offend thine ear,
> They do but sweetly chide thee, who confounds
> In singleness the parts that thou should'st bear.
> Mark, how one string, sweet husband to another,
> Strikes each in each by mutual ordering;
> Resembling sire and child and happy mother,
> Who all in one, one pleasing note do sing:

Whose speechless song, being many, seeming one,
Sings this to thee, — Thou single wilt prove none."

It is interesting to note that the other great music-lover among poets, Browning, uses almost the same note of praise, in contrasting musical combinations (chords) with simple tones or melodies. The passage is found in " Abt Vogler."

" Here is the finger of God ; a flash of the will that can ;
Existent behind all laws ; that made them, and lo ! they are.
And I know not if, save in this, such gift be allowed to Man,
That out of three sounds he frame, not a fourth sound, but a
    star.
Consider it well, each note of our scale in itself is naught,
It is everywhere in the world, loud, soft, and all is said.
Give it to me to use : I mix it with two in my thought,
And — there ! Ye have heard and seen. Consider and bow
    the head."

" The Passionate Pilgrim " can scarcely be called a Shakespearian work. Printed in 1599, by the unscrupulous publisher, William Jaggard, a man who seized his material wherever he could find it, and gave it to the public under whatever author's name would sell it best, it is one of the most tantalising works in literature,[1] for we know that our poet wrote some part of it, and cannot of surety say just which numbers belong to him.

---

[1] Two similar cases exist among great musical works. Mozart's 12th Mass, and his Requiem were both *partially* composed by him ; the question still puzzles the commentators, *which* parts are Mozart's.

There is one sonnet in this collection which has often been quoted (even in Germany) as a proof of Shakespeare's appreciation of the innate relations of poetry and music. It runs:

> " If Music and sweet Poetry agree,
> As they must needs, the Sister and the Brother,
> Then must the love be great 'twixt thee and me,
> Because thou lov'st the one and I the other.
> Dowland[1] to thee is dear, whose heavenly touch
> Upon the Lute doth ravish human sense;
> Spenser to me, whose deep conceit is such,
> As passing all conceit, needs no defence.
> Thou lov'st to hear the sweet melodious sound,
> That Phœbus' lute, the queen of music, makes;
> And I in deep delight am chiefly drowned,
> Whenas himself to singing he betakes.
> One god is god of both, as poets feign;
> One knight loves both, and both in thee remain."

It is a pity to spoil so much of good quotation and comment, but this poem, together with the charming " As It Fell upon a Day " (also frequently attributed to Shakespeare), is probably the work of Richard Barnfield, whose poetical volumes were published between 1594 and 1598. The thought embodied in the verse is, however, very much like that of Shakespeare, and it is not impossible that he had some hand in it.

---

[1] John Dowland, was the chief lutenist of the time; he was also an excellent composer for this instrument and in the vocal forms. He was born 1562, died 1626. His son, Robert Dowland, also became famous in the same field as his father.

The close connection between poetry and music, thus voiced in the sixteenth century, has had many echoes in our own time.   Wagner has said, "Music is the handmaid of Poetry," and "in the wedding of the two arts, Poetry is the man, Music the woman; Poetry leads and Music follows;" and Herbert Spencer himself, in his essay on "Education," thus arraigns modern compositions where music and poetry disagree:

"They are compositions which science would forbid.   They sin against science by setting to music ideas that are not emotional enough to prompt musical expression, and they also sin against science by using musical phrases that have no natural relation to the ideas expressed: even where these are emotional. They are bad because they are untrue, and to say they are untrue is to say they are unscientific."

Robert Franz, in a letter written, just before his death, to the author, says: "I am convinced that there is a much closer relationship between poetry and music than the average mind can comprehend."

The above are not the only instances of Shakespeare's love of counterpoint, or of the combination of poetry and music.   In "Richard II." (Act ii. Sc. I), the dying Gaunt sends message to the king thus:

"*Gaunt.*   O, but they say, the tongues of dying men
Enforce attention like deep harmony:
Where words are scarce, they are seldom spent in vain;
For they breathe truth, that breathe their words in pain.

He, that no more must say, is listen'd more
Than they, whom youth and ease have taught to glose;
More are men's ends mark'd, than their lives before:
The setting sun, and music at the close."

In "Henry V." (Act i. Sc. 2) Exeter compares good government to the interlacing of parts in well-constructed music.

" For government, though high, and low, and lower,
    Put into parts doth keep in one consent;
    Congruing in a full and natural close,
    Like music.

Through many other allusions one might trace this comprehension of the balance and symmetry of music, but the quotations already cited are the most important, although one may question the Shakespearian right to the citation from "The Passionate Pilgrim."

CHAPTER VI.

Musical Knowledge of Shakespeare (continued) — Surer in Vocal than in Instrumental Work — Technical Vocal Terms — " Setting " a Tune — Burdens — Division, Key, and Gamut — Plain-song.

THE statement made at the beginning of the preceding chapter, that Shakespeare was surer of his ground in the vocal than in the instrumental field, is borne out by the ease and frequency with which he employs terms taken from the singer's technique. If we may judge by a sentence placed in the mouth of Viola ("Twelfth Night," Act i. Sc. 2), the poet even knew of voices that were seldom heard in England in his time, and the duke, speaking to the heroine, in the fourth scene of the same act, describes her voice with —

> " thy small pipe
> Is as the maiden's organ, shrill, and sound
> And all is semblative a woman's part."

One of the scenes that is brimful of musical terms, and one in which almost all these terms belong to the singer's art, is found in "Two Gentlemen of Verona" (Act i. Sc. 2), where Lucetta endeavours, by trickery, to bring the note written by Proteus to the all too willing, yet seemingly recalcitrant, Julia. Lucetta lets the note drop, and picks it up in a manner to attract Julia's attention.

"*Julia.* What is't you took up so gingerly?

Lucetta. Nothing.

Julia. Why didst thou stoop, then?

Lucetta. To take a paper up, that I let fall.

Julia. And is that paper nothing?

Lucetta. Nothing concerning me.

Julia. Then let it lie for those that it concerns.

Lucetta. Madam, it will not lie where it concerns, Unless it have a false interpreter.

Julia. Some love of yours hath writ to you in rhyme.

Lucetta. That I might sing it, madam, to a tune: Give me a note: your ladyship can set.

Julia. As little by such toys as may be possible: Best sing it to the tune of 'Light o' love.'

Lucetta. It is too heavy for so light a tune.

Julia. Heavy? belike, it hath some burden then.

Lucetta. Ay; and melodious were it, would you sing it.

Julia. And why not you?

Lucetta. I cannot reach so high.

Julia. Let's see your song. — How now, minion?

Lucetta. Keep tune there still, so you will sing it out; And yet, methinks, I do not like this tune.

Julia. You do not?

Lucetta. No, madam, it is too sharp.

Julia. You, minion, are too saucy.

Lucetta. Nay, now you are too flat, And mar the concord with too harsh a descant: There wanteth but a mean to fill your song.

Julia. The mean is drown'd with your unruly bass.

Lucetta. Indeed, I bid the base for Proteus.

Julia. This babble shall not henceforth trouble me.

Here is a coil with protestation ! —   [*Tears the letter.*]
Go, get you gone : and let the papers lie :
You would be fingering them, to anger me.
    Lucetta. She makes it strange ; but she would be best
      pleased
To be so anger'd with another letter.   [*Exit.*"

This scene could easily give rise to an entire chapter of musical comment and elucidation.

        " Give me a note : your ladyship can set,"

proves Julia especially musical. To " set " a tune
meant to give its first note to the singers, without
aid of tuning-fork (which implement was only invented in 1711, by John Shore, an Englishman) or
instrument. Many are the rules given regarding
" setting " in the old instruction books ; we quote
from Playford's " Introduction to the Skill of
Musick."

    " Observe, that in the Tuning your Voice you strive to
have it clear. Also in the expressing your Voice, or Tuning
of Notes, let the Sound come clear from your Throat, and
not through your Teeth, by sucking in your Breath, for that
is a great obstruction to the clear utterance of the Voice.
    " Lastly, observe, that in Tuning your first note of your
Plain Song, you equal it so to the pitch of your Voice, that
when you come to your highest Note, you may reach it without squeaking, and your lowest Note without grumbling."

In the Puritan churches " setting a tune " was a
task of considerable importance and difficulty, since

instruments were seldom tolerated, least of all the organ, which smacked of the Church of Rome. An instance may be cited from Puritan days in America, regarding " setting ; " we quote from the diary of Samuel Sewall, of Boston, the date being December 28, 1705 :

"SIXTH DAY, Dec. 28th.

" Mr. Pemberton prays excellently, and Mr. Willard preaches from Ps. 66, 20, very excellently. Spake to me to set the Tune. I intended Windsor, and fell into High Dutch,[1] and then, essaying to set another Tune, went into a key much too high. So I prayed Mr. White to set it; which he did well, Lichf. tune. The Lord humble me and instruct me that I should be occasion of any interruption in the worship of God."

The above citation may readily show the difficulties of " setting " if one was not possessed of the rare faculty of absolute pitch.

The next line requiring attention is

" Best sing it to the tune of ' Light o' Love.' "

This tune seems to have been a favourite with Shakespeare, for he alludes to it again in a prominent manner in " Much Ado About Nothing," in

[1] The editor of the " Diary " falls into a quaint error in adding to the above: " From the context we infer that to ' fall into High Dutch ' was to sing at too low a pitch." As a matter of fact, " High Dutch " was the Puritan name for " Canterbury," and the worthy judge had actually gone into the wrong tune ; " Windsor " was the intended melody, and " Litchfield " the tune eventually set by " Mr. White."

Act iii. Sc. 4 (see chapter on dances), and in both cases he alludes to the lightness of the tune. Nor was our poet the only one who recognised the dainty character of the melody, for in Fletcher's "Two Noble Kinsmen," the jailer's daughter speaks of a horse with the simile:

"He gallops to the tune of 'Light o' Love.'"

Yet the melody itself is not rapid. Fortunately, it exists in its original state, and we reproduce it for the benefit of the reader who desires to note the fitness of Shakespeare's mention of it.

"LIGHT O' LOVE."
(Twice mentioned by Shakespeare.)
Slowly and with expression.

In both allusions Shakespeare speaks of a "burden" in the context. The burden [1] was a recurring phrase or figure which came in after each line or each couplet, sometimes at the end of each stanza. Nothing is more marked in connection with the old English music than the constant use of the burden, and it was an exception which Shakespeare noted, that "Light o' Love" went without a burden. Some of the refrains or burdens go back to a very remote antiquity. We have already seen that "Hey Troly, loly," an old Scottish ejaculation of sadness, gradually metamorphosed itself into "Tol de Rol" and "Fol de Rol," as used in bacchanalian music. Oldest of all the burdens was the phrase, "Derry, Derry down," or, "Hey Derry down." Etymologists have traced this phrase back to Norman England, to the Danish days, and even to the Saxon epoch, only to have it elude them at last. It is considered probable that the words are of Druidic origin.

Often the burden consisted simply of a repetition of the syllables "Fa la la" at the end of each line or verse ; in this case the song was called a "Fa-la." Morley and Hilton, both prominent in Shakespeare's time, wrote many beautiful "Fa-las." We present a facsimile of one of Morley's arranged as a duet by

[1] We shall find more about the "burden" in connection with the bacchanalian music of "Twelfth Night," and the songs of Ophelia in "Hamlet."

Playford.　The peculiar position of the two parts is explained by the fact that the singers sat, or stood, with the music between them, and faced each other, instead of being side by side.[1]

Of the running accompaniment of puns in the scene between Julia and Lucetta it is unnecessary to speak.　We now come to the line, —

"And mar the concord with too harsh a descant."

The word "descant" leads us back to the matter of Tybalt's fencing in the manner of the counting of prick-song.　In the preceding chapter we have explained the written descant which was called by this name.　Naturally, the freer descant which was improvised was of distinctly inferior quality, yet it speaks much for England's musical abilities that every cultured person was able to add a descant to any melody at a first hearing.　The very title of Morley's famous work on music, published in 1597, gives some insight into the two methods, for it runs,

"A Plaine and Easie Introduction to Practicall Musicke. Set downe in forme of a Dialogue: Devided into three Partes: The first teacheth to sing with all things necessary for the knowledge of a prickt Song.　The second teacheth of descante and to sing two parts in one upon a plain song or Ground, with other things for a Descanter," —

[1] Burdens and refrains will be further spoken of in Chapter X.

the Skill of Musick.

A. 2. Voc.   TREBLE.   *T. M.*

Ow is the Month of *Maying*, when merry

Lads are playing, *Fa la la la, &c.*

Each with his bonny Lass upon the greeny grass,

Fa la la la la la, *&c.*

Fa la la la la, &c.

Each with his bonny Lass upon the greeny grass,

Lads are playing, *Fa la la la, &c.*

Ow is the Month of *Maying*, when merry

T. M.   *BASSE.*   *A. 2. Voc.*

while the third part goes into the details of composition. In the second part, Morley has annotated his views on the matter of this extemporaneous addition of one or two parts to a ground. He speaks of it as follows :

" As for singing upon a plain-song, it hath byn in times past in England (as every man knoweth) and is at this day in other places, the greatest part of the usual Musicke which in any churches is sung, which indeed causeth me to marvel how men acquainted with musicke can delight to hear suche confusion, as of force must bee amongste so many singing extempore. But some have stood in an opinion, which to me seemeth not very probable, that is that men accustomed to descanting will sing together upon a plain-song without singing either false chords, or forbidden descant one to another, which till I see I will ever think unpossible. For, though they should all be most excellent men, and every one of their lessons by itself never so well framed for the ground, yet it is unpossible for them to be true one to another, except one man should cause all the reste to sing the same which he sung before them : and so indeed (if he have studied the canon beforehand) they shall agree without errors, else they shall never do it."

The art of free descant was taught even to the children of the Royal Chapel, a degree of musical education that must astonish the music teachers of the present age.

The lack of a "mean" or middle part to Lucetta's supposed harmony requires no especial explanation (see the pun on "singing a mean most meanly," "Love's Labour's Lost," Act v. Sc. 2), nor does the "unruly bass" take us far from modern part-singing, but the bidding of the base for Proteus suddenly takes the punning out of the domain of music into the realm of old English games. The sport was called "Base," or "Prisoner's Bars," and Shakespeare alludes to it again in "Cymbeline" (Act v. Sc. 3), with the lines, —

> "He with two striplings, lads more like to run
> The country base, than to commit such slaughter,
> Made good the passage."

The game was certainly as old as the time of Edward III., for it is mentioned in one of his edicts.[1]

The melody which formed the core around which the descant entwined itself was called the "plain-song." Shakespeare alludes to the plain-song in "Henry V." (Act iii, Sc. 2), where Falstaff's three worthies are pictured in the midst of battle.

> "*Bardolph.* On, on, on, on, on! to the breach, to the breach!
>
> *Nym.* 'Pray thee, corporal, stay; the knocks are too hot; and for mine own part, I have not a case of lives; the humour of it is too hot, that is the very plain-song of it.
>
> *Pistol.* The plain-song is most just; for humours do abound;
> Knocks go and come; God's vassals drop and die;
> > And sword and shield,
> > In bloody field,
> > Doth win immortal fame."

[1] See Strutt's "Sports and Pastimes" (Hone's Edition), page 78.

If the plain-song were given by the bass voice and were repeated over and over, to constantly varied descant, it was called a "ground-bass." Nothing delighted the old composers more than to show their ingenuity by writing, as prick-song, a set of such variations to the repeating "ground." We give a facsimile of a "ground-bass," with its changing descant, as composed by England's great composer, Henry Purcell.

But probably the surest proof of Shakespeare's vocal proficiency is found in his evident knowledge of "Gamut," or "Sol-fa-ing." This is the vocalist's ability to recognise the intervals between notes, and the pitch of the notes themselves, by syllables that have been attached to them. These syllables were first used in Italy, were the invention of Guido D'Arezzo, and came from the practical application of the first syllables of each line (except the last) of a hymn to St. John, the patron of singers, in which each phrase of the music began one degree higher than its predecessor. The words ran, —

> "Utqueant laxis
> Resonare fibris,
> Mira gestorum,
> Famuli tuorum,
> Solve polluti,
> Labii reatum,
> Sancte Johannes," —

[1]

An *EVENING HYMN.*

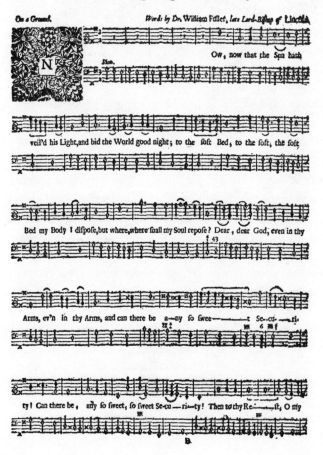

On a Ground.   *Words by Dr. William Fuller, late Lord-Bishop of Lincoln.*

Ow, now that the Sun hath

veil'd his Light, and bid the World good night; to the soft Bed, to the soft, the soft

Bed my Body I difpofe, but where, where fhall my Soul repofe? Dear, dear God, even in thy

Arms, ev'n in thy Arms, and can there be a—ny fo fwee————t Se—cu—ri-

ty! Can there be, any fo fweet, fo fweet Se-cu——ri—ty! Then to thy Re———ft, O my

[2]

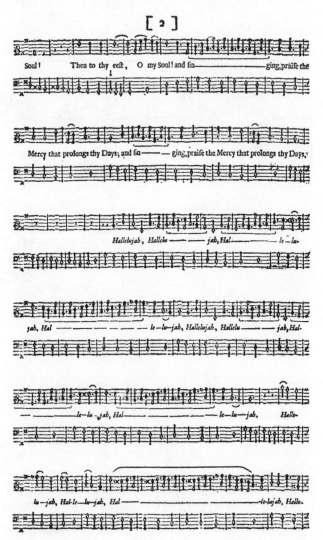

[3]

which may be translated, "That thy servants may be able to sing the praise of thy wondrous deeds with all their strength, cleanse their lips from all stain of sin, Oh! St. John."

To the six syllables, "si" was added at a later epoch, "ut" was changed to "do," and our vocal scale evolved. But in Shakespeare's day the singing of the syllables was not so plain a matter, for a new and more intricate system of nomenclature had been made, in which the syllable "mi" played a very important part and was the especial clue to modulation. Only the four syllables, "fa, sol, la, mi," were now used. We have already cited the music lesson in "The Taming of the Shrew" (quoted in Chapter III. because of its connection with the lute), in which Hortensio uses the vocal syllables in a very deft manner. If the reader will compare the following extract from Playford's "Introduction to the

Skill of Musick" (1664), with Hortensio's phrases, he will see how closely Shakespeare had studied the singer's phraseology :[1]

" Having observed the foregoing direction of proving your notes to know their places, you may easily know their names also, if you will follow this rule : first, observe that *Mi* is the principal or master note, which leads you to know all the rest ; for having found out that, the other follow upon course : and this *Mi* hath its being in four several places, but it is but in one of them at a time ; its proper place is in *B mi ;* but if *B fa*, which is a *B flat* (as is mentioned in Chap. 2) be put in that place, then it is removed into *E la mi*, which is its second place ; but if a *B flat* be placed there also, then it is in its third place, which is *A la mi re ;* if a *B flat* come there also, then it is removed into its fourth place, which is *D la sol re ;* so that in which of these it is, the next notes above it ascending are *Fa sol la*, *Fa sol la*, twice, and then you meet with your *Mi* again, for it is sound but once in eight notes. In like manner, the next notes below it descending are *La sol fa*, *La sol fa*, and then you have your *Mi* again : for your better understanding of which, observe the before-mentioned old metre, whose rules are plain, true, and easie."

We add a facsimile of the examples given, with the quaint verses alluded to by Playford. That Shakespeare understood the complicated system, is to our mind absolute proof of his technical musicianship ; no man not a singer would take the trouble to master the cumbrous nomenclature and awkward rules.[1]

[1] Beaumont and Fletcher's, or Jonson's allusions to music, are always more vague and less technical than Shakespeare's.

A very subtle technical point, connected with these syllables, is found in " King Lear " (Act i. Sc. 2), at the entrance of Edgar while Edmund is plotting against him. Edmund says :

" And pat he comes, like the catastrophe of the old comedy : My cue is villainous melancholy, with a sigh like Tom o' Bedlam. — O, these eclipses do portend these divisions ! fa, sol, la, mi."

Richard Grant White suggests that Edmund sings in order to appear at ease.   Burney, in his " History of Music," suggests that Shakespeare has purposely chosen the forbidden interval of music to illustrate the portent of evil.   Knight believes that the discordant sounds uttered by Edmund fit the scene, but are not meant as a comparison with the dislocation of events. The present writer cannot but believe that the poet who showed such familiarity with the vocal progressions, in the " Taming of the Shrew," here presented the worst possible interval of music (according to the theory of that time) as prognostication of the discords to come. We can conceive of no other reason for Shakespeare choosing exactly the progression which every composer of the epoch interdicted ; nor was this interdict a matter of passing fashion ; the old monks made a rhyme about this progression which was familiar to every musician of England, —

An Introduction to

ner, the Notes next below it deſcending
are *La ſol fa*, *La ſol fa*, and then you have
your *Mi* again : For your better underſtan-
ding of which, obſerve the before-mentioned old Metre, whoſe Rules are plain, true,
and eaſie.

> *No man can ſing true at firſt ſight,*
> *Unleſs he names his Notes aright :*
> *which ſoon is learnt, if that your* Mi
> *You know its Place where e'er it be.*

1. {   *If that no* Flat *be ſet in* B,
       Then in that Place ſtandeth your Mi.

Example.

Sol la Mi *fa* *ſol.* la *fa* *ſol*

2. { *B fa B mi.*   *But if your* *B *alone be* Flat,
     E la mi.   *Then* *E *is* Mi, *be ſure of that.*

Example.

Sol la *fa* *ſol* la Mi *fa* *ſol.*

3. *If*

the Skill of Muſick.

3. { *A la mi re.*

If both be Flat *, your* B *and* E,
Then *A *is* Mi *here you may ſee.*

Example.

La Mi *fa ſol la fa ſol la.*

4. { *D la ſol.*

If all be Flat, E, A, *and* B,
Then Mi *alone doth ſtand in* *D.

Example.

La *fa ſol la* Mi *fa ſol la*

The firſt three Notes above your Mi
Are fa ſol la, *here you may ſee ;*
The next three under Mi *that fall,*
Them la ſol fa *you ought to call.*

Example.

Sol la Mi *fa ſol la fa ſol fa la ſol fa* Mi *la ſol fa*

If you'll ſing true without all blame,
You call all Eights *by the ſame name.*

Exam-

" Mi contra Fa,
   Diabolus est in· Musica," —

fa,   sol,   la,   mi.

calling this set of notes " the Devil." [1]   We therefore
believe, with Burney, that this is one of the most
technical musical points in all Shakespeare.   Furness (Variorum Edition), however, presents several
opinions to the contrary. [2]

Less remarkable is the allusion to " sol-fa " in the
" Taming of the Shrew " (Act i. Sc. 2), where
Petruchio intimidates his servant :

" *Grumio*.   My master has grown quarrelsome : I should
      knock you first,
And then I know after who comes by the worst.
   Petruchio.   Will it not be ?
'Faith, sirrah, an you'll not knock, I'll wring it ;
I'll try how you can ' sol, fa,' and sing it.
                              [*He wrings Grumio by the ears.*
   Grumio.   Help, masters, help ! my master is mad."

In " Love's Labour's Lost," Act iv. Sc. 2, Holo-

[1] According to the gamut described above ; to-day the syllables
would be " fa, sol, la, si ; " they constitute a " tritone," *i. e.* a succession of three whole tones.

[2] Furness's own opinion, Vol. V., p. 55, is that Edmund sings
" Fa, sol, la, mi," — " just as Mistress Quickly sings ' and down,
down, adown-a' in " Merry Wives," i. 3. 44, when Doctor Caius is
approaching."

fernes uses the vocal syllables in singing, but this passage is unimportant.

In the disputed passage from "King Lear," the word "division" is used in a punning sense. The divisions of the royal family are patent enough, but in music "division" also had a particular meaning; it was the breaking of a melody, or its descant, into small notes, as, for example,[1]

Division of foregoing.

In 1659 Christopher Simpson published a work for viol, in which he says:

"Diminution, or division to a ground, is the breaking either of the base or of any higher part that is applicable thereto."

The modern musician would call it variation.

In the chamber-scene of "Romeo and Juliet" (Act iii. Sc. 5), Shakespeare uses the word "division," and once more in a punning way, for even in the most earnest scenes our poet cannot resist the temptation to play upon words. The passage occurs after Juliet pleads with her lover to stay, urging that it was the nightingale, and not the lark, whose notes they had heard. She at last yields to their separation with —

[1] See example of Purcell's "Ground Bass," page 103, for a fuller illustration of this.

"*Juliet.*   It is, it is, hie hence, be gone, away;
   It is the lark that sings so out of tune,
   Straining harsh discords, and unpleasing sharps.
   Some say, the lark makes sweet division;
   This doth not so, for she divideth us:
   Some say, the lark and loathed toad change eyes;
   O, now I would they had changed voices too!
   Since arm from arm that voice doth us affray,
   Hunting thee hence, with hunts-up to the day.
   O, now be gone; more light and light it grows."

The "Hunts-up" that Juliet refers to was a lively hunting-song in its origin, but in Elizabethan times any lively song fitted for the early morn, and even an *Aubade*, or morning love-song, was so called.   In Chapter X. will be found a fuller analysis of these, with a musical example.   Division is again spoken of in the following musical episode in "King Henry IV.," Part I. (Act iii. Sc. 1):

"*Mortimer.*   I will never be a truant, love,
Till I have learn'd thy language; for thy tongue
Makes Welsh as sweet as ditties highly penn'd,
Sung by a fair queen in a summer's bower,
With ravishing division to her lute.
   Glendower.   Nay, if you melt, then will she run mad.
                              [*Lady Mortimer speaks again.*
   Mortimer.   O, I am ignorance itself in this.
   Glendower.   She bids you,
Upon the wanton rushes lay you down,
And rest your gentle head upon her lap,
And she will sing the song that pleaseth you,
And on your eye-lids crown the god of sleep,

Charming your blood with pleasing heaviness,
Making such difference 'twixt wake and sleep,
As is the difference betwixt day and night,
The hour before the heavenly-harness'd team
Begins his golden progress in the east.
  Mortimer. With all my heart I'll sit, and hear her sing;
By that time will our book, I think, be drawn.
  Glendower. Do so:
And those musicians, that shall play to you,
Hang in the air a thousand leagues from hence;
Yet straight they shall be here: sit, and attend.

   · · · · · · · ·

               [*Glendower speaks some Welsh words,*
                      and then the music plays.
  Hotspur. Now I perceive, the devil understands Welsh;
And 'tis no marvel, he's so humourous.
By'r lady, he's a good musician.
  Lady Percy. Then should you be nothing but musical: for
you are altogether governed by humours. Lie still, ye thief,
and hear the lady sing in Welsh.
  Hotspur. I had rather hear Lady, my brach, howl in
Irish.
  Lady Percy. Wouldst thou have thy head broken?
  Hotspur. No.
  Lady Percy. Then be still."

The notes of music are often spoken of by Shake-
peare in a technical manner. The American reader
must bear in mind that the English nomenclature
is derived from the mediæval system which was used
before the division of music into measure; thus the
semibreve (meaning half of a short note) is the whole
note, the minim (meaning the smallest note,—

which it was, in the old monastic manuscripts) is the half-note, the crotchet is the quarter, the quaver the eighth. We have seen Don Pedro, in "Much Ado About Nothing," sneer at the "crotchets" of Balthazar, Mercutio allude to Tybalt's counting a minim while fencing (in "Romeo and Juliet)", and in "The Merry Wives of Windsor" we find Falstaff saying of Bardolph, —

> "His thefts were too open; his filching was like an unskilful singer, he kept not time, — "

whereupon Nym responds :

> "The good humour is to steal at a minim's rest."

The Folio gives this as a "*minute's* rest," but there is not much doubt that "minim" was intended.

To give all the quotations concerning tune and time, in which our poet has made some pun, play of words, or musical jest, would be to write a small concordance. Suffice it to say that in each case, not above mentioned, the meaning is obvious, and the words used in their modern sense.

CHAPTER VII.

The Dances of Shakespeare — Many Dances Sung — The Dump —
Other Dances. — England Fond of Lively Dances. — The Morris-
dance. — Masques — These Preceded Operas in England.

THE English were a dancing people, in the Elizabethan times, far more so than at present, yet there
was a great difference between them and the nations of continental Europe in Terpsichorean matters.

Most of the old dances had their origin in Spain,
where the Moors introduced the Arabic love of
pantomime combined with music, and gave rise
to a music that was graphic and well contrasted.
The majority of the stately dances came from this
source. While the aristocracy of Europe, with a
partial exception of the English, gave their adhesion
to the slow dances, the people took up only those
that were jovial and rapid. The jig, for example,
was to be found among the peasantry from Spain to
Ireland, while pavanes and sarabandes were much
more restricted in their use.

It may be necessary to state at the threshold of
this subject that many of the so-called "dances" of
the European courts were rather processionals than

anything else, and some of the aristocratic dances (as, for example, the passacaglia) were merely a series of posturings to musical accompaniment.   The dances of the peasantry, on the other hand, were almost always "round dances," and were of so violent a description that they were sometimes prohibited except on certain specified days or seasons.   Often these more common dances were given by couples, as in the waltz, polka, mazurka, etc., of to-day, but frequently they were danced by several participants taking each other's hands and swinging around in a large circle.   These " Reigen " have descended to the children, in present days, and are of the most remote antiquity.   The dance of the Hebrews around the golden calf, the dance of the ancient Egyptians around the bull-god Apis, the dances of the old sun-worshippers, sometimes around a human sacrifice, all belong to this family.

Naturally enough, we find the most ancient dances in England to be those which the peasantry enjoyed. We have already seen one of these old dances in " Sellinger's Round."   (See Chapter III.)

Among the oldest dances in England we find one that is frequently alluded to by Shakespeare, — the morris-dance.   Antiquaries unite in the belief that this was one of the Spanish dances that arose during the Moorish possession in the middle ages.   Its name is derived from " Morisco," a Moor, and it is not very far removed from the Spanish fandango of the present. It was known in France in the fifteenth century, and was there called " Morisque." In England its character underwent a change, and it seems to have united with an earlier dance, a sort of panto-mime, in which the deeds of Robin Hood and his Merry Men were celebrated. There is good reason, therefore, to suppose that, in spite of the importation of the dance from France or Spain, in the morris-dance was preserved one of the oldest pantomimes of England. Allusions to the morris-dance are found as early as the reign of Henry VII. The chief characters in the early representations were Robin Hood, Maid Marian, and Friar Tuck. There was also sometimes a clown or fool, and of course a musi-cian or two to accompany the dance.

The morris-dance became indissolubly associated with the May-day festivities, in old England. The dancers in the morris frequently indulged in the effort to " dance each other down," so that the ex-ercise often became a trial of physical endurance. Such trials are very common in the folk-dances of various nations, as the jig, the halling, the kamar-inskaia, in Ireland, Norway, and Russia. The morris-dance was frequently a sort of progress by leaps and twirls, and we read of dancers keeping this up all the way from one town to another, as William Kemp did in 1599, making the journey from London to Norwich in four weeks and dancing the morris for nine days. This same William Kemp, or Kempe, concerns the Shakespearian nearly, for he is asserted to have been the original Dogberry, in "Much Ado About Nothing," and Peter, in "Romeo and Juliet." He made a trip to France to perfect his dancing. He was the most popular clown and comedian of Shakespeare's time, so much so that the author of the "Return from Parnassus" says that "he is not counted a gentleman that knows not Will Kempe." A song was written about him, which was set to music by no less a composer than Thomas Weelkes. It ran:

> "Since Robin Hood, Maid Marian,
>   And Little John are gone a;
> The Hobby-horse was quite forgot,
>   When Kempe did dance alone a.
> He did labour after the Tabor
> For to dance, then into France
> He took pains
> To skip it.
> In hope of gains
> He will trip it,
> On the toe
> Diddle do."

He was a favourite at court and probably a personal friend of Shakespeare.

As a good example of the morris-dance we here reproduce a famous one of the seventeenth century, and one that is alluded to by Shakespeare in "Love's

WILLIAM KEMPE.

Labour's Lost " (Act iv. Sc. 2) where Holofernes says to Jaquenetta : " Trip and go, my sweet," " Trip and Go " being the title of one of the cheeriest of morris-dances.

"TRIP AND GO."

(A 17th century Morris Dance.)

Trip and go, heave and hoe, Up and down, to and fro,

From the Town To the Grove Two and two Let us rove, A

may - ing, a play - ing, Love hath no gainsaying, So

trip and go, trip and go, Merrily trip and go.

Shakespeare also mentions the dance and its season, very effectively, in "All's Well That Ends Well" (Act ii. Sc. 2), where the clown speaks of the fitness of his answers to the countess:

"As fit as a pancake for Shrove Tuesday, or a morris for a May-day."

In "Henry V." (Act ii. Sc. 4), the Dauphin speaks of the boldness with which the French should proceed against the English, with the words:

"And let us do it with no show of fear;
    No, with no more than if we heard that England
    Were busied with a Whitsun morris-dance."

That the morris-dance was known to Shakespeare, and that he may have seen it danced, often enough, may be taken for granted.

Oliphant, in his "Musa Madrigalesca" (p. 71), quotes Laneham's letter to Humphrey Martin, Mercer, in London, concerning the festivities at Kenilworth, in 1575, before Queen Elizabeth, in which occurred a morris-dance.

"Thus they were marshalled: first all the lusty lads and bold Bachelors of the parish, sutablie every wight with his blue buckram bride-lace upon a branch of green broom (because Rosemary is scant there) tied on his left arm, (for on that side lies the heart) in martial order ranged on before, two and two in a rank; some with a hat, some in a cap; some a coat, some a jerkin; some for lightness in his doublet and hose; some boots and no spurs, some spurs and no boots, and some *neither nother*. Then the Bridegroom foremost, in his tawney worsted jacket (for his friends were fain that he *should* be a Bridegroom before the Queen,) and a fair strawn hat with a capital crown, steeplewise on his head.

"Well, sir, after these a lively Morris dance according to the ancient manner; six dancers, Maid Marian, and the Fool. Then three pretty puzels[1] as bright as a breast of bacon, of thirty year old apiece, that carried three special spice-cakes of a bushel of wheat, (they had it by measure out of my Lord's bakehouse,) before the bride, with set countenance, and lips so demurely simpering as it had been a mare cropping a thistle. After these comes a freckle-faced, red-headed lubber, whose office was to bear the bride-cup all seemly besilvered and parcel (partly) gilt, adorned with a beautiful bunch of broom gaily begilded *for memory*. This gentle cupbearer yet had his freckled phizonemy somewhat unhappily infested as he went, by the busy flies that flocked about the bride cup for the sweetness of the sucket that it savoured of; but he like a tall fellow, withstood them stoutly, beat them away, killed them by scores, stood to his charge, and marched on in good order. Then followed the worshipful bride, led (after the country manner) between two ancient parishioners, honest townsmen; a thirty-year-old, of colour brown bay, not very beautiful indeed, but ugly, foul, and ill favoured; yet marvellous fain of the office, because she heard say she should dance before the Queen, in which feat she thought she would foot it as finely as the best."

Many of the old dances were sung. The very word "ballad" may have been derived from *ballare* (Italian), to dance, and some of the old song-dances

---

[1] Maids — from the French *pucelle*.

were called "ballets."   In one of Morley's "ballets,"
Thyrsis and Chloris are described :

> ". . . They danced to and fro, and finely flaunted it,
> And then both met again, and thus they chaunted it."

One of Weelkes's refrains runs —

> " All shepherds in a ring,
> Shall dancing ever sing."

It must have been a pretty sight to watch the
singers giving expression, not only to the character
of the music, but also to the words which accompanied many (but by no means all) of the old dances,
and Bottom is not inaccurate in " Midsummer-Night's
Dream" (Act v. Sc. 2), when he invites the duke to
" hear a Bergomask dance."   As long ago as the
time of the troubadours and minnesingers there
were dances with poetry attached to them, and in
France, especially, these dances were often of the
most graceful description.   We give an example of
such a dance which was popular in France before
Shakespeare's time ; this dance probably became
known even in the English courts, for the romanesca was a species of galliard, a dance to which
Shakespeare alludes more than once.

But there were also dances of more boisterous
character, with words attached.   We have already
spoken of the great antiquity of the circle dances

LA ROMANESCA.

Air de Danse.

Alltto modto. (Metr: ♩ = 88).

Aux échos des bois, Aux soupirs du feuil-
When the woods are gay, And the zephyrs are

la - ge; Mélez, charmants hautbois, Un doux ra-mage;
sighing; Then let the oboes play, Sweet notes replying;

Et par vos accords, Sur la ver-te fou-ge - re   Attirez
Echoes shall awake, At the tone so entrancing   And swiftly

Piano.

la bergê-re Qu'appellent mes transports. Mon cœur plein d'elle,
then advancing My love her path shall take. My heart is beating,

Veut atten-drir, . . Son cœur re-belle,   Ou bien mou-
When she is nigh, . Should she be fleeting,   Then I shall

rir!   O Made - lei - ne,   Cède aux a-
die!   Oh heed my singing,   Nor pain pro-

mours : .. Le lierre au chè-ne   S'unit tou-jours.
voke : .. The i - vy cling-ing   Still loves the oak.

Qu'a ma chan-son Vol-tigeant en ca-den-ce,   Ton pied mi-
Let my fond song Your kind heart be entrancing,   Nor tarry

gnon Vienne a-nimer la dan-se ;   Et qu'en bondissant, Ton cor-
long But now join in the dancing ;   As we bound along, In the

animez.

sa - ge d'a-beil - le,   D'un trésor naissant Entr'ou-
dance gaily swinging,   Ech-oes of the song In our

vre la mer - veille   Pour le tendre sou-ci . . Qui m'en-
hearts shall be ringing With light and tripping feet   in the

trai - ne,   J'implo-re ta merci, ...   O ma
measure,   We'll love the dance so sweet, .   And its

chaî - ne,   Laisse l'amour   nous enchaî - neraus -
treas - ure,   And heart to heart   in its ca-dence shall

si! . . . .
beat! . . . .

decres.

e   rall.

which seem to have been the heritage of the peasantry in all ages and climes. In England, any dance in which the dancers stood in a circle was called a "round," or a "roundel," which may explain the words of Titania ("Midsummer Night's Dream," Act ii. Sc. 2), —

"Come, now a roundel and a fairy song," —

which does not mean that the fairies are to sing a round (more generally called a "catch" in Shakespeare's day), but that they were to dance a circular dance with a poem attached, which was to be sung by the dancers themselves.

"Twelfth Night" and "Much Ado About Nothing," are the two plays that have the most interesting and the most copious allusions to dancing, and these allusions are so detailed and exact that one cannot help suspecting that Shakespeare was an adept in the art. In "Twelfth Night" (Act i. Sc. 3), Sir Toby Belch grows rapturous over his friend (Sir Andrew Aguecheek) and his dancing:

"*Sir Andrew*. I'll stay a month longer. I am a fellow o' the strangest mind i' the world; I delight in masques and revels sometimes altogether.

Sir Toby. Art thou good at these kickshaws, knight?

Sir Andrew. As any man in Illyria, whatsoever he be, under the degree of my betters, and yet I will not compare with an old man.

Sir Toby. What is thy excellence in a galliard, knight?

Sir Andrew. 'Faith, I can cut a caper.

Sir Toby. And I can cut the mutton to 't.

Sir Andrew. And, I think, I have the back-trick, simply as strong as any man in Illyria.

Sir Toby. Wherefore are these things hid? wherefore have these gifts a curtain before them? are they like to take dust, like mistress Mall's picture? why dost thou not go to church in a galliard? and come home in a coranto? My very walk should be a jig! . . . What dost thou mean? is it a world to hide virtues in? I did think, by the excellent constitution of thy leg, it was formed under the star of a galliard.

Sir Andrew. Ay, 'tis strong, and does indifferent well in a flame-coloured stock. Shall we set about some revels?

Sir Toby. What shall we do else? were we not born under Taurus?

Sir Andrew. Taurus? that's sides and heart.

Sir Toby. No, sir; it is legs and thighs. Let me see thee caper: ha! higher: ha, ha! — excellent!　　　　[*Exeunt.*"

We have here an entire constellation of dances, many of which the reader can find in the English or French suites of Bach. The galliard, to begin with the first of the list, was a lively and rather difficult dance. In the first prefatory letter to Barnaby Rich's " Farewell to the Military Profession " (Shakespeare Soc. reprint, p. 4) we read :

"Our galliardes are so curious, that thei are not for my daunsyng for thei are so full of trickes and tournes, that he which hath no more but the plaine Singuepace is no better accumpted of than a verie bongler."

The galliard was generally in 3-4 rhythm; Prætorius describes it as —

" An invention of the devil; . . . full of shameful and obscene gestures and immodest movements."

As the dance came from Rome it was sometimes called the " Romanesca," but in Italy and in France it was less boisterous than it became in England, as may be seen by the specimen of " Romanesca " which we have reproduced.

In an unquotable passage belonging to the same scene, our arch-vagabond makes reference to the " sink-a-pace," which is the " cinq-pas " (five-step), and also Barnaby Rich's " Singuepace," quoted above. This is also alluded to in " Much Ado About Nothing " (Act ii. Sc. 1), where Beatrice says to Hero :

" The fault will be in the music, cousin, if you be not wooed in good time : if the prince be too important, tell him there is measure in every thing, and so dance out the answer. For hear me, Hero : Wooing, wedding, and repenting, is as a Scottish jig, a measure, and a cinque-pace : the first suit is hot and hasty, like a Scottish jig, full as fantastical ; the wedding mannerly-modest, as a measure full of state and ancientry ; and then comes repentance, and, with his bad legs, falls into the cinque-pace faster and faster, till he sink into his grave."

We have now a large collection of dances upon our hands, for, between Sir Toby and Beatrice, five important ones have been mentioned. The " cinque-pace," for thus it was often Anglicised, was quaintly syncopated, so that Beatrice's connection of it with the wobbly gait of old age is a peculiarly apt one.

The cinque-pace is said to have been the original of the galliard.

The "measure" was stately and elegant, not unlike in its motions to the grace of the minuet. It is possible that the term arose from the dance called "passa-mezzo," which was very graceful but not as slow as the pavane. In "Twelfth Night" (Act v. Sc. 1), Sir Toby alludes to both of these dances in a single sentence:

"After a passy-measure or a pavin I hate a drunken rogue."

The pavane was the stateliest of all the 4-4 dances, and one can readily understand the dissipated Sir Toby hating both the elegant dance and its statelier sister.

KING HARRY THE VIII'S PAVYN.

It was natural that Shakespeare should indulge in many a pun on the word "measure," and this dance is repeatedly spoken of. In "Love's Labour's Lost" (Act v. Sc. 2), a series of puns is made upon the dance and the other meanings of the word "measure."

" *Rosaline.*   What would they, say they?

Boyet.   Nothing but peace, and gentle visitation.

Rosaline.   Why, that they have: and bid them so be gone.

Boyet.   She says, you have it, and you may be gone.

King.   Say to her, we have measured many miles,
To tread a measure with her on this grass.

Boyet.   They say that they have measured many a mile
To tread a measure with you on this grass.

Rosaline.   It is not so: ask them, how many inches
Is in one mile: if they have measured many,
The measure then of one is easily told.

Boyet.   If, to come hither, you have measured miles
And many miles; the princess bids you tell,
How many inches do fill up one mile.

Biron.   Tell her, we measure them by weary steps."

The same pun is made by the queen in "Richard II." Act iii. Sc. 4.

The coranto, or courante, may be found as the second dance in all of the suites of Bach and in many of those of Handel. It was a rapidly running dance, generally in 3-4 or in 3-8 rhythm.

The jig, or gigue, used by the old suite composers as the finale of this cycle form, was the most widely known dance of all, among the peasantry of every country. It existed from Spain (where there was also a slow gigue called the loure) to England and Ireland. The so-called Scotch jig had the wild impetuosity which we associate to-day with the Irish jig. One characteristic of this dance was its groups of three notes each, which suited best to 6-8 rhythm, although 12-8 and 3-8 were not impossible. Almost every period ended with a hearty stamp, and the jig became a test of endurance, as the morris-dance had been before it. The jig may be classed as the most rollicking and hearty of all the dances. Beatrice defines it correctly when she calls it " hot and hasty."

The jumping and capering which Sir Toby demands of Sir Andrew is characteristic of the English dancing of the olden days, activity counting for much more than grace in almost all the early dances.

In " Love's Labour's Lost " (Act iii. Sc. 1), we have another series of dances alluded to, and again are reminded of the singing to one's own dancing.

"*Armado.* Warble, child; make passionate my sense of hearing.

    Moth. ' Concolinel — '[1]   [*Singing.*

    Armado. Sweet air! — Go, tenderness of years; take this key, give enlargement to the swain, bring him festinately hither. I must employ him in a letter to my love.

    Moth. Master, will you win your love with a French brawl?

    Armado. How mean'st thou? brawling in French?

    Moth. No, my complete master: but to jig off a tune at the tongue's end, canary to it with your feet, humour it with turning up your eye-lids; sigh a note, and sing a note; some-

[1] This " Concolinel " is one of the mysteries of Shakespeare. It may be an old refrain or burden, but we can only guess at its meaning. " Bonnibel " (from the French " Bonne et Belle ") was often used as a refrain; which may have some connection with the subject.

time through the throat, as if you swallowed love with singing love; sometime through the nose, as if you snuffed up love by smelling love."

The brawl was the English spelling of the French *branle*. It was a dance in which the figures executed by the leading couple were imitated by a line of their followers; many of the mediæval dances were of this imitative character, and it is possible that the branle had a remote origin.

The canary was a species of gigue, quicker than the loure, yet slower than the true jig. Its rhythm was generally 3-8 or 6-8.

One of the Shakespearian allusions to the combination of singing and dancing brings back a melody which we have already met with, — the "Light o' Love." — ("Much Ado About Nothing," Act iii. Sc. 4).

> "*Beatrice*.   Good morrow, sweet Hero.
> *Hero*.   Why, how now! do you speak in the sick tune?
> *Beatrice*.   I am out of all other tune, methinks.
> *Margaret*.   Clap us into — ' Light o' love;' that goes without a burden; do you sing it, and I'll dance it.
> *Beatrice*.   Yea, ' Light o' love,' with your heels!"

Regarding the names of the dances quoted above, we may state that the galliard came from the word "gay;" the pavane from "pavone," a peacock; the branle from the French *branler*, to sway from side to side; courante from *courir*, to run; canary from the name of the islands, and gigue from *Geige*, the German name for the fiddle.

There is another, and an essentially English dance, that is spoken of by Shakespeare in a very graphic manner. The passage occurs in " Winter's Tale" (Act iv. Sc. 2), where the clown complains of the many commissions that he must carry out for his sister for the sheep-shearing festival.

" *Clown.* I cannot do't without counters. — Let me see ; what am I to buy for our sheep-shearing feast? Three pound of sugar; five pound of currants; rice, — What will this sister of mine do with rice? But my father hath made her mistress of the feast and she lays it on. She hath made me four-and-twenty nosegays for the shearers : three-man song-men all, and very good ones; but they are most of them means and bases : but one Puritan amongst them, and he sings psalms to hornpipes."

We have here the right dance in the wrong country ; one would as soon find Shakespeare's celebrated " seacoast in Bohemia " as discover any hornpipes there. The hornpipe is an ancient English dance. In old England, centuries ago, the shepherds used to play upon a long wooden pipe, which instrument gave rise to the much more developed English horn of the modern orchestra. The name of this ancient instru·ment, the horn-pipe, was transferred to the favourite dance of the shepherds, which was played upon it. The hornpipe had some of the characteristics of the jig and of the brawl. It ended with a stamping effect not unlike the conclusion of each period in a properly constructed jig.

Nowadays the hornpipe is considered especially a sailor's dance, but this was not the case in Shakespeare's time, nor in the century after, as one can readily perceive by examining the tune of " The British Grenadiers " (which is a hornpipe melody) or the brilliant hornpipe which ends Handel's " Concerto Grosso, No. 7," a work which is still occasionally heard in our chamber concerts. Before leaving the above quotation about the hornpipe we may notice the fact that the chorus was troubled then, as now, by a lack of high voices ; most of the singers are " means and bases." Regarding the " three-men song-men " we shall have more to say hereafter.

There was another composition, alluded to by Shakespeare, which was sometimes danced and sometimes sung without dancing, and even occasionally played as an instrumental composition. This was the " dump," which was slow and melancholy, and gave rise to the modern saying, " In the dumps," *i. e.* in melancholy mood.

It is probably the dump that Thomas Ford refers to, when he speaks (in 1607) of " pavens, galiards, almaines, toies, jiggs, *thumpes*, and such like." Steevens, the eminent Shakespearian commentator, considers the dump to have been an old Italian dance. Naylor, "Shakespeare and Music," page 23, defines it thus :

" The dumpe (from Swedish dialect, *dumpa*, to dance awkwardly) was a slow, mournful dance."

We may, however, suggest another etymology in this case, since the melody is supposed to come from southern Europe, and was sometimes a sorrowful tune without dancing; the Bohemian "dumka" fulfils all the demands of the dump, in that it is an elegy, is sometimes combined with dramatic action that may be called dancing, and is the saddest music imaginable. Some of the dumkas written by Dvorak, and used even in his symphonies, are sufficient proof that the dumka does not differ at all from the dump.

FIRST PERIOD OF "LADY CAREY'S DUMP."
(About 1600.)

Naturally Shakespeare alludes freely enough to such a characteristic melody. We have already quoted Proteus's advice to Thurio ("Two Gentlemen of Verona," Act iii. Sc. 2) to "tune a deploring dump," and Peter's paradox ("Romeo and Juliet," Act iv. Sc. 5), when he begs the musicians, "Oh, play some merry dump to comfort me," neither of which examples suggests dancing. We give an example of the character of the dump as well as of the pavane in Shakespeare's time.

All of the dances described above were freely danced in England by all conditions of men and women. In England and in the northern countries of continental Europe, even the aristocracy often indulged in the lively as well as in the more stately dances, and indeed generally seemed to prefer the former. In France, Italy, and Spain this was not the case, and the higher classes executed only the more elegant or more dignified dances.

Brandt, in his "Ship of Fools," speaks of the universal indulgence in dancing, as follows :

> "To it comes children, maydes, and wives,
> And flatering yonge men to see to have their pray,
> The hande in hande great falshode oft contrives,
> The old quean also this madness will assay ;
> And the olde dotarde, though he scantly may,
> For age and lamenes styrre eyther foote or hande,
> Yet playeth he the foole with other in the bande."

The last four lines at once bring up the picture of Sir Andrew Aguecheek ; it is evident that Shakespeare's portrait is not an overdrawn one.

A mode of entertainment, which combined dancing with pantomimic action and sometimes even with words which were spoken or sung, was the masque. Shylock's diatribe against masques ("Merchant of Venice," Act ii. Sc 5.) will be remembered, and has already been quoted in connection with the "wry-necked fife," but Shakespeare not only has many other allusions to this mode of entertainment, but actually introduced it complete upon his stage, in connection with his plays, as, for example, in "The Tempest," in "Timon of Athens," etc. (see Chapter XIII.).

"THE KYNG'S MASKE."

SARABAND.   Undoubtedly the Masque Music of Henry VIII.

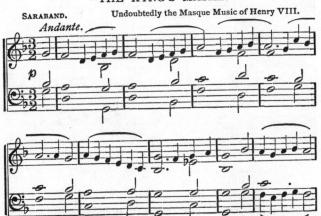

The description by Bacon, in Chapter I. of this
volume, may give the best idea of what these pageants were like.   The masque preceded the opera,

and probably came to England from Italy, although the latter country changed to opera immediately upon the invention of that kind of entertainment (1594–1600), while the chief masques of England were performed at a later epoch, the opera not being known in England during Shakespeare's lifetime.

According to Hall's "Chronicle" the first masque performed in England was at Greenwich, in 1512, "after the maner of Italie," and Holinshed says that there was not only a masque but a good comedy of Plautus performed in 1520. In 1530 a masque was performed in Whitehall. Burney, in his "History of Music" (Vol. III. p. 346), says :

"It is recorded in the folio edition of Ben Jonson's works, printed in 1640, that in 1617 his whole masque which was performed at the house of Lord Hay, for the entertainment of the French ambassador, was set to music after the Italian manner by Nic Laniere, who also painted the scenes."

Ferrabosco, Coperario, and other Italian masters set music to the early masques, and the English composers at once followed so good an example, such composers as Byrd, Robert Johnson, William and Henry Lawes, and a host of others setting Ben Jonson, Milton, Shakespeare, etc., to music in this form, a primitive opera without the recitative declamation which afterward obtained. No less a person than Inigo Jones designed the costumes and invented the machinery for some of the pageants. A masque given by the four Inns of Court, in London, in 1633, cost more than a thousand pounds. After the Restoration the masque seems to have degenerated into a mere fancy dress ball or masquerade.

Shakespeare's employment of the masque was quite in line with the taste of his time, which desired every species of pageant upon the stage. If the scenery was sadly deficient in the Shakespeare theatre, this was made up by the splendour of some of the costumes and the ingenuity of the machinery. Of this, however, we shall speak more at length in a later chapter.

Not only was dancing introduced in the Shakespearian plays, but even between the acts, and after the last act, some species of Terpsichorean revelry was added to the dramatic entertainment,[1] very much as the ballet is interpolated in operatic performances in Paris at present.

Only once does Shakespeare mention that round dance which the rustics loved, — the hay. It is in "Love's Labour's Lost" (Act v. Sc. 1) that Dull says :

"I'll make one in a dance or so; or I will play upon a tabor to the worthies, and let them dance the hay."

The hay, as well as the morris-dance, was associated with May-day festivities ; in fact, all kinds of

[1] See Chapter XIII.

musical and Terpsichorean sport were indulged in on that day, as may be judged from the following quotation from Spenser's "Shepherds' Calendar" (Eclogue v.) :

> " Siker this morrow, no longer ago,
> I saw a shole of shepherds outgo
> With singing, and shouting, and jolly cheer ;
> Before them yode a lusty Tabrere,
> That to the many a horn-pipe play'd,
> Whereto they dancen each one with his maid.
> To see these folks make such jouissance,
> Made my heart after the pipe to dance.
> Then to the greenwood they speeden them all,
> To fetchen home May with their musical :
> And home they bring him in a royal throne
> Crowned as king ; and his queen attone
> Was Lady Flora, on whom did attend
> A fair flock of fairies, and a fresh bend
> Of lovely nymphs — O that I were there,
> To helpen the ladies their May bush to bear ! "

We can sum up the style of the English dancing and its musical adjuncts with a quotation from an old pamphlet (1609), which says :

" The Courts of Kings for stately measures, the City for light heels and nimble footing ; Western men for gambols ; Middlesex men for tricks above ground ; Essex men for the Hey ; Lancashire for Hornpipes ; Worcestershire for Bagpipes ; but Herefordshire for a Morris dance, puts down not only all Kent, but very near three quarters of Christendom if one had line enough to measure it." (" Old Meg of Herefordshire for a Maid Marian.")

But it must be added that these " stately measures "
of the aristocracy, whether in England, Poland, Italy,
France, or any important European court, were
chiefly processional, and consisted in the dancers
imitating the steps and gestures of the first couple,
which explains Beatrice saying to Benedick (" Much
Ado About Nothing," Act ii. Sc. 2) : " We must
follow the leaders ! "

CHAPTER VIII.

In this chapter we propose to leave for awhile the technical references to music with which Shakespeare teems, and study the tributes which the poet has given to the art in general, the praises which he brings to it, and the enthusiasm which it evidently excites in him. Here the poet appeals not only to the musician, but to every person whose culture or refined instinct enables him to vibrate responsive to artistic beauty.

Perhaps no greater tribute to the power of music can be found than in Shakespeare's presentation of the psychical side of a character by its appreciation, half-appreciation, or non-appreciation of the art. The superficial critic will at once seize upon the well-known lines at the end of the following scene ("Merchant of Venice," Act v. Sc. 1), as the sum of it all:

"*Lorenzo.*   Why should we go in?
My friend Stephano, signify, I pray you,
Within the house, your mistress is at hand;
And bring you music forth into the air. —   [*Exit Stephano.*
How sweet the moonlight sleeps upon this bank!
Here will we sit, and let the sounds of music
Creep in our ears; soft stillness, and the night,
Become the touches of sweet harmony.
Sit, Jessica: Look, how the floor of heaven
Is thick inlaid with patines of bright gold;
There's not the smallest orb, which thou behold'st,
But in his motion like an angel sings,
Still quiring to the young-eyed cherubims:
Such harmony is in immortal souls;
But, whilst this muddy vesture of decay
Doth grossly close it in, we cannot hear it. —

Enter Musicians.

Come, ho, and wake Diana with a hymn;
With sweetest touches pierce your mistress' ear,
And draw her home with music.

   Jessica.   I am never merry, when I hear sweet music.
                                                              [*Music.*

   Lorenzo.   The reason is, your spirits are attentive:
For do but note a wild and wanton herd,
Or race of youthful and unhandled colts,
Fetching mad bounds, bellowing, and neighing loud,
Which is the hot condition of their blood;
If they but hear perchance a trumpet sound,
Or any air of music touch their ears,
You shall perceive them make a mutual stand,
Their savage eyes turn'd to a modest gaze,
By the sweet power of music: Therefore, the poet
Did feign, that Orpheus drew trees, stones, and floods;
Since nought so stockish, hard, and full of rage,

But music for the time doth change his nature :
The man that hath no music in himself,
Nor is not moved with concord of sweet sounds,
Is fit for treasons, stratagems, and spoils ;
The motions of his spirit are dull as night,
And his affections dark as Erebus :
Let no such man be trusted. — Mark the music."

We are not disposed to regard the last six lines of this sentence as absolute statement of fact ; it must be borne in mind that this sentiment is given to one of Shakespeare's lovers, and by no means the greatest of his kind. It is Lorenzo's ecstatic praise of music that we hear, and the poet has, perhaps purposely, made it somewhat extreme. The extravagant use made by commentators of this passage aroused the ire of one of the Shakespearian editors. Steevens, in commenting on the scene, bursts forth with this violent diatribe :

"The present passage, which is neither pregnant with physical and moral truth, nor poetically beautiful in an eminent degree, has constantly enjoyed the good fortune to be repeated by those whose inhospitable memories would have refused to admit or retain any other sentiment or description of the same author, however exalted or just. The truth is that it furnishes the vacant fiddler with something to say in defence of his profession, and supplies the coxcomb in music with an invective against such as do not pretend to discover all the various powers of language in inarticulate sounds."

It is in this connection that Steevens calls the sentence a "capricious sentiment," and intimates that Shakespeare only employed it to curry favour with his audience, with whom music was a fashion.

The attack is so extreme, especially as coming from the editor of the greatest music-lover among poets, that Furness (Variorum Edition, Vol. VII. p. 252) ventures to doubt its authenticity. Furness says:

> "It is difficult to decide, as we have had more than once to note, whether Steevens is in jest or earnest. I am by no means sure but that this attack on music was not a trap, whereby to lure some honest Goodman Dull into a defence of it."

One feels loath to differ from the most eminent of all Shakespearians, but such jesting would utterly unfit Steevens for any task like that of commentation, where not to be clear and reliable would be the deadliest of sins.[1] If, however, he intended a trap, he has caught plenty of victims, for a torrent of indignation was the result, — a torrent which has not spent its force even in the present day.

But it may be borne in mind that Shakespeare pictures Othello (Act iii. Sc. 1) as being averse to music, as may be seen from the following:

---

[1] The reader will find another anti-musical quotation from Steevens in Chapter X., which tends still further to discredit Furness's lenient suggestion.

> "*Enter* Cassio *and some Musicians.*
>
> *Cassio.* Masters, play here, I will content your pains.
> Something that's brief; and bid — good morrow, general.
>
> [*Music.*
>
> *Enter* Clown.
>
> *Clown.* Why, masters, have your instruments been at
> Naples, that they speak i' the nose thus?
> *Musicians.* How, sir, how?
>
> . . . .
>
> *Clown.* But, masters, here's money for you: and the gen-
> eral so likes your music, that he desires you, of all your loves,
> to make no more noise with it.
> *First Musician.* Well, sir, we will not.
> *Clown.* If you have any music that may not be heard, to't
> again: but, as they say, to hear music, the general does not
> greatly care.
> *First Musician.* We have none such, sir.
> *Clown.* Then put up your pipes in your bag, for I'll
> away: Go; vanish into air; away. [*Exeunt Musicians.*"

And, like the impetuous and tropical Othello, the courageous and impatient Harry Hotspur cares nothing
for the art; indeed, the second example is more pronounced than the first, for Othello "did not greatly
care" for music, while Percy evidently detests it, judging by the following citation from the first scene
of the third act of " Henry IV." (First Part).

> "*Glendower.* I can speak English, lord, as well as you;
> For I was train'd up in the English court:
> Where, being but young, I fram'd to the harp
> Many an English ditty, lovely well,
> And gave the tongue a helpful ornament:

A virtue that was never seen in you.

   Hotspur.   Marry, and I'm glad of it with all my heart;
I had rather be a kitten, and cry — mew,
Than one of these same metre ballad-mongers:
I had rather hear a brazen can'stick turn'd,
Or a dry wheel grate on an axle-tree;
And that would set my teeth nothing on edge.
Nothing so much as mincing poetry:
'Tis like the forced gait of a shuffling nag."

Yet the same citation shows, by the musical gifts of Glendower, that Shakespeare deemed musical appreciation or ability not incompatible with bravery and military prowess.[1]

Not all of those who care nothing for music are "fit for treason, stratagem, and spoils,"[2] for there is a very respectable list of notabilities who were tone-deaf. Among these we may mention Tennyson, Charles Lamb, Addison, Doctor Johnson (who thought it necessary to apologise for Shakespeare's love of music), Dean Swift, and a host of others. But Shakespeare seems to intimate, at least, that a lack of musical appreciation is to be viewed with suspicion, for in "Julius Cæsar" (Act i. Sc. 2)

---

[1] Note also Lucentio's definition of the use of music ("Taming of the Shrew," Act iii. Sc. 1), quoted in Chapter III., beginning "Preposterous ass," for a lesser estimate of music.

[2] Closely akin to the Shakespearian line, is that quoted by Morley (1598); he says: "I ever held this sentence of the poet as a canon of my creed, — That whom God loveth not, they love not Musick."

Cæsar speaks of a dislike of plays and of music as being one of his causes of distrust of Cassius.

" *Cæsar.* Let me have men about me that are fat;
Sleek-headed men, and such as sleep o' nights :
'Yond Cassius has a lean and hungry look;
He thinks too much : such men are dangerous.
    Antonius. Fear him not, Cæsar, he's not dangerous;
He is a noble Roman, and well given.
    Cæsar. Would he were fatter : — But I fear him not:
Yet if my name were liable to fear,
I do not know the man I should avoid
So soon as that spare Cassius. He reads much;
He is a great observer, and he looks
Quite through the deeds of men : he loves no plays,
As thou dost, Antony : he hears no music."

It is a point worth noting that, whenever Shakespeare points his jests at music, he is sure to bring forth some of his most earnest tributes to the art in the same play. "Twelfth Night," as may be seen in other chapters, is full of the ribald side of music, yet no play is richer in earnest musical allusions. The very first lines of this comedy are devoted to a eulogy of music.

" ACT. I.

SCENE I. *An Apartment in the Duke's Palace.*

Enter DUKE, CURIO, Lords ; Musicians *attending.*

    Duke. If music be the food of love, play on,
Give me excess of it ; that, surfeiting,
The appetite may sicken, and so die. —

> That strain again — it had a dying fall :
> O, it came o'er my ear like the sweet sound
> That breathes upon a bank of violets,
> Stealing, and giving odour. — Enough ; no more :
> 'Tis not so sweet now, as it was before."

The last word of the fifth line of the above has set the commentators by the ears, for many prefer to read it as " south " (*i. e.* the south wind), which is the more poetical metaphor, but seems to find no good warrant in the original edition. We owe the altered reading — " the sweet south " — to Pope. Rowe would have us read " the sweet wind ; " Steevens gives his adhesion to " south," and thinks that the passage might have been inspired by a similar tribute to the southwest wind in Sydney's " Arcadia ; " Knight and White agree in choosing " sound," and it is worth noticing that Shakespeare nowhere gives any laudation of the south wind, but connects it with fog, rain, and bad weather. The subject is not within our province, yet we may cite the above opinions as an instance of one of the many battles that have been fought over Shakespearian texts.

Fortunately, the rest of the citation is easy of definition, for " dying fall " means only a cadence played diminuendo. Bacon, in his " Sylva Sylvarum," speaks of a " fall from a discord to a concord."

To return to our musical tributes ; we need not as

yet leave " Twelfth Night." In Act ii. Sc. 4, our ducal music-lover again bursts forth in praise of the art.

> " *Duke.* Give me some music. — Now, good morrow, friends. —
>
> Now, good Cesario, but that piece of song,
> That old and antique song we heard last night;
> Methought it did relieve my passion much;
> More than light airs and recollected terms,
> Of these most brisk and giddy-pacéd times: —
> Come, but one verse.
>
>   *Curio.* He is not here, so please your lordship, that should sing it.
>
>   *Duke.* Who was it?
>
>   *Curio.* Feste, the jester, my lord; a fool, that the lady Olivia's father took much delight in; he is about the house.
>
>   *Duke.* Seek him out, and play the tune the while.
>
>   [*Exit Curio. — Music.*
>
> Come hither, boy: If ever thou shalt love,
> In the sweet pangs of it, remember me:
> For, such as I am, all true lovers are;
> Unstaid and skittish in all motions else,
> Save in the constant image of the creature
> That is beloved. — How dost thou like this tune?
>
>   *Viola.* It gives a very echo to the seat
> Where love is throned."

When Feste, the most important and musical of Shakespeare's clowns, enters, there is further musical comment:

> " *Re-enter* CURIO *and* Clown.
>
>   *Duke.* O fellow, come, the song we had last night! —
> Mark it, Cesario; it is old and plain.

The spinsters and the knitters in the sun,
And the free maids, that weave their thread with bones,
Do use to chant it; it is silly sooth,
And dallies with the innocence of love,
Like the old age.

    Clown. Are you ready, sir?
    Duke. Ay; pr'ythee, sing.   [*Music.*

SONG.[1]

   Clown. ' Come away, come away, death,
        And in sad cypress let me be laid;
         Fly away, fly away, breath;
        I am slain by a fair, cruel maid.
        My shroud of white, stuck all with yew,
            O prepare it;
        My part of death no one so true
            Did share it.

        Not a flower, not a flower sweet,
        On my black coffin let there be strewn:
         Not a friend, not a friend greet
        My poor corpse, where my bones shall be thrown:
        A thousand thousand sighs to save,
            Lay me, O, where
        Sad true lover ne'er find my grave,
            To weep there.'

   Duke. There's for thy pains.
   Clown. No pains, sir; I take pleasure in singing, sir.
   Duke. I'll pay thy pleasure then.
   Clown. Truly, sir, and pleasure will be paid, one time or
another."

---

   [1] The original setting of this important song is unfortunately
lost.

Again, however, we find a stumbling-block. "Recollected terms" makes a very dubious meaning. If, as Knight suggests, the word "tunes" be substituted, the passage is easy of comprehension. White believes that the phrase means carefully studied expressions, which is rather far-fetched. It is possible (although we broach the new reading with diffidence) that the word is "re-collected," which would imply second-hand, used over terms.

The cry for "the old age," *i. e.* "the good old times," is quaint enough, coming so long ago. Yet one can find the same thought expressed much before Shakespeare's time, for Aristophanes, a half-dozen centuries before our era, also cried out for "the good old times;" in fact, Adam and Eve seem to be the only parties who did not compare the past with the present, to the disadvantage of the latter.

Cleopatra (Act ii. Sc. 5) speaks of music as the —

> "moody food
> Of us that trade in love," —

and, by the way, directly after, invites Charmian to a game of billiards, a little more than a thousand years before anything like billiards was invented! But Cleopatra defies chronology, and desires her stays cut at a time when they did not exist!

It may be regarded as one of the æsthetic points

of Shakespeare, that he describes the musician's mel-
ancholy.   The passage is found in "As You Like
It" (Act iv. Sc. 1), and is spoken by the cynical
Jaques:

> "I have neither the scholar's melancholy, which is emula-
> tion; nor the musician's, which is fantastical; nor the court-
> ier's, which is proud; nor the soldier's, which is ambitious;
> nor the lawyer's, which is politic; nor the lady's, which is
> nice; nor the lover's, which is all these."

Naturally so poetic a nature as that of Shakespeare
would speak of evening as music's most fitting frame.
In "The Merchant of Venice" (Act v. Sc. 1), Portia
speaks to Nerissa of this fitness:

> "Music! hark!
> *Nerissa.*   It is your music, madam, of the house.
> *Portia.*   Nothing is good, I see, without respect;
> Methinks, it sounds much sweeter than by day.
> *Nerissa.*   Silence bestows that virtue on it, madam.
> *Portia.*   The crow doth sing as sweetly as the lark,
> When neither is attended; and, I think,
> The nightingale, if she should sing by day,
> When every goose is cackling, would be thought
> No better a musician than the wren.
> How many things by season season'd are
> To their right praise, and true perfection! —
> Peace, hoa! the moon sleeps with Endymion,
> And would not be awak'd!   [*Music ceases.*"

And in "Much Ado About Nothing" (Act ii. Sc.
3), Claudio voices very nearly the same sentiment.

"*Don Pedro.* Come, shall we hear this music?
    Claudio. Yea, my good lord : — How still the evening is,
As hush'd on purpose to grace harmony ! "

The music of the sea does not escape the genius of
our great poet. He does not, to be sure, go as far as
Walt Whitman, with his stirring lines :

" To-day a rude and brief recitative
Of ships sailing the seas,
Each with its special flag or ship signal,
Of unnamed heroes in the ships,
Of waves spreading and spreading, far as the eye can reach,
Of dashing spray, and the winds piping and blowing ;
And out of these a song for the sailors of all nations ;
Fitful, like a surge."

Nevertheless, "The Tempest" has many allusions
to marine music, of better character and more refined
style than the broad bacchanalian touches which are
found in that great work ; Oberon, too, in "Midsummer Night's Dream" (Act ii. Sc. 1), speaks of the
music of the sea :

" My gentle Puck, come hither: Thou remember'st
    Since once I sat upon a promontory,
    And heard a mermaid, on a dolphin's back,
    Uttering such a dulcet and harmonious breath,
    That the rude sea grew civil at her song ;
    And certain stars shot madly from their spheres,
    To hear the sea-maid's music."

And in the "Comedy of Errors" (Act iii. Sc. 2), we
find the lines :

"O, train me not, sweet mermaid, with thy note,
    To drown me in thy sister's flood of tears;
Sing, syren, for thyself, and I will dote:
    Spread o'er the silver waves thy golden hairs."

Naturally, too, the music of the spheres is mentioned more than once by Shakespeare, who lived in an epoch which held to the derivation of the symmetry of music from natural causes. In "Twelfth Night" (Act iii. Sc. 1), Olivia says to the supposed Cesario (Viola) that she would rather hear his suit "than music from the spheres;" in "Antony and Cleopatra," the heroine speaks of the Antony she had dreamed of:

"His voice was propertied
    As all the tunéd spheres, and that to friends;
But when he meant to quail and shake the orb,
    He was as rattling thunder."

In "Pericles" (Act v. Sc. 1), the following allusion to the music of the spheres is found:

"*Pericles.*   But what music?
    Pelicanus.   My lord, I hear none.
    Pericles.   None?
The music of the spheres: list, my Marina.
    Lysimachus.   It is not good to cross him; give him way.
    Pericles.   Rarest sounds!
Do ye not hear?
    Lysimachus.   Music? my lord, I hear —
    Pericles.   Most heavenly music;
It nips me unto list'ning, and thick slumber
Hangs on mine eyelids; let me rest.   [*He sleeps.*"

In "As You Like It" (Act ii. Sc. 5), Duke, senior, says of Jaques:

> " If he, compact of jars, grows musical,
>   We shall have shortly discord in the spheres."

The theory of the music made by the motions of the planets had its origin in ancient Egypt, where music was closely connected with astronomy. Pythagoras, pupil of the Egyptian priests, stole their theories and promulgated them in Greece as his own, whence the music of the spheres was generally known as a Pythagorean theory. The earliest notes used in ancient Greece, about six centuries before Christ, were the planetary signs, the sun being the central and controlling note. In the sixteenth century more than one system was built upon this poetic idea. The author possesses an old edition of the works of Zarlino (1562), wherein not only diagrams of the proportions of the spheres are applied to music, but even the tempo is sought for in nature, the Italian writer suggesting that the speed of music be counted by the *pulse of a healthy man!*

Among the various tributes to the power of music which we have culled, we find one, however, which intimates that this power can be employed either for good or evil. It will be noted that this description of the art occurs in connection with a song. The scene occurs in " Measure for Measure," at the beginning of the fourth act.

" MARIANA *discovered sitting; a boy singing.*

SONG.

' Take, oh take those lips away,
    That so sweetly were forsworn;
And those eyes, the break of day,
    Lights that do mislead the morn:
But my kisses bring again,
                    bring again,
    Seals of love, but seal'd in vain,
                    seal'd in vain.'

Mariana.   Break off thy song, and haste thee quick away;
Here comes a man of comfort, whose advice
Hath often still'd my brawling discontent.   [*Exit boy.*

Enter DUKE.

I cry you mercy, sir ; and well could wish,
You had not found me here so musical :
Let me excuse me, and believe me so, —
My mirth it much displeased, but pleased my woe.
    Duke.   'Tis good : though music oft hath such a charm,
To make bad good, and good provoke to harm."

The apology for being musical, the statement that music can pervert good into evil, is very different from the Shakespeare of the foregoing musical eulogies. Music can become evil only by association with improper words or vicious surroundings. The *cancan* from Offenbach's " Belle Helene," might bring up evil associations in the mind of any one familiar with that opera, but it would suggest only innocent hilarity, gradually growing into frenzy, to a person who knew it simply as instrumental music. There is no instrumental music that can be considered harmful *per se*. That the reader may judge of the song which moved the duke to so peculiar an arraignment of music, we reprint the early setting of the poem by Dr. John Wilson.[1] There is strong reason to suppose that this music was used upon the stage in "Measure for Measure" during the lifetime of Shakespeare.

TAKE THOSE LIPS AWAY.

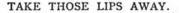

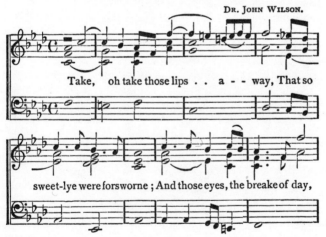

Take, oh take those lips . . a - - way, That so

sweet-lye were forsworne ; And those eyes, the breake of day,

---

[1] Possibly this is the "Jack Wilson" spoken of in "Twelfth Night." (See Variorum Edition, Furness.)

Lights, that do mis-leade the morne : But my kiss - es

bring againe, Seales of love, but seal'd in vaine.

CHAPTER IX.

The Bacchanalian Music of Shakespeare — Early English Drinking-songs — Skelton's Ale-song —Tavern Life and Customs —
Catches — Ancient Rounds — " Three-men's Songs."

THE era of drinking-songs did not begin with
Shakespeare, nor did they end with his time; if the
reader will consult Ritson's famous "Collection of
English Songs" he will find English drinking-songs
of all epochs and styles.   Probably the oldest English drinking-song of any literary merit is to be found
in "A ryght pithy, pleasaunt and merie comedie;
intytuled Gammer Gurton's Nedle.   London 1575."
This wild song (by no means the basest of the
author's licentious writings) was probably written
by the John Skelton referred to in Chapter V.
Scott has, we think erroneously, attributed the song
to John Still ; it was originally marked " by Mr. S."
and there is little doubt but this vague signature
referred to the man most capable, at this epoch, of
producing such an effusion.   The drinking-song, which
was the prototype of many that followed, ran thus :

"Backe and syde go bare, go bare,
 Both foote and hande go colde :

But bellye, God sende thee good ale ynoughe,
Whether it be newe or olde.
I cannot eat but lytle meate,
My stomacke is not good,
But sure I thinke that I can drinke
With him that weares a hood.

" Thoughe I go bare, take ye no care,
  I am nothinge acolde ;
  I stuff my skyn so full within,
  Of joly good ale and olde.
    Backe and syde go bare, go bare, etc.

" I love no rost, but a nut-browne toste,
  And a crab laid in the fyre ;
  A little breade shall do me stead,
  Much breade I not desyre.
  No frost nor snow, nor winde I trowe,
  Can hurte mee if I wolde ;
  I am so wrapt, and throwly lapt,
  Of joly good ale and olde.
    Backe and syde go bare, go bare, etc.

" And Tyb my wyfe, that as her lyfe,
  Loveth well good ale to seeke ;
  Full oft drynkes shee, tyll ye may see
  The teares run downe her cheeke ;
  Then doth shee trowle to mee the bowle,
  Even as a mault-worme shuld ;
  And sayth, sweete hart, I tooke my part
  Of this joly good ale and olde.
    Backe and syde go bare, go bare, etc.

" Now let them drynke, till they nod and winke,
  Even as good felowes shoulde doe :

> They shall not mysse to have the blisse,
> Good ale doth bringe men to.
> And all poore soules that have scowred boules,
> Or have them lustely trolde,
> God save the lyves of them and their wyves,
> Whether they be yonge or olde.
>   Backe and syde go bare, go bare, etc."

There is little doubt but that Shakespeare enjoyed this branch of literature. At Stratford-on-Avon the visitor is shown a chair whereon the poet is said to have sat at the tavern and joined in the jovial singing there. Vicar Ward's account (first made public fifty years after the event), that —

" Shakespeare, Drayton and Ben Jonson had a merrie meeting, and it seems drank too hard, for Shakespeare died of a feavour ther contracted," —

may or may not be true, but such an event would not be greatly out of character with the times nor with the company which Shakespeare enjoyed, the rollicking Bohemian circle of Elizabethan and Jacobean days. Cowley died, subsequently, from about the same cause, and his boon companions were of much more dignified station.

If Shakespeare did not copy his drinking-songs from Skelton, he gave to his clowns and vagabonds a certain device which one can find in the earlier poet, — the habit of throwing in the refrain or a line from a catch or song here and there. We find this custom used in Skelton's "Moral Plays." a good half-century before the poet's days.

If Shakespeare was familiar with the tavern at Stratford-on-Avon, he was probably still more so with the taverns in London, for these were not merely places of refreshment, but became the clubs of the time, as the coffee-houses were at a later period, houses where friend met friend, a rendezvous of social intercourse. At the Mermaid Tavern, in Bread Street, many of the poets and dramatists of the epoch were wont to congregate, and, although we can find no distinct record of the fact, it is extremely probable that Shakespeare often formed one of the gathering. Most minute are the details which Shakespeare gives us of the life in these resorts.

The jests were not always of the highest order in these taverns, and a practical joke was prized above almost any other form of wit. On the wall there was often a picture of two asses' heads, or fools' heads with cap and bells, with a legend of "We be three," or "When shall we three meet again?" In "Twelfth Night" (Act ii. Sc. 3), the clown Feste asks of Sir Toby, "Did you never see the picture of 'we three'?" and Sir Toby at once catches the implied meaning, responding, "Welcome, ass!" as the guests in the tavern did when any simpleton inquired for the third ass spoken of in the inscription, yet invisible in the picture.

The music in the tavern was most frequently made by the convivial friends who met together there, for every gentleman was expected to be able to bear his part in vocal music if he had anything like "a voice;" but there were also strolling musicians, held in low esteem, who would enter these houses and seek for temporary employment in playing for some company unable to furnish their own musical recreation. Such music was called a "noise," occasionally. In that most graphic bit of tavern-life, the fourth scene of the second act of "King Henry IV." (Second part), the drawer bids his companion —

"See if thou canst find out Sneak's noise; Mistress Tear-sheet would fain hear some music."

In Ben Jonson's "Silent Woman" (Act iii. Sc. 1), we read :

"*Dauphine*. Well, there be guests and meat now; how shall we do for music?
Clerimont. The smell of the venison, going through the streets, will invite one noise of fiddlers or other.
Dauphine. I would it would call the trumpeters hither.
Clerimont. Faith, there is hope; they have intelligence of all feasts. There is good correspondence betwixt them and the London cooks; 'tis twenty to one but we have them."

And Fletcher also alludes to musicians' "noise" in several of his plays.

The musicians themselves were scarcely regarded as anything else than mendicants. Gosson, in his

"Short Apologie of the Schoole of Abuse," London, 1587, says:

> "London is so full of unprofitable pipers and fiddlers, that a man can no sooner enter a tavern, than two or three cast of them hang at his heels, to give him a dance before he depart."

They thrust themselves upon any company that gathered for conviviality with, "Will you have any music, gentlemen?" and seem to have been as difficult to shake off as Neapolitan beggars. In the thirty-ninth year of Elizabeth (1597), a law was promulgated against these humble sons of the Muses, by which all minstrels, "wandering abroad," were classed as "rogues, vagabonds, and sturdy beggars," and were promised severe punishment. A little later on, Cromwell reinforced the edict with : —

> "Any persons commonly called Fidlers or Minstrels who shall at any time be taken playing, fidling, and making music in any inn, ale-house, or tavern, or shall be taken proffering themselves, or desiring, or intreating any . . . to hear them play or make music in any of the places aforesaid shall be adjudged and declared to be rogues, vagabonds and sturdy beggars."

Yet sometimes in Elizabeth's day these itinerant musicians received fat fees. One anonymous writer, who brought out a pamphlet called the "Actor's Remonstrance," in 1643, says that they sometimes received twenty shillings for two hours' playing ; but as this was written a full generation after the epoch, and the statement is not backed up by any proof, we may assume (especially taking the Elizabethan statute into consideration) that the strolling players were held of very low caste, and eked out but a scanty livelihood.

When music was sent for, as in the case cited above, it was generally to play in the best room of the tavern, and this room frequently received some especial name. The larger taverns seem to have had more than one room with such name.[1] Shakespeare brings in this nomenclature in "Measure for Measure" (Act ii. Sc. 1), where the clown alludes to the "Bunch of Grapes," not a tavern, but an especial room in it ; in the Boar's Head Tavern (Act ii. Sc. 4, of First Part of "King Henry IV.") we find Poins (or Pointz) alluding to "the Half-moon ;" and other instances of this custom might readily be cited.

If the revellers made their own music, they genererally sang catches together, and these compositions were of the liveliest description, often (as will be seen in the next chapter) containing some jest or *double-entendre.* We reproduce a few of the poems that constituted the text of the old catches :

[1] See the tavern-scene in Fletcher's "Captain" (Act iv. Sc. 2) for a very graphic presentation of this matter.

I

" If any so wise is,
    That sack he despises,
    Let him drink his small beer and be sober.
    Whilst we drink sack and sing
    As if it were Spring,
    He shall droop like the trees in October.

" But be sure, overnight,
    If this dog do you bite,
    You take it henceforth for a warning ;
    Soon as out of your bed,
    To settle your head,
    Take a hair of his tail in the morning."

2

" She that will eat her breakfast in bed,
    And spend the morn in dressing of her head,
    And sit at dinner like a maiden bride,
    And nothing do all day but talk of pride :
    Jove of his mercy may do much to save her,
    But what a case is he in that shall have her ? "

3

" Never let a man take heavily the clamour of his wife,
    But be ruled by me, and lead a merry life.
    Let her have her will in everything,
    If she scolds then laugh and sing,
            Hey derry, derry derry ding."

Shakespeare's own characters occasionally appear
in early catches, as may be seen by the reproduction
of the catch by George Holmes, who was not the
organist of Lincoln, but an anterior musician, living
possibly in the time of Charles I.

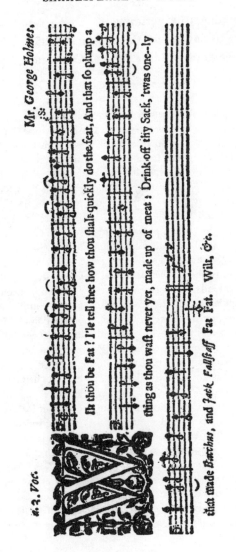

Regarding the performance of the catch, we can present to our reader the explicit directions given by John Playford in his "Musical Companion," printed in 1672.

"I thought it necessary for information of some Songsters who are not well acquainted with the Nature and Manner of Singing of Catches, to give them these Directions: First, a Catch is a Song for three Voyces, wherein the several Parts are included in one; or, as it is usually tearmed, Three Parts in One. Secondly, the manner of Singing them is thus, The First begins and Sings the Catch forward, and when he is at that Note over which this (:S:) Mark or Signature is placed, the Second begins and Sings forward in like manner, and when he is singing that Note over which the said Signature is, the Third begins and Sings, following the other, each Singing it round two or three times over, and so conclude.

"This kind of *Musick* hath for many Years past been had in much estemation by the most Judicious and Skilful Professors of *Musick*, for the Excellency of the Composition and Pleasant Harmony; and no late *Musick* that I have met with affords so much Delightful Recreation, though some fond Ignorant Novices in *Musick* have cry'd them down, because the height of their Skill is not able to understand them. But being unwilling so much good *Musick* should be buried in oblivion, it has made me adventure them once more into the World, for the benefit of future Ages: And I am sure they will be welcome at this time to many Judicious Persons, to whom I recommend them; for this is a Catching Age, all kinds of Catches and Catchers are abroad, *Catch that Catch can*, *Catch that Catch may*, *Thine Catch it, and mine Catch it;* But these harmless *Catches*, my wish is, those that Catch them with delight to Learn and for Instruction, may hereby reap both Pleasure and Delight: But those that Catch at them with detraction, (as that is a Catching disease) may Catch only the Fruits of their own Envy and Malice." [1]

Catches, although generally in three parts, were by no means always so, as may be seen in the collection entitled "Pammelia," published in 1609, in which all numbers of voices up to ten parts enter in the different catches and canons. We give a reproduction of a four-part catch from "Sympson's Compendium of Musick" (1678). The punning character of many of the catches may be seen in certain ones which are sung even to-day, as for example, Doctor Callcott's "Ah, how Sophia," which, in rapid singing, becomes "A house afire," or the celebrated catch about Burney's "History of Music," in which "Burney's history" becomes "Burn his history," by a similar change of tempo. Shakespeare's was emphatically a punning age, and any pun, if it were never so bad, was tolerated and laughed at in the reign of "Good Queen Bess," as may be seen by the fanciful title and preface of the collection of catches last mentioned, the first collection ever printed.

"PAMMELIA. [2]

" Musick's Miscellanie, or mixed varietie of pleasant Roundelays, and delightful Catches of three, four, five, six, seven,

---

[1] We may add to the above that many catches had some " catch," or double meaning in the words, these *double-entendres* often being quite indelicate.

[2] From two Greek words signifying *Miscellaneous Harmony*.

Contrivance of Canon.

§ 11. *Of Catch or Round.*

I Muſt not omit another ſort of Canon," in more
requeſt and common uſe (though of leſs dignity) than all thoſe which we have mentioned ;
and that is a Catch or Round : Some call it a Canon in *Uniſon* ; or a Canon conſiſting of Periods.
The contrivance whereof is not intercate : for, if
you compoſe any ſhort Strain, of three or four
Parts, ſetting them all within the ordinary com-
paſs of a Voice ; and then place one Part at the
end of another, in what order you pleaſe, ſo as
they may aptly make one continued Tune ; you
have finiſhed a Catch :

Example.

eight, nine, ten parts in one. None so ordinary as musical; none so musical as not to all very pleasing and acceptable. London: printed by William Barley for R. B. and H. W., and are to be sold at the Spread Eagle at the great north door of St. Pauls, 1609.

" To the well disposed to read, and to the merry disposed to sing. Amongst other liberal arts, music for her part hath always been as liberal in bestowing her liberal gifts as any one whatsoever; and that in such rare manner for diversity, and ample measure for multiplicity, as more cannot be *ex*pected, except it were more than it is *re*spected : yet in this kind only, it may seem somewhat niggardly and unkind in never as yet publicly communicating, but always privately retaining, and as it were envying to all, this more familiar mirth and jocund melody. But it may be music hath hitherto been defective in this vein, because this vein indeed hath hitherto been defective in music: and, therefore, that fault being now *mended*, this kind of music also is now com*mended* to all men's kind acceptation. This did I willingly undertake, and have easily *eff*ected, that all might equally partake of that which is so generally *aff*ected. *Catches* are so generally affected, I take it, *quia non superant captum*, because they are so consonant to all ordinary musical capacity, being such indeed as all such whose love of music exceeds their skill cannot but commend ; such also, as all such whose skill in music exceeds their love of such slight and light fancies, cannot either contemn or condemn : good art in all for the more musical ; good mirth and melody for the more jovial ; sweet harmony mixed with much variety ; and both with great facility. Harmony to please, variety to delight, facility to invite thee. Some toys, yet musical without absurdity ; some very musical, yet pleasing without difficulty ; *light*, but not without music's *delight ;* music's pleasantness, but not without easiness : what seems old is at least renewed ; art having *re*formed what pleasing tunes injurious time and ignorance had *de*formed. The only *in*tent is to give general *con*tent, *com*posed

by art to make thee *dis*posed to mirth.   Accept, therefore,
kindly what is done willingly, and published only to please
good company."

During the same year (1609) a second volume,
entitled "Deuteromelia," appeared, and its preface,
quoted in connection with "Three-men's Songs," is
more weakly punning than the preface to "Pammelia."   It will be found in the latter part of the
present chapter.   Ravenscroft is believed to have
been the compiler of both volumes, and therefore the
author of the hideous prefaces.

In "The Tempest" Shakespeare brings in some
of his most ribald tavern music ; this is natural
enough with three such vagabonds as Trinculo,
Stephano, and Caliban, and of course the three-part
catch is present.   In Act iii. Sc. 2, Stephano, who,
like many of Shakespeare's vagabonds, is very musi-
cally inclined, says (before he starts a catch) :

" Come on, Trinculo, let us sing.
[*Sings*] ' Flout 'em and skout 'em, and skout 'em and flout 'em ;
Thought is free.'
    Caliban.   That's not the tune.

                [*Ariel plays the tune on a tabor and pipe.*
    Stephano.   What is this same ?
    Trinculo.   This is the tune of our catch, played by the
picture of No-Body.
    Stephano.   If thou beest a man, shew thyself in thy like-
        ness ;
If thou beest a devil, take it as thou list.
    Trinculo.   O, forgive me my sins !

Stephano. He that dies, pays all debts: I defy thee —
Mercy upon us!

Caliban. Art thou afeard?

Stephano. No, monster, not I.

Caliban. Be not afeard; the isle is full of noises,
Sound, and sweet airs, that give delight, and hurt not.
Sometimes a thousand twangling instruments
Will hum about mine ears: and sometimes voices,
That, if I then had waked after long sleep,
Will make me sleep again: and then, in dreaming,
The clouds, methought, would open, and shew riches
Ready to drop upon me; that, when I waked,
I cried to dream again.

Stephano. This will prove a brave kingdom to me, where
I shall have my music for nothing."

While in Act ii. Sc. 2, Stephano gives some of the
worst tavern music of his time:[1]

" *Enter* STEPHANO *singing; a bottle in his hand.*

Stephano. 'I shall no more to sea, to sea,
      Here shall I die ashore:' —
This is a very scurvy tune to sing at a man's funeral;
Well, here's my comfort.   [*Drinks.*
' The master, the swabber, the boatswain, and I,
  The gunner, and his mate,
Loved Mall, Meg, and Marian, and Margery,
  But none of us cared for Kate:
  For she had a tongue with a tang,
  Would cry to a sailor, " Go hang!"
She loved not the savour of tar nor of pitch,
Yet a tailor might scratch her where'er she did itch,

---

[1] In Furness (Variorum Edition) an article is quoted which claims
this to be the most graphic of sea-songs.

   Then to sea, boys, and let her go hang.'
This is a scurvy tune too: But here's my comfort.

                          [*Drinks.*"

And Caliban also sings solos of a grotesque class.
Against this amount of vulgar music we have the
delicate music of Ariel, sometimes tender, sometimes
playful, forming one of the finest of artistic contrasts.
Small wonder that the lyrics of this play have inspired music in many composers, and have been
set in innumerable forms ever since the poet's lifetime.   Unfortunately, however, the original settings
of most of the beautiful poems, the melodies which
Shakespeare himself was accustomed to hear, seem
irretrievably lost.   Doctor Bridge has, however,
unearthed two of the poems, set by Johnson (1612),
harmonised (1659) by Wilson.

WHERE THE BEE SUCKS.

THE TEMPEST.   R. JOHNSON. 1612.
Lively.

Where the bee sucks, there suck I : .... In a cowslip's

bell I lie ; There I couch when owls do cry On the

bat's back I do fly Af - ter sum-mer mer-ri - ly.

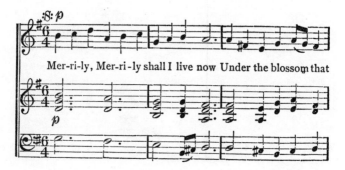

Mer-ri-ly, Mer-ri-ly shall I live now Under the blossom that

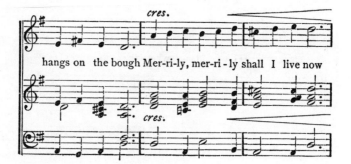

hangs on the bough Mer-ri-ly, mer-ri-ly shall I live now

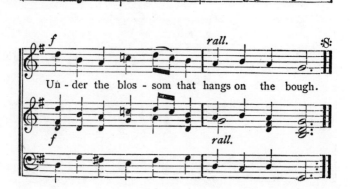

Un - der the blos - som that hangs on the bough.

FULL FATHOM FIVE.

THE TEMPEST.   R. JOHNSON. 1612.

But doth suffer a sea-change Into something rich and strange.

Un poco Animato e marcato.

Sea-nymphs hourly ring his knell: Hark!   now I

hear them, Hark! now I hear them,—Ding - dong,   bell.

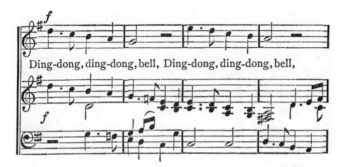

Ding-dong, ding-dong, bell, Ding-dong, ding-dong, bell,

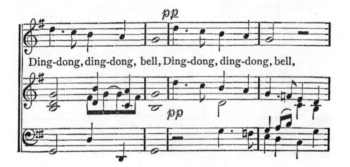

Ding-dong, ding-dong, bell, Ding-dong, ding-dong, bell,

Ding-dong, ding-dong, bell Ding-dong, ding-dong, bell.

Exactly as "The Tempest" presents three vagabonds singing the three-part music, the catches, and
bacchanalian songs of the time, so does "Twelfth
Night" introduce us to a trio of scamps (Feste, the
clown, being the most decent of the three), who troll
out their lays in a similar manner. And, as in "The
Tempest" we find the earnest side of music balanced
against its coarser phases, so in the wilder comedy do
we have lyrics, such as "Oh, Mistress Mine" and
"Come away, come away, Death," as well as the lofty
tributes to the power of music already noted. As
the music of the dissipated trio (Sir Toby Belch,
Sir Andrew Aguecheek, and the clown) introduces
a number of burdens, we shall examine them more
at length in the next chapter in connection with
the subject of the old refrains. Suffice it to say
here that many a character seems introduced forcibly
and without reason into Shakespeare's plays, whose
presence will be readily understood if the reader
remembers that three were necessary to sing the
regulation catch or other merry music which the
dramatist desired. Thus, for example, the otherwise
uncalled-for appearance of the two pages in "As You
Like It" (Act v. Sc. 3). Touchstone and Audrey
are together, when two pages enter, the first saluting
with, "Well met, honest gentlemen." It is not long
before we discover why these two wanderers have
walked upon the stage. The scene goes on:

" *Touchstone.* By my troth, well met: Come, sit, sit, and a song.

Second Page. We are for you: sit i' the middle.[1]

First Page. Shall we clap into 't roundly without hawking, or spitting, or saying we are hoarse; which are the only prologues to a bad voice?

Second Page. I' faith, i' faith; and both in a tune, like two gipsies on a horse.

SONG.

I.

It was a lover, and his lass,
 With a hey, and a ho, and a hey nonino,
That o'er the green corn-field did pass,
 In the spring time, the only pretty ring time,
When birds do sing, hey ding a ding, ding;
Sweet lovers love the spring.

II.

Between the acres of the rye,
 With a hey, and a ho, and a hey nonino,
These pretty country folks would lie.
 In spring time, etc.

III.

This carol they began that hour,
 With a hey, and a ho, and a hey nonino,
How that a life was but a flower.
 In spring time, etc.

IV.

And therefore take the present time,
 With a hey, and a ho, and a hey nonino,

---

[1] Alluding to the old English rhyme:
  " Hey-diddle-diddle,
   The fool in the middle."

For love is crowned with the prime.
    In spring time, etc.

Touchstone.   Truly, young gentlemen, though there was no great matter in the ditty, yet the note was very untuneable.

First Page.   You are deceived, sir; we kept time, we lost not our time.

Touchstone.· By my troth, yes; I count it but time lost to hear such a foolish song. God be with you; and God mend your voices! Come, Audrey.   [*Exeunt.*"

The song which is framed in so much of comment fortunately is preserved to us in its original setting. We present it with its contemporaneous music.

"IT WAS A LOVER AND HIS LASS."

Quoted by Chappell from an old MS. bearing date A. D. 1639, in Advocate's Library, Edinburgh.

It was a lov-er and his lasse With a hey, with a ho, with a hey now ne no, And a hey . . . no nee, no, no, no.

That o'er the greene corne field did passe In Spring tyme, in

Spring tyme, in Spring tyme, the on-lie prettie ring tyme, When

Birds doo sing, Hey ding a ding a ding, Hey ding a ding a

ding, Hey ding a ding a ding, Suiet Lovers love the Spring.

The antiquity of three-part rounds and catches is very great. One of the rounds that is sung in England and America to-day, the well-known —

> " Turn again, Whittington,
> Thou worthy citizen,
> Lord Mayor of London," —

was composed as long ago as 1453, when Sir John Norman was Lord Mayor of London, and, instead of marching in procession through the city streets, on the morning of St. Simon and Jude's Day, took his pageant along the Thames, by water. The watermen, grateful for such an innovation, made the round —

> " Row the boat, Norman, row,
> Heave ho, and rum below, [1]
> Row to thy leman," —

of which we append the music. The oldest piece of skilful music now extant is the round, "Sumer is icumen in," preserved in manuscript in the British Museum and dating probably from A. D. 1215. "Three Blind Mice" is a catch (originally sung with vulgar words) of the Shakespearian epoch, and other familiar rounds are equally old.

[1] " Heave ho and rum below" was one of the oldest and most employed refrains : it appears in many of the old ballads and romances.

ROW THE BOAT, NORMAN, ROW.

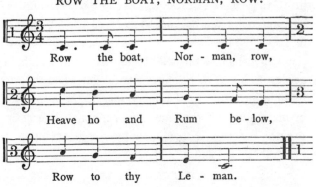

Row   the boat,   Nor - man,   row,

Heave   ho   and   Rum   be - low,

Row   to   thy   Le - man.

Shakespeare alludes to the habit of singing many of the lighter songs in three parts. We have already cited the clown, in " Winter's Tale " (Act iv. Sc. 2), giving an allusion to " three-men song-men," and in the same play (Act iv. Sc. 3) we find Autolycus vending ballads which were to be sung in three parts. The title of " Three Merry Men be We," spoken of in " Twelfth Night," also suggests the three-part singing which was in such vogue. Naylor, in his " Shakespeare and Music " (p. 83), gives several examples of the use of the term "three-men" as applied to vocal music.

Nevertheless, Oliphant, whose researches are entitled to some respect, believes that the term "Freemen's Songs," is not a corruption of " Three-men's Songs," although in this he stands in opposition to many authorities, from Ritson to Naylor. In his " Musa Madrigalesca " (p. 242), he cites the following preface to the second book of catches, published in 1609. As it is another example of the wretched punning which was held to be such a delightful accomplishment in Shakespeare's day, and of the forcible introduction of unnecessary Latin (also found in many plays of the time), we reproduce the entire preface, together with Oliphant's comments upon it.

" DEUTEROMELIA,

"Or the second part of Music's Melodie, or melodious music of pleasant roundelays; K. H. mirth, or Freemen's songs, and such delightful catches. *Qui canere potest canat.* Catch that catch can. *Ut mel os, sic cor melos afficit et reficit.* London: printed for Thomas Adams, dwelling in Paul's Church-yard, at the sign of the White Lion, 1609.

"'Mirth and music to the cunning catcher,
    Derth and physic to the coney-catcher.'

" *Secundæ cogitationes* are ever, they say, *meliores*, and why may not then *secundæ cantiones* as well be *dulciores?* I *presume* they are so; and that makes me *resume this vein*, with hope that I shall not *consume in vain* my labour therein. For, first, the kind acceptation of the former impression, is as a new invitation to this latter edition; though not of the same things, yet of things of the same condition: full of the same delectation, made to please as the other were; made truly musical with art by my *correction*, and yet plain and capable with ease by my *direction.*

" Neither can he that is the most able musician say, but

that of these most men, almost all men are capable, that are not altogether unmusical; neither can he that is most spiteful say, but they are very delightful, aye, and someway *gainful* too (yet more *painful* to me, I am sure, than *gainful*); but tho' there be but little to be *gotten* by them, yet pity were it such mirth should be *forgotten* of us; and therefore, to make an end, I say no more, but

> " ' . . . Si quid novisti dulcius istis,
> Candidus imperti; si non, his utere mecum; '

either *commend* me or *come mend* me, and so I *end* me, as *resolute* as thou art *dissolute*."

Oliphant's comments on the above are:

" From the foregoing preface it is, I think, quite clear that *Deuteromelia* is a second publication by the editor of Pammelia. The terms *K. H. mirth* and *Freemen's songs* have given rise to considerable discussion. It is supposed that the former stands for *King Henry's mirth;* that is, songs or catches of a merry nature, which were favourites with that jovial prince. I think it likely to be so, but am not aware of anything either for or against the matter, except conjecture.

" How the meaning of *Freemen's songs* could ever appear doubtful, I know not, nor can I imagine how Warren could be guilty of such a stupid mistake as to suppose that *Freeman* was the name of a composer; for in his collection is inserted *Of all the birds that I ever see*, (which is one of the three part *Freemen's songs* in Deuteromelia), with the name prefixed of *Nicholas Freeman*, 1667 ! nearly sixty years after the original publication. Ritson has some absurd notion of *Freemen* being a mistake for *Three-men*, because Shakspeare speaks of *Three-men-song men*, that is, men who could sing songs of three parts: but if he ever saw the book of which I am now writing, he must there have found also Freemen's songs to

four voices, which sets that matter at rest. Drayton, in his
' Legend of Thomas Cromwell, Earl of Essex,' puts the following verses in that nobleman's mouth:

> " ' Of *Freemen's Catches* to the Pope I sing,
>   Which wan much license to my countrymen;
> Thither the which I was the first to bring,
>   That were unknown in Italy till then.'

" He went to Italy in the year 1510."

Nevertheless, the weight of evidence seems to be
in favour of the derivation from "Three men," and
the overwhelming majority of catches and "Freemen's Songs" are in *three* parts, as we shall see in
the succeeding chapter.

CHAPTER X.

Bacchanalian Music, continued — A Scottish Melody Used by
Shakespeare — Table-music in Elizabethan Days — Refrains
of Catches and Ballads — Hunt's-ups — Serenades — Morning
Songs.

WE have already seen that the chief bacchanalian
music of Shakespeare is to be found in "Twelfth
Night," while the leading tavern-scenes are to be
discovered in the two parts of "King Henry IV."
Nevertheless, to our collection of musical vagabonds
must be added a rascal of much deeper dye, a man
who seems a living proof that the music-maker, as
well as the music-hater, "is fit for treason, stratagem,
and spoils," — Iago. The scene ("Othello," Act ii.
Sc. 3) where the crafty Iago, by simulated good-fel-
lowship, leads Cassio to his intoxication and ruin
runs:

> "*Iago*.　Some wine, ho!
>> 'And let me the canakin clink, clink;　　[*Sings*.
>> And let me the canakin clink:
>>> A Soldier's a man;
>>> A life's but a span;
>>> Why then, let a soldier drink.'
> Some wine, boys!　　　　　　　　[*Wine brought in.*
>> *Cassio*.　'Fore Heaven, an excellent song.

Iago. I learned it in England, where (indeed) they are most potent in potting; your Dane, your German, and your swag-bellied Hollander, — Drink, ho! — are nothing to your English.

Cassio. Is your Englishman so expert in his drinking?

Iago. Why, he drinks you, with facility, your Dane dead drunk.

. . . .

Iago. O sweet England!
  'King Stephen was a worthy peer,
    His breeches cost him but a crown;
  He held them sixpence all too dear,
    With that he call'd the tailor — lown

  He was a wight of high renown,
    And thou art but of low degree:
  'Tis pride that pulls the country down,
    Then take thine auld cloak about thee.'

Some wine, ho!

Cassio. Why, this is a more exquisite song than the other.

Iago. Will you hear it again?

Cassio. No; for I hold him to be unworthy of his place, that does those things."

Of the first song the original music is not traceable,[1] but the second snatch of rollicking music can be traced home; it was sung to an old Scottish melody.

[1] A somewhat similar catch, however, by Doctor Byrd, is given in the collection called "Pammelia" (1609), running:

    "Come drink to me,
    And I to thee,
    And then shall we
    Full well agree.

   "I've loved the jolly tankard
    Full seven winters and more;
   I loved it so long,
    That I went upon the score.

We give the melody both with its original and its Shakespearian words.

In the preceding chapter we have seen the music of the tavern called a "noise," and the name was by no means misapplied, for much of this minstrelsy was of the loudest description. Not only was this the case, but table-music (*i. e.* music played during meals) in general was liked in proportion to its loudness by many of the less cultivated patrons, even those of high rank. Writing of Queen Elizabeth's table-music, an authority says: [1]

"Elizabeth used to be regaled during dinner with twelve trumpets and two kettle-drums; which, together with fifes, cornets, and side-drums, made the hall ring for half an hour together."

It may be incidentally mentioned that the word "table-music" was also used in another sense in the seventeenth century. Two, three, four, or more singers would often sit at a table, instead of standing, while executing their music; such compositions as were printed with the intention of being thus sung

> "Who loveth not the tankard,
> He is no honest man;
> And he is no right soldier,
> That loveth not the can.

> "Tap the cannikin, trole the cannikin,
> Toss the cannikin, turn the cannikin.
> Hold now, good son, and fill us a fresh can,
> That we may quaff it round from man to man."

[1] P. Hentzner's "Itinerarium," p. 53.

TAKE THY OLD CLOAK ABOUT THEE.

This   winter's weather   wax-eth cold,   And
King   Stephen was   a   worthy peer,   His

frost doth freese on   ev - 'ry hill, And   Boreas blowes his
breeches cost   him   but   a crown, He held them six-pence

blasts soe bold,   That   all our kye   are like to spill:
all   too dear,   With that he called   the tailor "lown"

Then   Bell my wife,   who   loves   no strife,   She
He   was   a wight   of   high   re-nown,   And

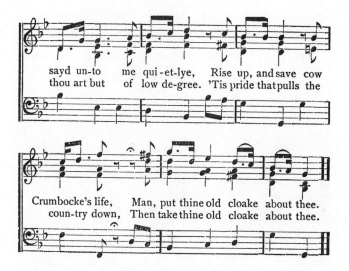

sayd un-to me qui-et-lye, Rise up, and save cow
thou art but of low de-gree. 'Tis pride that pulls the

Crumbocke's life, Man, put thine old cloake about thee.
coun-try down, Then take thine old cloake about thee.

were called "table-music." We have given an example of Morley's "Now is the Month of Maying," arranged for two voices in this manner. (See Chapter
VI.) The book was laid on the table between the
two singers, each of whom could read his part from
his own side of the table, as they sat opposite each
other.

We now quote a scene from "Twelfth Night,"
which may be regarded as the most typical one connected with the music of the tavern in all the works
of Shakespeare, although it occurs, not in an inn, but
in the house of Olivia. The reader will bear in mind
what has already been stated regarding the loudness

of most of this music, and will readily comprehend the indignation of Olivia, Malvolio, and Maria. It is the third scene of the second act of the great comedy.

" Enter Clown.

Sir Andrew.　Here comes the fool, i' faith.

Clown.　How, now, my hearts? Did you never see the picture of we three?

Sir Toby.　Welcome, ass. Now let's have a catch.

Sir Andrew.　By my troth, the fool has an excellent breast. I had rather than forty shillings I had such a leg, and so sweet a breath to sing, as the fool hath. In sooth, thou wast in very gracious fooling last night, when thou spokest of Pigrogromitus, of the Vapians passing the equinoctial of Queubus; 'twas very good, i' faith. I sent thee sixpence for thy leman. Hadst it?

Clown.　I did impeticos thy gratillity; for Malvolio's nose is no whipstock: My lady has a white hand, and the myrmidons are no bottle-ale houses.

Sir Andrew.　Excellent! Why, this is the best fooling, when all is done. Now, a song.

Sir Toby.　Come on; there is sixpence for you: let's have a song.

Sir Andrew.　There's a testril of me too; if one knight give a —

Clown.　Would you have a love-song, or a song of good life?

Sir Toby.　A love-song, a love-song.

Sir Andrew.　Ay, ay; I care not for good life.

SONG.

Clown.　O mistress mine, where are you roaming?
　　　　　O, stay and hear; your true love's coming,
　　　　　　That can sing both high and low:

Trip no farther, pretty sweeting;
Journey's end in lovers' meeting,
   Every wise man's son doth know.

Sir Andrew.   Excellent good, i' faith!
Sir Toby.   Good, good.

Clown.   What is love? 'tis not hereafter;
Present mirth hath present laughter;
   What's to come, is still unsure:
In delay there lies no plenty;
Then come kiss me, sweet-and-twenty.
   Youth's a stuff will not endure.

Sir Andrew.   A mellifluous voice, as I am true knight.

Sir Toby.   A contagious breath.

Sir Andrew.   Very sweet and contagious, i' faith.

Sir Toby.   To hear by the nose, it is dulcet in contagion. But shall we make the welkin dance indeed? Shall we rouse the night-owl in a catch, that will draw three souls out of one weaver?[1] shall we do that?

Sir Andrew.   An you love me, let's do't: I am a dog at a catch.

Clown.   By'r lady, sir, and some dogs will catch well.

Sir Andrew.   Most certain: let our catch be, 'Thou knave.'

Clown.   'Hold thy peace, thou knave,' knight? I shall be constrain'd in't to call thee knave, knight.

Sir Andrew.   'Tis not the first time I have constrain'd one to call me knave. Begin, fool; it begins, 'Hold thy peace.'

Clown.   I shall never begin, if I hold my peace.

---

[1] Schmidt says that the weavers in Elizabethan times were mostly refugees from the Netherlands, and therefore Calvinists, who were much addicted to psalm-singing.

Sir Andrew. Good, i' faith! Come, begin.

[*They sing a catch.*

Enter MARIA.

Maria. What a catterwauling do you keep here! If my lady have not called up her steward, Malvolio; and bid him turn you out of doors, never trust me.

Sir Toby. My lady's a Cataian, we are politicians; Malvolio's a Peg-a-Ramsey, and 'Three merry men be we.' Am not I consanguineous? Am I not of her blood? Tilly-vally, lady! 'There dwelt a man in Babylon, lady, lady!'

[*Singing.*

Clown. Beshrew me, the knight's in admirable fooling.

Sir Andrew. Ay, he does well enough, if he be disposed, and so do I too; he does it with a better grace, but I do it more natural.

Sir Toby. 'O, the twelfth day of December,'— [*Singing.*

Maria. For the love o' God, peace.

Enter MALVOLIO.

Malvolio. My masters, are you mad? or what are you? Have you no wit, manners, nor honesty, but to gabble like tinkers at this time of night? Do you make an alehouse of my lady's house, that ye squeak out your coziers' catches without any mitigation or remorse of voice? Is there no respect of place, persons, nor time, in you?

Sir Toby. We did keep time, sir, in our catches. Sneck up!

Malvolio. Sir Toby, I must be round with you. My lady bade me tell you, that, though she harbours you as her kinsman, she's nothing allied to your disorders. If you can separate yourself and your misdemeanours, you are welcome to the house; if not, an it would please you to take leave of her, she is very willing to bid you farewell.

Sir Toby. 'Farewell, dear heart, since I must needs be gone.'

Maria. Nay, good Sir Toby.

Clown. ' His eyes do show his days are almost done.'

Malvolio. Is't even so?

Sir Toby. ' But I will never die.'

Clown. Sir Toby, there you lie.

Malvolio. This is much credit to you.

Sir Toby. ' Shall I bid him go?'   [*Singing.*

Clown. ' What an if you do?'

Sir Toby. ' Shall I bid him go, and spare not?'

Clown. ' O, no, no, no, no, you dare not.'

Sir Toby. Out o' time? sir, ye lie. — Art any more than a steward? Dost thou think, because thou art virtuous, there shall be no more cakes and ale?

Clown. Yes, by Saint Anne; and ginger shall be hot i' the mouth too."

This scene is as full of musical allusions as an egg of meat; not even the music-teaching scene in "The Taming of the Shrew," or the musical dialogue between Lucetta and Julia in "Two Gentlemen of Verona," can compare with it in point of constant musical metaphor; it is the most continuously musical scene to be found in Shakespeare. A certain prolixity of comment may therefore be permitted. "The fool has an excellent breast," speaks of Feste's good vocal qualities. Shakespeare demanded a good vocalist in this part, for it must be remembered that the clown appears not only in the catch-music of this scene (and in the love-song), but in tender and earnest music that draws forth the most enthusiastic encomium from the duke. Knight, prob-

ably the most musical of the Shakespearian commentators, cites Warton and Tusser as using the
word "breast" in this sense, the latter saying, —

> "Thence for my *voice*, I must (no choice)
>   Away, of force, like posting-horse.
> For sundry men, had placards then
>   Such child to take ;
> The better *breast*, the lesser rest,
> To serve the quire, now there, now here," —

which refers to the impressment of children in the
royal choirs.

If Knight is to be called the most musical of the
commentators, Doctor Johnson and Steevens may be
pilloried as the least so. We have already seen
Johnson apologising for Shakespeare's musical tendencies ; Steevens writes himself down an — antagonist of music, in the following comment upon the
above line : [1]

"I suppose this cant term ["breast"] to have been current
among the musicians of the age. All professions have in
some degree their jargon ; and the remoter they are from
liberal science, and the less consequential to the general inter-
ests of life, the more they strive to hide themselves behind
affected terms and barbarous phraseology."

As regards the love-song, "Oh, Mistress Mine,"
it exists in the form in which Shakespeare was

[1] Another proof that Furness's lenient judgment of Steevens
was a too kindly view of the case.

wont to hear it sung. "Twelfth Night" was probably written in 1599, or 1600, and is mentioned in
John Manningham's "Diary" (in the British Museum)
Feb. 2, 1601 (2); the tune of this song is to be
found in Morley's "Consort Lessons," printed in
1599, and was composed before this time, since it
is also found in Queen Elizabeth's "Virginal Book,"
arranged by Byrd. We give the song with the
harmonies of the latter musician. The words have
been set some twenty times since this original
version!

"O MISTRESS MINE."

O Misstress mine, Where are you roaming? O Misstress mine,

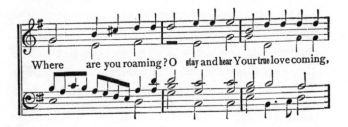

Where are you roaming? O stay and hear Your true love coming,

That can sing both high and low: Trip
no further, pret - ty sweet - ing, Jour-ney's end
in Lovers meeting Ev - e - ry Mother's Son . . doth know.

The next musical point is the punning on the
words of the catch, "Hold thy Peace." The original music of this catch is given by both Burney and
Hawkins, although neither cite their source of derivation. We print this catch that the reader may see
for himself the comical word-play which Shake-

speare has wreathed around it. The catch was probably begun slowly, gradually taken quicker and quicker, until it ended as if it were an actual tavern brawl.

CATCH.

"Twelfth Night."

Hold thy peace and I prithee, hold thy peace,

Thou knave, hold thy peace, thou knave,

Thou knave

The next musical point that claims attention is Sir Toby's sentence, beginning " My lady's a Ca-taian." Sir Toby is in that highly convivial frame of mind which accompanies the early stages of inebriation, and the refrains and burdens of many different songs jumble themselves together in his brain. " Peg-a-Ramsey " was an old tune with very lively words attached. From the character of some of these it would seem that a " Peg-a-Ramsey " might mean a scold, a nagging person.

"PEG–A–RAMSEY."

Moderate Time.

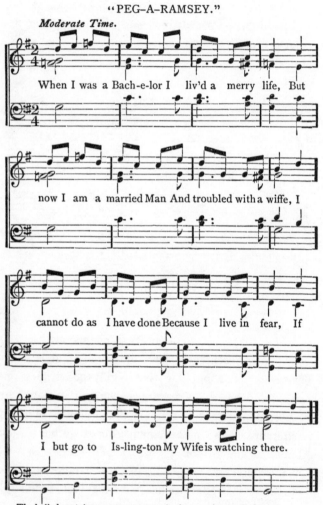

When I was a Bach-e-lor I liv'd a merry life, But
now I am a married Man And troubled with a wiffe, I
cannot do as I have done Because I live in fear, If
I but go to Is-ling-ton My Wife is watching there.

The ballad contains numerous verses in the same hen-pecked spirit.

" Three merry men be we " was taken from the old ballad of " Arthur a Bland," or " Hey down a down," a musical tale of a jolly tanner of Nottinghamshire, who goes into the forest and meets Robin Hood. The pair have a lusty bout of quarterstaff, in which both are badly bruised. Robin Hood finally begs Arthur to join his band, which the latter does. He proves to be a relative of Little John, one of the most celebrated of the outlaws ; when they are met together the verse ensues :

> " The Robin Hood took them both by the hands,[1]
> And danc'd round about the oke tree :
> For three merry men, and three merry men,
> And three merry men we be.

> " And ever hereafter, as long as we live,
> We three will be as one ;
> The wood it shall ring, and the old wife sing,
> Of Robin Hood, Arthur and John."

The old melody still exists, and we append it. " Tilly-vally " may possibly be the burden of some old ballad, although White suggests that it might have been a cant term of disparagement ; in this all is conjecture. The next phrase alludes to an old ballad of which Bishop Percy, in his " Reliques,"

---

[1] These lines can be cited in favour of either the " three-men's-song " or the " free-men's-song " theory, alluded to in the preceding chapter.

TUNE OF "THREE MERRY MEN BE WE."

Boldly.

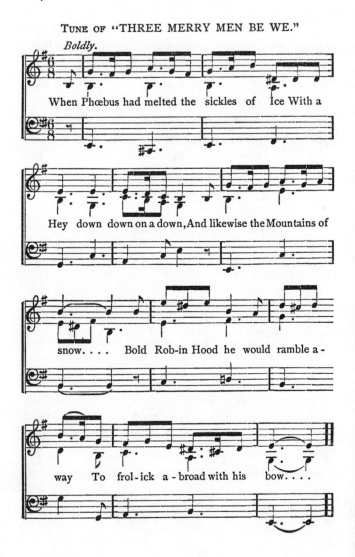

When Phœbus had melted the sickles of Ice With a

Hey down down on a down, And likewise the Mountains of

snow.... Bold Rob-in Hood he would ramble a-

way To frol-ick a-broad with his bow....

quotes a single verse. The ballad is to be found
entire in the Pepys collection, but is prolix and dull.
The verse alluded to by Sir Toby runs:

> " There dwelt a man in Babylon
> Of reputation great by fame;
> He took to wife a fair woman,
> Susanna she was called by name:
> A woman fair and virtuous;
> Lady, Lady:
> Why should we not of her learn thus
> To live godly?"

The song was called " Constant Susanna." " Lady,
lady," was a common refrain in many of the old
ballads; Mercutio sings it in " Romeo and Juliet"
(Act ii. Sc. 4). " Oh, the twelfth day of December "
has not been satisfactorily traced; it was probably a
ballad of some kind.

The absolute fidelity to nature of this entire scene
is remarkable; it is the half-drunken man, exactly
as one may find him to-day, whose readiest vent of
high spirits is in song; nothing can stop him, nothing check his torrent of fragmentary harmony. As
to the gabbling " like tinkers," it may be recalled
that the tinkers had a rough music of their own,
frequently alluded to by the old dramatists as a type
of coarse music. " Now God be with old Simeon,"
the catch particularly affected by this strolling fra-
ternity, has already been spoken of in Chapter IV.

"Cozier's catches" carries out the same simile, for a "cozier" was a person who botched his work, — generally a poor tailor or cobbler.

There now follows a musical scene which is *sui generis;* an entire song is interwoven by Shakespeare into the action. Sir Toby's bewildered mind is ready to catch any passing impression, provided it lead to music, on which at the moment his thoughts are most intent. As Malvolio comes to the words, "She is very willing to bid you farewell," he is at once reminded of a song by Robert Jones, a famous lutenist and composer for that instrument and for the voice. The song is entitled "Corydon's Farewell to Phyllis." It appears in "The First Booke of Ayres, composed by Robert Jones," folio. Printed for T. Este, 1601. It is given by Rimbault in his "Musical Illustrations of Ancient English Poetry." We give the music and dialogue as they were interspersed in the Shakespearian performances.

CORYDON'S FAREWELL TO PHILLIS.

Fare-well, dear love; since thou wilt needs be-gone,

not? Oh no, no, no, no, no, You dare   not.

The real poem, which Shakespeare has here parodied, ran as follows:

" Farewell, dear Love, since thou wilt needs be gone,
    Mine eyes do shew, my life is almost done.
        Nay, I will never die, so long as I can spie
        There be many mo, though that she doe goe,
            There be many mo, I fear not:
            Why then let her goe, I care not.

" Farewell, farewell; since this I find is true,
    I will not spend more time in wooing you;
        But I will seek elsewhere, if I may find love there.
        Shall I bid her goe? what and if I doe?
            Shall I bid her goe and spare not?
            O no, no, no, I dare not.

" Ten thousand times farewell; — yet stay a while: —
    Sweet, kiss me once; sweet kisses time beguile.
        I have no power to move.   How now am I in love?
        Wilt thou needs be gone?   Go then, all is one.
            Wilt thou needs be gone?   Oh, hie thee!
            Nay, stay, and do no more deny me.

" Once more adieu, I see loath to depart
    Bids oft adieu to her, that holds my heart.

But seeing I must lose thy love, which I did choose,
Goe thy way for me, since that may not be.
    Goe thy ways for me.   But whither?
    Goe, oh, but where I may come thither.

" What shall I doe? my love is now departed.
  She is as fair, as she is cruel-hearted.
    She would not be intreated, with prayers oft repeated;
    If she come no more, shall I die therefore?
      If she come no more, what care I?
      Faith, let her goe, or come, or tarry."

There is another instance of the interweaving of part of a song through the action, in this same play of " Twelfth Night."   It occurs in the second scene of the fourth act, where the following dialogue, partly sung, is found :

> " *Clown.* Hey Robin, jolly Robin,   [*Singing.*
>   Tell me how thy lady does.
>
> *Malvolio.* Fool —
> *Clown.* My lady is unkind, perdy.
> *Malvolio.* Fool —
> *Clown.* Alas! why is she so?
> *Malvolio.* Fool, I say —
> *Clown.* She loves another. Who calls, ha?"

Doctor Farmer has conjectured that the song should begin thus :

> " Hey, jolly Robin, tell to me
>   How does thy lady do?
> My lady is unkind, perdy,
>   Alas! why is she so?"

But Percy ("Reliques," Book II., No. 4) gives the old song from which the quotations are taken. It was probably written in the time of Henry VIII. The words run :

> " A Robyn,
>   Jolly Robyn,
> Tell me how thy leman doeth,
>   And thou shalt knowe of myn.
>
> " My lady is unkynde, perde.
>   Alack! why is she so?
> She loveth an other better than me;
>   And yet she will say no.
>
> " I fynde no such doublenes;
>   I fynde women true;
> My lady loveth me dowtles,
>   And will change for no newe.
>
> " Thou art happy while that doeth last:
>   But I say, as I fynde,
> That women's love is but a blast,
>   And torneth with the wynde.
>
> " Suche folkes can take no harme by love,
>   That can abide their torn.
> But I alas can no way prove
>   In love, but lake and morne.
>
> " But if thou wilt avoyde thy harme,
>   Lerne this lessen of me :
> At others fieres thy selfe to warme,
>   And let them warme with the."

A favourite catch, with a refrain, may be added to all these fragments of musical allusion. It is spoken of in "The Taming of the Shrew" (Act iv. Sc. 1) as follows :

"*Curtis.* Therefore, good Grumio, the news?

Grumio. Why 'Jack, boy! ho boy!' and as much news as thou wilt."

This is a direct quotation from an old catch which we here append :

CATCH. "JACK, BOY, HO! BOY!"

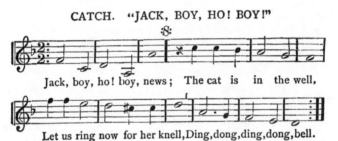

Jack, boy, ho! boy, news; The cat is in the well, Let us ring now for her knell, Ding, dong, ding, dong, bell.

The "dildos and fadings," which the servant speaks of in "Winter's Tale"[1] (Act iv. Sc. 3), were also refrains to songs, as may be seen from the following refrain to Ophelia's "How Should I Your True Love Know:"

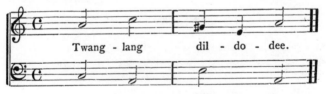

Twang - lang dil - do - dee.

[1] See also Chapter XI.

Another burden which is alluded to in "The Taming of the Shrew" is found in Petruchio's remark to Katherine (Act ii. Sc. 1), — "We will be married o' Sunday." This phrase may be a mere coincidence, or it may have been taken from an old song which ran —

> " To church away!
>   We will have rings
>   And fine array,
>   With other things,
>   Against the day,
>   For I'm to be married o' Sunday."

Richard Grant White quotes the above song, but as he gives no source of derivation, and as he often follows fanciful theories, we give the citation for what it is worth.

Hunting-music is found in some of Shakespeare's plays, and a hunt's-up was often used as a bright song with which to awaken favoured individuals in the early morning. One of the best of these songs is found in "As You Like It" (Act iv. Sc. 2).

" *Enter* JAQUES *and* Lords, *in the habit of Foresters.*

Jaques. Which is he that killed the deer?
First Lord. Sir, it was I.
Jaques. Let's present him to the duke, like a Roman conqueror; and it would do well to set the deer's horns upon his head, for a branch of victory. — Have you no song, forester, for this purpose?
Second Lord. Yes, sir.

Jaques. Sing it; 'tis no matter how it be in tune, so it make noise enough.

SONG.

 1. What shall he have that kill'd the deer?

 2. His leather skins and horns to wear.

  1. Then sing him home:

     [*The rest shall bear this burden.*

 Take thou no scorn, to wear the horn;

 It was a crest, ere thou wast born.

  1. Thy father's father wore it;

  2. And thy father bore it:

[*All.*] The horn, the horn, the lusty horn,

  Is not a thing to laugh to scorn."

In this scene the words, "The rest shall bear this burden," have caused some trouble to the commentators, for, by an odd mistake, they have been interpolated into the body of the song, whereas they are almost of a certainty a mere direction to the singers to join in the "burden" of the song. Some commentators, Knight and White, for example, would have the line, "Then sing him home," also read as a mere stage-direction, but this is at least debatable ground.[1] We give the music of this song, or "catch," as it was probably heard on Shakespeare's stage. It is reprinted from Playford's "Musical Companion" (1672), but Playford had copied it from Hilton's earlier works, as he states in his preface. Another debatable case occurs in "The Merchant of Venice" (Act iii. Sc. 2):

[1] See Furness for a full debate as to the matter of the burden.

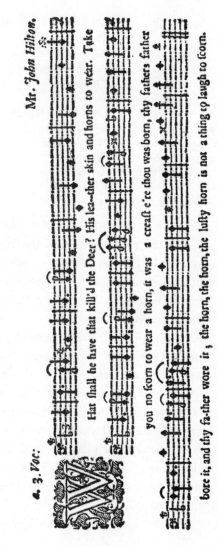

" *Music whilst* Bassanio *comments on the caskets to himself.*

SONG.[1]

1. Tell me, where is fancy bred,
   Or in the heart, or in the head?
   How begot, how nourished?
   Reply, reply.
2. It is engender'd in the eyes,
   With gazing fed; and fancy dies
   In the cradle where it lies:
   Let us all ring fancy's knell;
   I'll begin it — Ding, dong, bell.
   All. Ding, dong, bell."

Johnson, most unmusical of commentators (a man who ought never to have edited Shakespeare), held that the words, "Replie, Replie," were merely a stage-direction that a second voice should reply to the first. The repetition of the word makes this position very untenable; yet many editions have since appeared in which the word is merely attached as a heading to the second stanza, or omitted altogether.

Serenades formed a very popular branch of music in the sixteenth and seventeenth centuries, and Shakespeare speaks of them with some frequency. There is a sentence in the Second Part of "Henry IV." (Act iii. Sc. 2), in which Falstaff derides Shallow, saying :

---

[1] The original melody used here has not been discovered.

" He came ever in the rearward of the fashion, and sung those tunes . . . that he heard the carmen whistle, and sware they were his fancies, or his Good-nights."

The "fancies" spoken of here were probably fantasies or improvisations, while the "Good-nights" were serenades. In a preceding chapter we have seen Thurio serenading Sylvia ("Two Gentlemen of Verona," Act iv. Sc. 2) with "a deploring dump," which was quite in the character of evening music. But there was also another species of ambulatory love-song, which has been miscalled a serenade; we mean the bright and joyous song with which the olden-time lover awoke his mistress. This morning-

A "HUNTS-UP," OR MORNING SONG.
(17th Century.)

Vivace.

The Hunt is up, the Hunt is up, And now it is al - most day, And he that's at home In

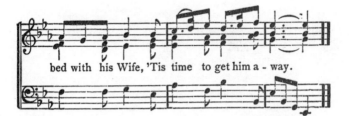

bed with his Wife, 'Tis time to get him a - way.

song, called "aubade" by the French composers and "alba" by the ancient troubadours, was exactly the opposite of the pensive and soothing serenade. Fynes Moryson, in his "Itinerary" published in 1617, says that it was a custom *peculiar to England,* that if a gentleman had company at a highway inn, he would be offered music (which he might freely take or refuse), and, if solitary, the musicians would give him the *good-day* with music in the morning.[1] It is such a morning-song that Cloten brings to Imogen in the third scene of the second act of "Cymbeline." The song is, as usual, set in a framework of comment.

" *Cloten.* It's almost morning, is't not?

First Lord. Day, my lord.

Cloten. I would this music would come: I am advised to give her music o' mornings; they say, it will penetrate. —

Enter Musicians.

Come, on; tune: . . . First a very excellent good-conceited thing; after a wonderful sweet air, with admirable rich words to it, and then let her consider.

[1] Quoted by Chappell, "Old English Ditties."

SONG.

'Hark! hark! the lark at heaven's gate sings.
　　And Phœbus 'gins arise,
His steeds to water at those springs
　　On chaliced flowers that lies;
And winking Mary-buds begin
　　To ope their golden eyes;
With every thing that pretty bin: [1]
　　My lady sweet, arise;
　　　　Arise, arise.'

So, get you gone: if this penetrate, I will consider your music
the better: if it do not, it is a vice in her ears, which horse-
hairs, and cat-guts, nor the voice of unpaved eunuch to boot,
can never amend.   [*Exeunt Musicians.*"

The original musical setting of this poem is lost,
but it has received a setting worthy of Shakespeare
by one of the greatest of German masters, — Schubert. Of this musical setting and of the circumstances of its production, we shall speak in a later
chapter.

---

[1] Much controversy has arisen about the word "lies," in this
connection. The use of this instead of its nominative was common enough in Shakespeare's time. The word "bin," substituted
for "is" by Hanmer, has also caused comment both favourable and
otherwise. Shakespeare unquestionably wrote "is," and the forced
rhyme, old-fashioned term, and grammatic license seem unnecessary, yet "bin" will probably be used in many editions in *sæcula
sæculorum.*

CHAPTER XI.

THE ballad is the peculiar artistic heritage of the Northern nations. Wherever the theatre was well developed the ballad languished, for it had no mission to perform in national literature which could not be as adequately, or even more thoroughly, accomplished by means of the drama. Even ancient Greece, with all its literary and musical activity, possessed no ballads, the epos being the nearest approach to this form. In later days, Italy and France cared little for this vein of musical narrative, while Germany, Scandinavia, and England presented the deeds of national heroes to the public which craved the recital, in the shape of ballad or saga.

If the terms are used strictly, there should be a strong discrimination between " ballad " and " song," for the ballad was a tale of events, set to music, while the song dealt with emotions only. Of course, there are many instances where the one form goes into the domain of the other, temporarily. The old English chroniclers were often glad to incorporate the legendary information received through a ballad, into their histories. The "Anglo-Saxon Chronicle" contains at least two complete historical ballads, and fragments of nearly a dozen more are incorporated into the body of the work, and William of Malmesbury frankly acknowledges his indebtedness to the traditional ballads of the countryside, in his history of King Edward (the son of Alfred the Great), a confession which many of his brother chroniclers would have been obliged to make, had they been as honest as he.

A royal ballad was composed as early as 1017, when King Canute burst into song, upon the river Ely, upon a summer evening. The pious chronicler of Ely gives the words of the first stanza of this ballad, but the music has disappeared. The English bears the mark of the twelfth, rather than of the eleventh century.

> " Merie sungen the muneches binnen Ely,
>   Tha Cnut ching reu ther by:
>   Roweth, cnites, noer the land,
>   And here we thes muneches saeng.
>
> " Merry sang the monks by Ely,
>   As Canute, King, rowed thereby.
>   Row knights, near the land,
>   And hear we these monks sing."

We present a facsimile of one of the black-letter ballads of the fifteenth century, from a manuscript in the Sloane collection in the British Museum. Mr. Thos. Wright has added to it a short glossary, which is also appended. The reader will note an allusion to the "division" of melody as explained in Chapter VI.

xx

Kyrie, so kyrie, Iankyn syngyt merie, with aleyson.

As I went on zol day
in owre profeſſyon /
Know I joly Iankyn
be his mery ton /
Iankyn be=gan the offys
on the zol day /
And zyt me thynkyt it dos me good
ſo merie gan he ſay /
kyrieleyſon.
Iankyn red the pyſtyl
ful fayre and ful wel /
And zyt me thinkyt it dos me good /
as euere haue I ſel.

Jankyn at the sanctus
       crakit a merie note /
And zyt me thinkyt it dos me good /
       I payid for his cote.

Jankyn crakit nots /
       an hunderid on a knot /
And zyt he hakkyt hem smallere
       than worts to the pot.

                    k.

Jankyn at the Angnus
       beryt the pax brede /
He twynkelid / but sayd nowt
       and on myn fot he trede.

Benedicamus domino /
       Cryst fro schame me schylde /
Deo gracias ther=to /
       alas I go with schylde.

                    k.

Gloss. *kyrie aleyson* (κυριε ελεισον) 'Lord, have mercy on us,' a part of the liturgy — *zol*, yule, christmas — *ton*, tone — *offys*, office, service — *zyt*, yet — *red*, read — *pystyl*, epistle — *sel*, bliss, happiness — *crakit*, cracked — *hakkyt*, hacked — *worts*, herbs — *beryt*, bore — *nowt*, nought, nothing — *trede*, trode — *schylde*, shield — *schylde*, child.

Many of the ballads which are well-known in England to-day have an antiquity scarcely inferior to the one cited above. "For He's a Jolly Good Fellow," for example (known in America as "We Won't Go Home Till Morning"), can be traced through the the French "Malbrooke" to the old crusader "Mambron," and its melody was heard in Palestine in the twelfth century. Oddly enough, the tune took root in the East, and can be heard to-day in many an Oriental city. The fellaheen of Egypt claim the tune as their own, and so it is, if eight centuries of possession can make it so. "There Were Three Crows Sat on a Tree," "Lord Lovell," and several other popular ballads of the day can also be traced, in varying shapes, to a remote past.

It is natural, therefore, to find the ballad playing a prominent part, in many ways, in the Shakespearian drama. If the ballad appears in the action less frequently than the lyrical song, it is none the less used, at times, with peculiar fitness and occasionally with a power that is phenomenal. To this last category belong the ballads that Ophelia sings during her fits of madness. Nothing can be more pathetic than the introduction of light and inconsequential ballad music in these moments of darkness and agony. Just as a single candle might throw into more terrible contrast the blackness of some vast cavern, just as the mirth and revelry expressed in the "Ça Ira" and the "Carmagnole" made more frightful the scenes in the French Reign of Terror, which they accompanied, so the woes of Ophelia are emphasised and doubly impressed upon the auditor by the ribald music that she sings.

Fortunately, in this case we have the very music which Shakespeare employed. When Drury Lane Theatre was burned, in 1812, the old transcription of the melodies, which had been handed down from the original sources, was lost; an enthusiastic musician, however, to whom all Shakespearians owe thanks, Doctor Arnold, sought out Mrs. Jordan, who had often played the part of Ophelia, and from her lips transcribed the tunes that she had so frequently sung. Mr. Linley also wrote down the melodies from memory, having heard Miss Field (afterward Mrs. Forster) sing the tunes in the above mentioned theatre. The two versions agree well enough for one to prove the other, but the Arnold transcription (which we reproduce for our readers) is probably the more authentic. The scenes in which the ballads occur are as follows :

"*Re-enter* HORATIO *with* OPHELIA.

Ophelia.   Where is the beauteous majesty of Denmark?
Queen.   How now, Ophelia?
Ophelia.   ' How should I your true love know
                From another one?

By his cockle hat and staff,
And his sandal shoon?'   [*Singing.*

Queen.   Alas, sweet lady, what imports this song?
Ophelia.   Say you? nay, pray you, mark.

'He is dead and gone, lady,   [*Sings.*
He is dead and gone;
At his head a green-grass turf,
At his heels a stone.'

O, ho.

Queen.   Nay, but Ophelia—
Ophelia.   Pray you, mark.

'White his shroud as the mountain snow.'   [*Sings.*

Enter KING.

Queen.   Alas, look here, my lord.
Ophelia.   'Larded all with sweet flowers,
Which bewept to the grave did go,[1]
With true-love showers.'

King.   How do you, pretty lady?
Ophelia.   Well, God 'ield you! They say the owl was a
baker's daughter. Lord, we know what we are, but know not
what we may be. God be at your table.

King.   Conceit upon her father.
Ophelia.   Pray, let us have no words of this; but when
they ask what it means say you this:

'Good morrow, 'tis Saint Valentine's day,
All in the morning betime,
And I a maid at your window,
To be your Valentine:"

[1] Knight, Pope, Steevens, and others give this "did *not* go,"
arguing that Polonius was not a youth, hence *no* true-love showers.

Regarding the "cockle hat and staff," Warburton says (Vol. VIII. p. 224) that these are the distinguishing marks of a pilgrim. The chief places of devotion being beyond sea, the pilgrims were wont to put cockle-shells in their hats to denote the intention or performance of their devotion. The allusion to the owl and the baker's daughter is explained by an old ballad (of which we have, however, never seen a copy), in which the tale is told of the Saviour going to a baker's shop and asking bread; he was given a

And how should I your true love know, From many another one? O by his cock-le Hat, and Staff, And by his San-dal Shoon. Twang, lang, dil-do, dee.

Gaily.

Good mor-row, 'tis St. Valen-tine's Day, All

in the morning be - time, ... And I a

rall.

Maid at your window To be your Val-en - tine.

Mournfully.

And will he not come a - gain, And will he not

come a - gain? No, no, no, he is dead. Gone

to his Death bed, And he nev-er will come a - gain.

large lump of dough by the baker, but the daughter, thinking the portion too large, took away half. When the portion of Christ was put in the oven it began to swell larger and larger, while the baker's daughter began to hoot and cry and was turned into an owl. The song about St. Valentine's Day is commented upon by Halliwell thus :

"This song alludes to the custom of the first girl seen by a man on the morning of this day being considered his Valentine, or True-love."

The custom is of great antiquity in England, but probably did not have its origin there; indeed it can be traced back to the Roman *Lupercalia*, and probably arose from the ancient idea that birds chose their mates on February 14th, St. Valentine's Day. There is nothing in the life of the saint that would seem to make him sponsor for the amatory character of the festivities.

The later part of the scene (the fifth of the fourth act) soon follows:

"*Enter* OPHELIA, *fantastically dressed with straws and flowers.*

Laertes. O heat, dry up my brains! tears, seven times salt,
Burn out the sense and virtue of mine eye! —
By Heaven, thy madness shall be paid with weight,
Till our scale turn the beam. O rose of May!
Dear maid, kind sister, sweet Ophelia! —
O Heavens! is't possible, a young maid's wits
Should be as mortal as an old man's life?
Nature is fine in love: and, where 'tis fine,
It sends some precious instance of itself
After the thing it loves.

Ophelia. 'They bore him barefaced on the bier;
　　　　Hey no nonny, nonny hey nonny:
　　　　And in his grave rain'd many a tear;' —
Fare you well, my dove!

Laertes. Hadst thou thy wits, and didst persuade revenge,
It could not move thus.

Ophelia. You must sing, 'Down a-down, an you call him a-down-a.' O, how the wheel becomes it! It is the false steward, that stole his master's daughter.

Laertes. This nothing's more than matter.

Ophelia. There's rosemary, that's for remembrance; pray you, love, remember; and there is pansies, that's for thoughts.

Laertes. A document in madness; thoughts and remembrance fitted.

Ophelia. There's fennel for you, and columbines: — there's rue for you; and here's some for me: — we may call it, herb of grace o' Sundays: — you may wear your rue with a difference. — There's a daisy: — I would give you some violets; but they withered all, when my father died: — They say, he made a good end, —

    ' For bonny sweet Robin is all my joy.'   [*Sings.*

Laertes.   Thought and affliction, passion, hell itself,
            She turns to favour, and to prettiness.
Ophelia.   [*Sings*] ' And will he not come again?
            And will he not come again?
                No, no, he is dead,
                Go to thy death-bed,
            He never will come again.
            His beard was as white as snow,
            All flaxen was his poll:
                He is gone, he is gone,
                And we cast away moan;
            God 'a mercy on his soul!'
And of all Christian souls!   I pray God.   God be wi' you.
                                    [*Exit Ophelia.*
Laertes.   Do you see this, O God!"

The reader will note how the burdens follow each other in this scene. "Hey no nonny, nonny, hey nonny," is followed by "Down a down, an you call him a-down-a," which is very similiar to what Mistress Quickly sings in the third scene of the first act of "The Merry Wives of Windsor," and Ophelia praises the refrain with "O, how the wheel becomes it," meaning that the burden fits well to its song, and not, as Knight suggests, that it was adapted to be sung by spinners at the wheel.[1] The ballad of which this appears to be the burden, *i. e.* the false steward who stole his master's daughter, has eluded attempts at identification thus far. The fragment, "For bonny sweet Robin is all my joy," is found in the old volume known as "Queen Elizabeth's Virginal Book." It seems to have been very popular in Shakespeare's day, for Fletcher alludes to the tune as "Bonny Robin," in "Two Noble Kinsmen," and several ballads were sung to its melody. We give the melody as it was commonly sung, with a single line of the words, — all that remains of the original poetry. As it appears in William Ballet's Lute-book, a valuable manuscript in the library of Trinity College, Dublin (and older than the Elizabethan volume cited above), under the title "Robin Hood Is to the Greenwood Gone," it is possible that this was one of the many ballads made upon the old English popular hero.

[1] Bishop Hall's censure of ballads in 1597 runs :

"Some drunken rhymer thinks his time well spent
If he can live to see his name in print;
Who, when he once is fleshèd to the presse,
And sees his handsell have such faire successe,
Sung to the wheele and sung unto the payle,
He sends forth thraves of ballads to the sale."

In "Much Ado About Nothing" (Act i. Sc. 1) Benedick refers contemptuously to "a ballad-maker's pen."

In the last ballad, or rather song, which Ophelia sings, the line, "God 'a mercy on his soul," has been changed in some editions to "Gramercy on his soul;" the Folio gives the latter, the Quartos the former reading.

But there is something far deeper to study, in this scene, than mere quibbles about readings, or the tracing of burdens to their original context, or even the tunes of the ballads themselves, beautiful as their effect must have been (and still is) upon the stage; it is the wonderful subtlety with which these snatches of song illustrate the insanity of the unhappy heroine. We have already alluded to the added power which their contrast gives to the pathos of the action, but there is a touch more subtile than this in the song of Valentine's Day. The second stanza of this becomes rather coarse and indelicate, and is the most decided proof of the entire alienation of the chaste Ophelia's mind. Physicians know that often the estranged mind becomes the opposite of its sane self, the silent become garrulous, the religious become blasphemous, and here we have the gentle Ophelia becoming ribald and vulgar. It has been asked, however, how could such a maiden have learned such songs? To this we reply that it was not necessary that she should have *learned* them; it would suffice that she should have heard them, or even once have been shocked by them. The author was recently told of the case of an insane servant girl (by Dr. Charles R. Walker, of Concord, Mass.) who, in her delirium, spoke entire Latin sentences. She had been in the family of a scholar who sometimes read Virgil aloud to his wife and daughter, and had caught the sound of the verses unconsciously.

It is interesting to compare the songs of Edgar, simulating madness, in "King Lear," with these jangling fragments of prettiness; here, too, we find broken bits of tunes and inconsequential sentences.

"Pillicock sat on Pillicock-hill,
     Halloo, halloo, loo, loo."

"Saint Withold footed thrice the wold;
   He met the night-mare, and her nine-fold;
      Bid her alight
      And her troth plight,
      And aroint thee, witch, aroint thee."

"But mice, and rats, and such small deer,
   Have been Tom's food for seven long year."

These are parts of the ravings of the pseudo-lunatic, and Staunton rightly conjectures that they should be sung rather than recited, the latter being the case with most representations of the character. All of the citations given above, and the other similar fragments, which it is not necessary to quote, are fragments of musical ballads and songs, sometimes of nursery rhymes which had a dozen varying tunes at the caprice of the singer.

The mad-scenes in "King Lear" are not comparable with the subtle ones in "Hamlet," save in the one point that in both plays agony is emphasised by a frivolous background. The melodies attached to Edgar's songs are unfortunately not preserved to us, but it may be interesting, in this connection, to state that England was particularly fond of "mad-songs" (see Hawkins's "History of Music," Vol. II. p. 825), and Tom o' Bedlam was a regular character in the seventeenth century. The madman upon the stage was regarded as a sort of clown, of a particularly spicy character; the audience generally laughed heartily at the mad-scenes, and one is not astonished to find the fool, in "King Lear," capping Edgar's verse (Act iii. Sc. 6).

> "*Edgar.*   Come o'er the bourn, Bessie, to me:
> *Fool.*   Her boat hath a leak,
>   And she must not speak
>   Why she dares not come over to thee."

The song, "Come O'er the Bourn, Bessie," was entered at Stationer's Hall, in 1562.

It is quite possible that Shakespeare in the mad-scenes made a concession to the popular taste of his time. This would place the Ophelia songs on a lower level than that which is generally assigned them, and would also deteriorate the effect of the scenes in "King Lear," just alluded to. Inferential evidence that this may have been the case may be found in Fletcher's "Two Noble Kinsmen" (Act iv. Sc. 3), where the gaoler's daughter appears in a distraught condition, and gives fragments of songs quite in the Ophelian manner, and also becomes highly indelicate in her language. The rustic revellers and the schoolmaster, in this scene, think it great sport to find a madwoman to join in their morris-dance, and the whole scene was evidently intended to pro‹ voke the *mirth* of the audience.

We may suppose, however, that Shakespeare made use of the fondness of his public for a mad-scene, and turned the hilarity into a more worthy channel. Fletcher's gaoler's daughter certainly seems but a vulgar caricature of Ophelia.

We can turn from the fragmentary musical mutter‹ ings of Edgar, with much delight, to the rollicking picture of ballad-singing given in connection with Autolycus, in "Winter's Tale." Here we have a minstrel such as England possessed regiments of in the ancient times; such as were persecuted by law, hounded by the Church (see Chapter IX.), yet remained to the end a set of jolly, Bohemian repro-bates. The scenes in which Autolycus is prominent are here given (Act iv. Sc. 2) :

> "*A Road near the Shepherd's Cottage.*
>
> *Enter* AUTOLYCUS, *singing.*
>
> ' When daffodils begin to peer, —
>   With, heigh ! the doxy over the dale, —
> Why, then comes in the sweet o' the year;
>   For the red blood reigns in the winter's pale.
>
> ' The white sheet bleaching on the hedge, —
>   With, heigh ! the sweet birds, O, how they sing ! —
> Doth set my pugging tooth on edge;
>   For a quart of ale is a dish for a king.

> ' The lark, that tirra-lirra chants, —
>   With, hey! with, hey! the thrush and the jay, —
> Are summer songs for me and my aunts,
>   While we lie tumbling in the hay.'

I have served prince Florizel, and, in my time, wore three-pile; but now I am out of service;

> ' But shall I go mourn for that, my dear?
>   The pale moon shines by night;
> And, when I wander here and there,
>   I then do most go right.

> ' If tinkers may have leave to live,
>   And bear the sow-skin budget;
> Then my account I well may give,
>   And in the stocks avouch it.'

My traffic is sheets; when the kite builds, look to lesser linen. My father named me Autolycus; who being, as I am, littered under Mercury, was likewise a snapper-up of unconsidered trifles. With die and drab, I purchased this caparison; and my revenue is the silly cheat: Gallows and knocks are too powerful on the highway; beating and hanging are terrors to me; for the life to come, I sleep out the thought of it. — A prize! a prize!"

After this delightful lyric (the music of which has unfortunately disappeared) the clown enters and is cheerfully robbed by Autolycus, who departs at the end of the scene, singing:

> " Jog on, jog on, the footpath way,
>   And merrily hent the stile-a;
> A merry heart goes all the day,
>   Your sad tires in a mile-a."

and of this an old melody still exists; we herewith
append it.   The tune is traced as far back as 1650,
and probably is the one known to Shakespeare nearly
a half-century before.   The next scene of the play
introduces Autolycus again.

Moderate Time.

Jog on, jog on the foot - path way, And
mer - ri - ly hent the stile a, A mer - ry heart goes
all the day, Your sad tires in a mile a.

" *Enter a* SERVANT.

Servant. O master, if you did but hear the pedler at the door, you would never dance again after a tabor and pipe; no, the bagpipe could not move you: he sings several tunes faster than you'll tell money; he utters them as he had eaten ballads, and all men's ears grew to his tunes.

Clown. He could never come better; he shall come in: I love a ballad but even too well; if it be doleful matter, merrily set down, or a very pleasant thing indeed, and sung lamentably.

Servant. He hath songs, for man or woman, of all sizes; no milliner can so fit his customers with gloves: he has the prettiest love-songs for maids; so without bawdry, which is strange; with such delicate burdens of ' dildos and fadings,' ' jump her and thump her;' and where some stretch-mouthed rascal would, as it were, mean mischief, and break a foul jape into the matter, he makes the maid to answer, ' Whoop, do me no harm, good man;' puts him off, slights him, with ' Whoop, do me no harm, good man.'

Polixenes. This is a brave fellow.

Clown. Believe me, thou talkest of an admirable conceited fellow. Has he any unbraided wares?

Servant. He hath ribands of all the colours i' the rainbow; points, more than all the lawyers in Bohemia can learnedly handle, though they come to him by the gross; inkles, caddisses, cambrics, lawns: why, he sings them over, as they were gods or goddesses: you would think, a smock were a she angel: he so chants to the sleeve hand, and the work about the square on't.

Clown. Pr'ythee, bring him in; and let him approach singing.

Perdita. Forewarn him, that he use no scurrilous words in his tunes.

Clown. You have of these pedlers, that have more in 'em than you'd think, sister.

Perdita. Ay, good brother, or go about to think.

Enter AUTOLYCUS, *singing.*

‘ Lawn, as white as driven snow;
  Cyprus, black as e’er was crow;
  Gloves, as sweet as damask roses;
  Masks for faces, and for noses;
  Bugle bracelet, necklace-amber;
  Perfume for a lady’s chamber;
  Golden quoifs, and stomachers,
  For my lads to give their dears;
  Pins, and poking sticks of steel,
  What maids lack from head to heel:
  Come, buy of me, come: come buy, come buy,
  Buy, lads, or else your lasses cry:
  Come, buy.’

Clown. If I were not in love with Mopsa, thou shouldst take no money of me; but being enthrall’d as I am, it will also be the bondage of certain ribands and gloves.

Mopsa. I was promised them against the feast; but they come not too late now.

Clown. What hast here? ballads?

Mopsa. Pray now, buy some: I love a ballad in print a-life; for then we are sure they are true.

Autolycus. Here’s one to a very doleful tune, how a usurer’s wife was brought to bed of twenty moneybags at a burden; and how she longed to eat adders’ heads, and toads carbona- doed.

Mopsa. Is it true, think you?

Autolycus. Very true, and but a month old.

Dorcas. Bless me from marrying a usurer!

Autolycus. Here’s the midwife’s name to ’t, one mistress Taleporter; and five or six honest wives, that were present: Why should I carry lies abroad?

Mopsa. ’Pray you now, buy it.

Clown. Come on, lay it by: And let’s first see more ballads; we’ll buy the other things anon.

Autolycus. Here's another ballad. Of a fish that appeared upon the coast, on Wednesday the four-score of April, forty thousand fathom above water, and sung this ballad against the hard hearts of maids. . . . The ballad is very pitiful, and as true.

Dorcas. Is it true too, think you?

Autolycus. Five justices' hands at it; and witnesses, more than my pack will hold.

Clown. Lay it by too: Another.

Autolycus. This is a merry ballad; but a very pretty one.

Mopsa. Let's have some merry ones.

Autolycus. Why, this is a passing merry one; and goes to the tune of 'Two maids wooing a man:' there's scarce a maid westward, but she sings it; 'tis in request, I can tell you.

Mopsa. We can both sing it; if thou'lt bear a part, thou shalt hear; 'tis in three parts.

Dorcas. We had the tune on 't a month ago.

Autolycus. I can bear my part; you must know, 'tis my occupation: have at it with you.

SONG.

A. Get you hence, for I must go;
    Where, it fits not you to know.
D. Whither? *M.* O, whither? *D.* Whither?
M. It becomes thy oath full well,
    Thou to me thy secrets tell:
D. Me too, let me go thither.

M. Or thou go'st to the grange or mill:
D. If to either, thou dost ill.
A. Neither. *D.* What neither? *A.* Neither.
D. Thou hast sworn my love to be:
M. Thou hast sworn it more to me;
    Then whither go'st? say, whither?

Clown. We'll have this song out anon by ourselves: My father and the gentlemen are in sad talk, and we'll not trouble them. Come, bring away thy pack after me. Wenches, I'll buy for you both. Pedler; let's have the first choice. — Follow me, girls.

Autolycus. And you shall pay well for 'em. [*Aside.*

> 'Will you buy any tape,
>   Or lace for your cape,
>   My dainty duck, my dear-a?
>   Any silk, any thread,
>   Any toys for your head,
>   Of the new'st, and finest, finest, wear-a?
>   Come to the pedler;
>   Money's a medlar,
>   That doth utter all men's ware-a.'

> [*Exeunt Clown, Autolycus, Dorcas, and Mopsa.*"

We have already spoken of the refrains of the old ballads; "dildos and fadings" allude to these refrains. Malone, Theobald, and Tyrwhitt agree that "fadings" meant an old Irish dance. Malone was told by Irish antiquaries that it was derived from "Rinca Fada," "The Long Dance," and he quotes a song from "Sportive Wit" (1666), which implies that it was rustic in character.

> "The courtiers scorn us country clowns,
>   We country clowns do scorn the court;
>   We can be as merry upon the downs,
>   As you at midnight, with all your sport,
>   With a fading, with a fading."

Knight (Vol. II. p. 383), gives a full account of the style of this dance. The "jape" was a violent explosion of mirth, and in this connection we have another Shakespearian jest, for the clown suggests that Autolycus reproves evil-meaning mirth with "Whoop, do me no harm, good man," which would be like trying to extinguish a fire with oil, for the ballad with this refrain was decidedly not fit for publication. Furness says (Variorum Edition, Vol. XI. p. 208) :

"Indeed, the humour, in the whole of this speech by the clown, would be relished by an Elizabethan audience, to whom the praise bestowed by the clown on the decency of the ballad would be at once recognised as one of the jokes."

Naylor, in his "*Shakespeare and Music,*" gives the following melody, of which the last words only are presented, as being a popular tune of the 16th century.

AUTOLYCUS.

[Whoop, do me no harm, good man.]

The "ballad of a fish" affords an instance of microscopic commentary. Halliwell, not content

with the fact that Shakespeare is satirising the
entire class of sensational ballads, tries to show
that there was a ballad about a "monstruous fish,"
published about seven years before this play was
written.   He devotes five long pages to a number
of fish ballads ("Oh, Flesh, Flesh, how art thou
fishified!") and other "monstruosities."   The fact
of such humble folk as are here represented joining
in a three-part song might be an exaggeration for
Bohemia in the epoch, but was possible in England,
and we may repeat that, whether the scene be in
Bohemia or elsewhere, it is only England, and Elizabethan and Jacobean England, that is represented.
The original music of the songs of Autolycus in
this scene has unfortunately been lost.

Among the old ballads of England we frequently
find some which present the plots of some of Shakespeare's plays in so direct a fashion that one might
readily imagine the poet borrowing points from them,
in spite of the generally adverse verdict of the commentators.   The ballad of "Gernutus, the Jew of
Venice," runs so close to the "Merchant of Venice,"
that it has been supposed that Shakespeare, here
at least, drew part of his drama from the old song-
recital.   Furness believes this not to have been the
case, and certain added incidents which are not
found in the ballad, and are to be discovered in an
old Italian novel by Ser Giovanni, would indicate

that the play and the ballad both came from the same source. We give the ballad entire, from Percy's "Reliques," and also its melody as discovered by Doctor Rimbault.

GERNUTUS, THE JEW OF VENICE.

In Ve - nice towne not long a - go A
With - in that ci - ty dwelt that time, A

cru - el Jew did dwell, Which liv - ed all on
merchant of great fame, Which be - ing dis - tressed

u - su - rie, As I - ta - lian writ - ers tell.
in his need Un - to Ger - nu - tus came!

"A new Song, shewing the crueltie of Gernutus, a Jewe, who lending to a merchant an hundred crowns, would have a pound of fleshe, because he could not pay him at the time appointed.   To the tune of 'Black and Yellow.'"

THE FIRST PART.

In Venice towne not long agoe
   A cruel Jew did dwell,
Which lived all on usurie,
   As Italian writers tell.

Gernutus called was the Jew,
   Which never thought to dye,
Nor ever yet did any good
   To them in streets that lie.

His life was like a barrow hogge,
   That liveth many a day,
Yet never once doth any good
   Until men will him slay.

Or like a filthy heap of dung,
   That lieth in a whoard;
Which never can do any good,
   Till it be spread abroad.

So fares it with the usurer,
   He cannot sleep in rest,
For feare the thiefe will him pursue
   To plucke him from his nest.

His hearte doth thinke on many a wile,
   How to deceive the poore;
His mouth is almost ful of mucke,
   Yet still he gapes for more.

His wife must lend a shilling,
    For every weeke a penny,
Yet bring a pledge that is double worth,
    If that you will have any.

And see, likewise, you keepe your day,
    Or else you loose it all:
This was the living of the wife,
    Her cow she did it call.

Within that citie dwelt that time
    A marchant of great fame,
Which being distressed in his need,
    Unto Gernutus came:

Desiring him to stand his friend
    For twelve month and a day;
To lend to him an hundred crownes;
    And he for it would pay

Whatsoever he would demand of him,
    And pledges he should have:
" No " (quoth the Jew with flearing lookes),
    "Sir, aske what you will have,

" No penny for the loane of it
    For one you shall pay;
You may doe me as good a turne,
    Before my dying day.

" But we will have a merry jeast,
    For to be talked long:
You shall make me a bond," quoth he,
    " That shall be large and strong:

" And this shall be the forfeyture,
    Of your owne fleshe a pound:

If you agree, make you the bond,
　　And here is a hundred crownes."

"With right good will!" the marchant says:
　　And so the bond was made.
When twelve month and a day drew on,
　　That backe it should be payd,

The marchant's ships were all at sea,
　　And money came not in;
Which way to take, or what to doe
　　To thinke he doth begin.

And to Gernutus strait he comes,
　　With cap and bended knee;
And sayde to him, "Of curtesie,
　　I pray you beare with mee.

"My day is come, and I have not
　　The money for to pay:
And little good the forfeyture
　　Will doe you, I dare say."

"With all my heart," Gernutus sayd,
　"Commaund it to your minde:
In thinges of bigger waight then this
　　You shall me ready finde."

He goes his way; the day once past,
　　Gernutus doth not slacke
To get a sergiant presently,
　　And clapt him on the backe.

And layd him into prison strong,
　　And sued his bond withall;
And when the judgement day was come,
　　For judgement he did call.

The marchant's friends came thither fast,
　With many a weeping eye,
For other means they could not find,
　But he that day must dye.

THE SECOND PART.

"Of the Jew's crueltie: setting foorth the mercifulnesse of
the Judge towards the Marchant. To the tune of 'Blacke
and Yellow.'"

Some offered for his hundred crownes
　Five hundred for to pay;
And some a thousand, two or three,
　Yet still he did denay.

And at the last ten thousand crownes
　They offered, him to save:
Gernutus sayd, "I will no gold,
　My forfeite I will have.

"A pound of fleshe is my demand,
　And that shall be my hire."
Then sayd the judge, "Yet, good my friend,
　Let me of you desire

"To take the flesh from such a place,
　As yet you let him live:
Do so, and lo! an hundred crownes
　To thee here will I give."

"No, no," quoth he, "no, judgment here;
　For this it shall be tride;
For I will have my pound of fleshe
　From under his right side."

It grieved all the companie
　His crueltie to see,

For neither friend nor foe could helpe
  But he must spoyled bee.

The bloudie Jew now ready is
  With whetted blade in hand,
To spoyle the bloud of innocent,
  By forfeit of his bond.

And as he was about to strike
  In him the deadly blow,
" Stay " (quoth the judge) " thy crueltie ;
  I charge thee to do so.

" Sith needs thou wilt thy forfeit have,
  Which is of flesh a pound,
See that thou shed no drop of bloud,
  Nor yet the man confound.

" For if thou doe, like murderer
  Thou here shalt hanged be :
Likewise of flesh see that thou cut
  No more than longes to thee.

" For if thou take either more or lesse,
  To the value of a mite,
Thou shall be hanged presently,
  As is both law and right."

Gernutus now waxt franticke mad,
  And wotes not what to say ;
Quoth he at last, " Ten thousand crownes
  I will that he shall pay ;

" And so I graunt to set him free."
  The judge doth answere make ;
" You shall not have a penny given ;
  Your forfeyture now take."

At the last he doth demaund
    But for to have his owne :
" No," quoth the judge, " doe as you list,
    Thy judgement shall be showne.

" Either take your pound of flesh," quoth he,
    " Or cancell me your bond : "
" O cruell judge," then quoth the Jew,
    " That doth against me stand ! "

And so with griping grieved mind
    He biddeth them farewell :
Then all the people prays'd the Lord,
    That ever this heard tell.

Good people, that doe heare this song,
    For trueth I dare well say,
That many a wretch as ill as hee
    Doth live now at this day ;

That seeketh nothing but the spoyle
    Of many a wealthey man,
And for to trap the innocent
    Deviseth what they can.

From whome the Lord deliver me,
    And every Christian too,
And send to them like sentence eke
    That meaneth so to doe.

Nor is the " Merchant of Venice" the only play
which comes near to an anterior ballad ; " King Lear "
also has its prototype in this shape. In this case
there is no sure evidence that the ballad preceded
the play. The melody, which we also present, is the
old melody known as " Flying Fame," which was very

popular in the seventeenth century, but cannot be traced to a definite date of origin.

KING LEAR AND HIS THREE DAUGHTERS.

King Lear once rul - ed in this land, With prince - ly pow'r and peace; And had all things with hearts con - tent, That might his joys in - crease.

A lamentable song of the death of King Leir and his three Daughters. To the tune of "When Flying Fame."

King Leir once ruled in this land
With princely power and peace,

And had all things with hearts content,
 That might his joys increase.
Amongst those things that nature gave,
 Three daughters fair had he,
So princely seeming beautiful,
 As fairer could not be.

So on a time it pleas'd the king
 A question thus to move,
Which of his daughters to his grace
 Could shew the dearest love:
" For to my age you bring content,"
 Quoth he, " then let me hear,
Which of you three in plighted troth
 The kindest will appear."

To whom the eldest thus began:
 " Dear father, mind," quoth she,
" Before your face, to do you good,
 My blood shall render'd be.
And for your sake my bleeding heart
 Shall here be cut in twain,
Ere that I see your reverend age
 The smallest grief sustain."

" And so will I," the second said;
 " Dear father, for your sake,
The worst of all extremities
 I'll gently undertake:
And serve your highness night and day
 With diligence and love;
That sweet content and quietness
 Discomforts may remove."

" In doing so, you glad my soul,"
 The aged king repli'd;

" But what sayst thou, my youngest girl,
  How is thy love ally'd ? "
" My love " (quoth young Cordelia then),
  " Which to your grace I owe,
Shall be the duty of a child,
  And that is all I'll show."

" And wilt thou shew no more," quoth he,
  " Than doth thy duty bind ?
I well perceive thy love is small,
  When as no more I find.
Henceforth I banish thee my court;
  Thou art no child of mine;
Nor any part of this my realm
  By favour shall be thine.

" Thy elder sisters loves are more
  Than well I can demand;
To whom I equally bestow
  My kingdome and my land,
My pompal state and all my goods,
  That lovingly I may
With those thy sisters be maintain'd
  Until my dying day."

Thus flattering speeches won renown,
  By these two sisters here;
The third had causeless banishment,
  Yet was her love more dear.
For poor Cordelia patiently
  Went wandring up and down,
Unhelp'd, unpity'd, gentle maid,
  Through many an English town:

Untill at last in famous France
  She gentler fortunes found;

Though poor and bare, yet she was deem'd
    The fairest on the ground:
Where when the king her virtues heard,
    And this fair lady seen,
With full consent of all his court
    He made his wife and queen.

Her father, old King Leir, this while
    With his two daughters staid;
Forgetful of their promis'd loves,
    Full soon the same decay'd;
And living in Queen Ragan's court,
    The eldest of the twain,
She took from him his chiefest means,
    And most of all his train.

For whereas twenty men were wont
    To wait with bended knee,
She gave allowance but to ten,
    And after scarce to three,
Nay, one she thought too much for him;
    So took she all away,
In hope that in her court, good king,
    He would no longer stay.

" Am I rewarded thus," quoth he,
    " In giving all I have
Unto my children, and to beg
    For what I lately gave?
I'll go unto my Gonorell:
    My second child, I know,
Will be more kind and pitiful,
    And will relieve my woe."

Full fast he hies then to her court;
    Where when she heard his moan,

Return'd him answer, that she griev'd
  That all his means were gone,
But no way could relieve his wants;
  Yet if that he would stay
Within her kitchen, he should have
  What scullions gave away.

When he had heard, with bitter tears,
  He made his answer then;
" In what I did, let me be made
  Example to all men.
I will return again," quoth he,
  " Unto my Ragan's court;
She will not use me thus, I hope,
  But in a kinder sort."

Where when he came, she gave command
  To drive him thence away:
When he was well within her court,
  (She said) he would not stay.
Then back again to Gonorell
  The woeful king did hie,
That in her kitchen he might have
  What scullion boys set by.

But there of that he was deny'd
  Which she had promis'd late:
For once refusing, he should not,
  Come after to her gate.
Thus twixt his daughters for relief
  He wandred up and down,
Being glad to feed on beggars food
  That lately wore a crown.

And calling to remembrance then
  His youngest daughters words,

That said, the duty of a child
　　Was all that love affords —
But doubting to repair to her,
　　Whom he had banish'd so,
Grew frantic mad; for in his mind
　　He bore the wounds of woe.

Which made him rend his milk-white locks
　　And tresses from his head,
And all with blood bestain his cheeks,
　　With age and honour spread.
To hills and woods and watry founts,
　　He made his hourly moan,
Till hills and woods and senseless things
　　Did seem to sigh and groan.

Even thus possest with discontents,
　　He passed o're to France,
In hopes from fair Cordelia there
　　To find some gentler chance.
Most virtuous dame! which, when she heard
　　Of this her father's grief,
As duty bound, she quickly sent
　　Him comfort and relief.

And by a train of noble peers,
　　In brave and gallant sort,
She gave in charge he should be brought
　　To Aganippus' court;
Whose royal king, with noble mind,
　　So freely gave consent
To muster up his knights at arms,
　　To fame and courage bent.

And so to England came with speed,
　　To repossesse King Leir,

And drive his daughters from their thrones
    By his Cordelia dear.
Where she, true-hearted, noble queen,
    Was in the battel slain ;
Yet he, good king, in his old days,
    Possest his crown again.

But when he heard Cordelia's death,
    Who died indeed for love
Of her dear father, in whose cause
    She did this battle move,
He swooning fell upon her breast,
    From whence he never parted ;
But on her bosom left his life
    That was so truly hearted.

The lords and nobles, when they saw
    The end of these events,
The other sisters unto death
    They doomed by consents ;
And being dead, their crowns they left
    Unto the next of kin :
Thus have you seen the fall of pride,
    And disobedient sin.

We cite one more example of an old English ballad
related to the Shakespearian drama.   As in the case
of the one quoted above, it is difficult to determine
whether the play or the ballad came first, yet, we
may suppose, had the tragedy preceded the ballad,
the song writer would have availed himself of some
of the leading incidents which are conspicuous by
their absence in his effort.   The same point may be

argued in favour of the precedence of the other two ballads given, to the plays with which they seem related. But it would be hazardous to fix a definite date for such fugitive compositions as these; the reader must seek his own verdict by comparison, in this case. The author does not consider them valuable Shakespearian data, but presents them (from Bishop Percy's " Reliques " and Rimbault's " Musical Illustrations) " as good examples of the old English ballad style in its fullest prolixity and musical monotony.

THE LAMENTABLE AND TRAGICAL HISTORY OF TITUS ANDRONICUS.

To the tune of " Fortune."

TITUS ANDRONICUS'S COMPLAINT.

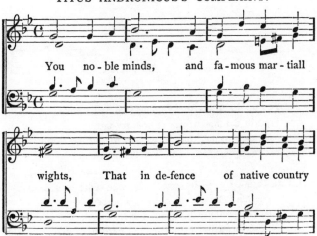

fights, Give eare to me, that ten yeares fought for Rome, Yet reapt dis- grace at my re - turn-ing home.

You noble minds, and famous martiall wights,
That in defence of native country fights,
Give eare to me, that ten yeares fought for Rome,
Yet reapt disgrace at my returning home.

In Rome I lived in fame fulle three-score yeares,
My name beloved was of all my peeres;
Full five-and-twenty valiant sonnes I had,
Whose forwarde vertues made their father glad.

For when Romes foes their warlike forces bent,
Against them stille my sonnes and I were sent;
Against the Goths full ten yeares weary warre
We spent, receiving many a bloudy scarre.

Just two-and-twenty of my sonnes were slaine
Before we did returne to Rome againe:
Of five-and-twenty sonnes, I brought but three
Alive, the stately towers of Rome to see.

When wars were done, I conquest home did bring,
And did present my prisoners to the king,
The Queene of Goths, her sons, and eke a Moore,
Which did such murders, like was nere before.

The emperour did make this queene his wife,
Which bred in Rome debate and deadlie strife;
The Moore, with her two sonnes, did growe soe proud,
That none like them in Rome might bee allowd.

The Moore soe pleas'd this new-made empress' eie,
That she consented to him secretlye
For to abuse her husbands marriage-bed,
And soe in time a blackamore she bred.

Then she, whose thoughts to murder were inclinde,
Consented with the Moore of bloody minde
Against myselfe, my kin, and all my friendes,
In cruell sort to bring them to their endes.

Soe when in age I thought to live in peace,
Both care and griefe began then to increase:
Amongst my sonnes I had one daughter bright,
Which joy'd and pleased best my aged sight.

My deare Lavinia was betrothed than
To Cesars sonne, a young and noble man:
Who, in a hunting by the emperours wife
And her two sonnes, bereaved was of life.

He, being slaine, was cast in cruel wise
Into a darksome den from light of skies:
The cruell Moore did come that way as then
With my three sonnes, who fell into the den.

The Moore then fetcht the emperour with speed,
For to accuse them of that murderous deed;
And when my sonnes within the den were found,
In wrongfull prison they were cast and bound.

But nowe behold what wounded most my mind:
The empresses two sonnes, of savage kind,
My daughter ravished without remorse,
And took away her honour, quite perforce.

When they had tasted of soe sweete a flowre,
Fearing this sweete should shortly turn to sowre,
They cutt her tongue, whereby she could not tell
How that dishonoure unto her befell.

Then both her hands they basely cutt off quite,
Whereby their wickednesse she could not write,
Nor with her needle on her sampler sowe
The bloudye workers of her direfull woe.

My brother Marcus found her in the wood,
Staining the grassie ground with purple bloud,
That trickled from her stumpes and bloudlesse armes:
Noe tongue at all she had to tell her harmes.

But when I sawe her in that woefull case,
With teares of bloud I wet mine aged face:
For my Lavinia I lamented more
Then for my two-and-twenty sonnes before.

When as I sawe she could not write nor speake
With grief mine aged heart began to breake;
We spred an heape of sand upon the ground,
Whereby those bloudy tyrants out we found.

For with a staffe, without the helpe of hand,
She writt these wordes upon the plat of sand:
" The lustfull sonnes of the proud emperesse
Are doers of this hateful wickednesse."

I tore the milk-white hairs from off mine head,
I curst the houre wherein I first was bred;
I wisht this hand, that fought for countrie's fame,
In cradle rockt, had first been stroken lame.

The Moore, delighting still in villainy,
Did say, to sett my sonnes from prison free,
I should unto the king my right hand give,
And then my three imprisoned sonnes should live.

The Moore I caus'd to strike it off with speede,
Whereat I grieved not to see it bleed,
But for my sonnes would willingly impart,
And for their ransome send my bleeding heart.

But as my life did linger thus in paine,
They sent to me my bootlesse hand againe,
And therewithal the heades of my three sonnes,
Which filld my dying heart with fresher moanes.

Then, past reliefe, I upp and downe did goe,
And with my teares writ in the dust my woe:
I shot my arrowes towards heaven hie,
And for revenge to hell often did crye.

The empresse then, thinking that I was mad,
Like Furies she and both her sonnes were clad,
(She nam'd Revenge, and Rape and Murder they)
To undermine and heare what I would say.

I fed their foolish veines a certaine space,
Untill my friendes did find a secret place,
Where both her sonnes unto a post were bound,
And just revenge in cruell sort was found.

I cut their throates, my daughter held the pan
Betwixt her stumpes, wherein the bloud it ran:
And then I ground their bones to powder small,
And made a paste for pyes streight therewithall.

Then with their fleshe I made two mighty pyes,
And at a banquet served in stately wise,
Before the empresse set this loathsome meat;
So of her sonnes own flesh she well did eat.

Myselfe bereav'd my daughter then of life,
The empresse then I slewe with bloudy knife,
And stabb'd the emperour immediatelie,
And then myself: even soe did Titus die.

Then this revenge against the Moore was found:
Alive they sett him halfe into the ground,
Whereas he stood until such time he starv'd:
And soe God send all murderers may be serv'd.

More interesting than these dreary verses of a bygone time are the ballads which, as we have seen, Shakespeare introduced upon his own stage. Often a mere passing allusion was made to this or that popular tune, without introducing the ballad itself. We have seen Sir Toby naming catch after catch, yet only singing one complete specimen. Peter, in "Romeo and Juliet," mentions three songs, yet sings only the fragment of a single one. In like manner we find allusion made, in "Love's Labour's Lost" (Act i. Sc. 2), to one of the old ballads of a pre-Shakespearian time:

"*Armado.* Is there not a ballad, boy, of the King and the Beggar?

Moth. The world was very guilty of such a ballad some three ages since: but, I think, now 'tis not to be found, or, if it were, it would neither serve for the writing, nor the tune.

Armado. I will have the subject newly writ o'er, that I may example my digression by some mighty precedent. Boy, I do love that country girl, that I took in the park with that rational hind Costard; she deserves well.

Moth. To be whipped; and yet a better love than my master. [*Aside.*

Armado. Sing, boy; my spirit grows heavy in love.

Moth. And that's great marvel, loving a light wench.

Armado. I say, sing.

Moth. Forbear, till this company be past."

Nor is this the only Shakespearian allusion to the ballad of "King Cophetua and the Beggar Maid," for in " Romeo and Juliet " (Act ii. Sc. 2), Mercutio says :

> " Her purblind son and heir,
>   Young Adam Cupid, he that shot so true,
>   When King Cophetua loved the beggar-maid."

It is very probable that the second line of this sentence was taken from the first line of the second stanza of the following poem. Also in the Second Part of "Henry IV." (Act v. Sc. 3) Falstaff says to Pistol :

> " Oh base Assyrian knight, what is thy news?
>   Let King Cophetua know the truth thereof."

Other of the old dramatists occasionally drew their metaphors from the same source, — the following ballad, which Percy quotes from Richard Johnson's "Crown Garland of Goulden Roses," 1612.

A SONG OF A BEGGAR AND A KING.

I read that once in Affrica
    A princely wight did raine,
Who had to name Cophetua,
    As poets they did faine.
From natures lawes he did decline,
For sure he was not of my minde,
He cared not for women-kind,
    But did them all disdaine.
But marke what hapned on a day;
As he out of his window lay,
He saw a beggar all in gray,
    The which did cause his paine.

The blinded boy that shootes so trim
From heaven downe did hie,
He drew a dart and shot at him,
In place where he did lye:
Which soone did pierse him to the quicke,
And when he felt the arrow pricke,
Which in his tender heart did sticke,
He looketh as he would dye.
" What sudden chance is this," quoth he,
" That I to love must subject be,
Which never thereto would agree,
But still did it defie ? "

Then from the window he did come,
And laid him on his bed ;
A thousand heapes of care did runne
Within his troubled head.
For now he meanes to crave her love,
And now he seekes which way to proove
How he his fancie might remoove,
And not this beggar wed.
But Cupid had him so in snare,
That this poor beggar must prepare
A salve to cure him of his care,
Or els he would be dead.

And as he musing thus did lye,
He thought for to devise
How he might have her companye,
That so did 'maze his eyes.
" In thee," quoth he, " doth rest my life;
For surely thou shalt be my wife ;
Or else this hand with bloody knife,
The Gods shall sure suffice."
Then from his bed he soon arose,
And to his pallace gate he goes ;

Full little then this begger knowes
  When she the king espies.

" The gods preserve your majesty,"
  The beggers all gan cry ;
" Vouchsafe to give your charity,
  Our childrens food to buy."
The king to them his purse did cast,
And they to part it made great haste ;
This silly woman was the last
  That after them did hye.
The king he cal'd her back againe,
And unto her he gave his chaine ;
And said, " With us you shal remaine
  Till such time as we dye.

" For thou," quoth he, " shalt be my wife,
  And honoured for my queene ;
With thee I meane to lead my life,
  As shortly shall be seene :
Our wedding shall appointed be,
And every thing in its degree ;
Come on," quoth he, " and follow me,
  Thou shalt go shift thee cleane.
What is thy name, faire maide ? " quoth he.
" Penelophon, O King," quoth she ;
With that she made a lowe courtsèy ;
  A trim one as I weene.

Thus hand in hand along they walke
  Unto the king's pallace :
The king with courteous, comly talke
  This begger doth embrace.
The begger blusheth scarlet red,
And straight againe as pale as lead,

But not a word at all she said,
  She was in such amaze.
At last she spake with trembling voyce,
And said, " O King, I doe rejoyce
That you wil take me for your choyce,
  And my degree so base."

And when the wedding day was come,
  The king commanded strait
The noblemen, both all and some,
  Upon the queene to wait.
And she behaved herself that day
As if she had never walkt the way;
She had forgot her gowne of gray,
  Which she did weare of late.
The proverbe old is come to passe,
The priest, when he begins his masse,
Forgets that ever clerke he was;
  He knowth not his estate.

Here you may read Cophetua,
  Through long time fancie-fed,
Compelled by the blinded boy
  The begger for to wed:
He that did lovers lookes disdaine,
To do the same was glad and faine,
Or else he would himselfe have slaine,
  In storie, as we read.
Disdaine no whit, O lady deere,
But pitty now thy servant heere,
Least that it hap to thee this yeare,
  As to that king it did.

And thus they led a quiet life
  During their princely raine,

> And in a tombe were buried both,
>   As writers sheweth plaine.
> The lords they tooke it grievously,
> The ladies tooke it heavily,
> The commons cryed pitiously,
>   Their death to them was paine,
> Their fame did sound so passingly,
> That it did pierce the starry sky,
> And throughout all the world did flye
>   To every princes realme.

We need no apology for the quotation of this ballad in full, for Shakespeare makes abundant use of
it in the latter part of "Love's Labour's Lost."
Armado certainly keeps his promise of having the
subject "newly writ o'er," for his entire declaration
of love (Act iv. Sc. 1) is derived from the foregoing ballad.

"*Boyet.*   This letter is mistook, it importeth none here;
It is writ to Jaquenetta.
   Princess.   We will read it, I swear:
Break the neck of the wax, and every one give ear.
   Boyet. (*Reads*) "By Heaven, that thou art fair, is most infal-
lible; true, that thou art beauteous; truth itself, that thou art
lovely.   More fairer than fair, beautiful than beauteous, truer
than truth itself, have commiseration on thy heroical vassal!
The magnanimous and most illustrate king Cophetua set eye
upon the pernicious and indubitate beggar Zenelophon; [1] and
he it was that might rightly say, 'veni, vidi, vici;' which to
anatomize in the vulgar, (O base and obscure vulgar!) videli-
cet, he came, saw and overcame: he came, one; saw, two;

---

[1] Shakespeare probably intends an error here.

overcame, three. Who came? the king; Why did he come? to see: Why did he see? to overcome: To whom came he? to the beggar: What saw he? the beggar: Who overcame he? the beggar. The conclusion is victory; On whose side? the king's: The captive is enriched; On whose side? the beggar's; the catastrophe is a nuptial; On whose side? the king's?—no, on both in one, or one in both. I am the king; for so stands the comparison: thou the beggar; for so witnesseth thy lowliness. Shall I command thy love? I may. Shall I enforce thy love? I could. Shall I entreat thy love? I will. What shalt thou exchange for rags? robes; For tittles, titles: For thyself, me. Thus, expecting thy reply, I profane my lips on thy foot, my eyes on thy picture, and my heart on thy every part.

Thine, in the dearest design of industry.

DON ADRIANO DE ARMADO."

Another interesting introduction of a fragment of a ballad occurs in "Hamlet" (Act ii. Sc. 2), while the prince is feigning insanity, and here, as Shakespeare was fond of doing in his most piquant moments, we have the words of the poem strung along through the action :

"*Hamlet.* 'O Jephtha, judge of Israel,'—what a treasure hadst thou!

Polonius. What a treasure had he, my lord?

Hamlet. Why—' One fair daughter, and no more,
The which he loved passing well.'

Polonius. Still on my daughter. [*Aside.*

Hamlet. Am I not i' the right, old Jephtha?

Polonius. If you call me Jephtha, my lord, I have a daughter that I love passing well.

Hamlet. Nay, that follows not.

Polonius. What follows then, my lord?

Hamlet. Why, ' As by lot, God wot,' and then, you know,
' It came to pass, As most like it was,'— The first row of the
pious chanson will shew you more; for look, my abridgment
comes.

Enter Four or Five Players."

Although only the first part of this ballad is alluded
to here, it may be worth while to reprint as much of
it as Bishop Percy has discovered, for the sake of the
quaintness of the versification and the general *naïveté*
of the story.

> Have you not heard these many years ago,
>   Jeptha was judge of Israel?
> He had one only daughter and no mo,
>   The which he loved passing well.
>   And as by lott,
>   God wot,
>   It so came to pass,
>   As Gods will was,
> That great wars there should be,
> And none should be chosen chief but **he**.
>
> And when he was appointed judge,
>   And chieftain of the company,
> A solemn vow to God he made,
>   If he returned with victory,
>   At his return,
>   To burn
>   The first live thing.
>
>   .   .   .   .
>
> That should meet with him then,
> Off his house when he should return agen.

It came to pass, the wars was o'er,
   And he returned with victory;
His dear and only daughter first of all
   Came to meet her father foremostly:
         And all the way
         She did play
      On tabret and pipe,
      Full many a stripe,
With note so high,
For joy that her father is come so nigh.

But when he saw his daughter dear
   Coming on most foremostly,
He wrung his hands, and tore his hair,
   And cryed out most piteously:
      " Oh! it's thou," said he,
      " That have brought me
        Low,
   And troubled me so
   That I know not what to do.

" For I have made a vow," he sed,
  " The which must be replenished; "
 .   .   .   .
      " What thou hast spoke
        Do not revoke,
     What thou hast said;
     Be not afraid;
   Altho' it be I,
   Keep promises to God on high.

" But, dear father, grant me one request,
   That I may go to the wilderness,
Three months there with my friends to stay;
   There to bewail my virginity;

> And let there be,"
>   Said she,
>   " Some two or three
>   Young maids with me."
> So he sent her away,
>   For to mourn, for to mourn, till her dying day.

With one other ballad, which Shakespeare seems
to have enjoyed and to have quoted more than once,
we leave this branch of a subject that is apt to grow
dangerously prolix, because of the great length of
the old ballad-writers, and their carelessness of poetic
subtleties and refinements. " Greensleeves " comes
to the front twice in the comedy of " The Merry
Wives of Windsor." It is spoken of by Falstaff
(Act v. Sc. 5).

" Let the sky rain potatoes; let it thunder to the tune of
' Green Sleeves; ' hail kissing-comfits and snow eringoes; let
there come a tempest of provocation, I will shelter me here.
                                    [*Embraces Mrs. Ford.*"

But a far wittier jest than "thundering to the tune
of ' Greensleeves,' " is found in the first scene of the
second act of the same play. It is where Mistress
Ford and Mistress Page compare their love-letters.
As Mrs. Ford shows her own, she says :

" We burn day-light : — here, read, read; perceive how I
might be knighted. I shall think the worse of fat men, as
long as I have an eye to make difference of men's liking : and
yet he would not swear; praised woman's modesty; and gave

such orderly and well-behaved reproof to all uncomeliness, that I would have sworn his disposition would have gone to the truth of his words: but they do no more adhere and keep place together, than the hundredth Psalm to the tune of 'Green Sleeves.' What tempest, I trow, threw this whale, with so many tuns of oil in his belly, ashore at Windsor? How shall I be revenged on him?"

Here we find a most musicianly jest: the disagreement of Falstaff's words with his actual nature is compared to the disagreement of poetry with its musical setting. One finds plenty of such disagreements in the musical repertoire, but only the conscientious musician is shocked by them. Rossini presented the weeping mother, full of anguish and sorrow, standing beside the cross, by the most cheerful and brilliant music, in "Cujus Animam;" Donizetti pictured the heart-broken Lucia and the furious Edgar both to the same mellifluous strains, in the charmingly melodic sextette in "Lucia di Lammermoor." But thinkers in music do not tolerate such juggleries, and such widely separated personalities as Herbert Spencer (essay on "Education"), and Richard Wagner, have attacked such *mesalliances*. Here we find Shakespeare also giving an implied arraignment of such unfitness. The jest might be modernised into — "Falstaff's words and deeds no more fit together than Gray's 'Elegy' to the tune of Offenbach's 'Cancan.'"

Since Shakespeare has twice alluded to the old ballad, it is interesting to study what is known of it. It seems to have been very popular in the Elizabethan time, for Beaumont and Fletcher speak of it in " The Loyal Subject," it was attacked by Elderton in 1580, and numerous different sets of words were sung to it during the Shakespearian epoch, and in later times. It is spoken of as "a new tune," in 1580 and in 1584. It seems to have been of rather questionable character in its earliest stages. Of course a large part of the flavour of Shakespeare's jest arises from the yoking together a godly subject and a tune that had been associated with immorality. Chappell, in his " National Music " (p. 39), cites many different settings of the tune to all kinds of words, from Scriptural to political. It is, however, unquestionable that Shakespeare had in mind the wantonness of this ditty, in its original state, when he causes Mistress Ford to make her jest, for it thus becomes one of the most perfect musical metaphors in his works. Naylor ("Shakespeare and Music," p. 75) wastes his time in trying to fit " All people that on earth do dwell " (the hundredth psalm) to a tune of Hawkins, and proving that the accents come out wrong ; but the jest is much more spicy than a mere matter of accents.

We reproduce the tune of " Greensleeves " as it was sung in Shakespeare's time.

"GREENSLEEVES."

At the beginning of this chapter we found Shake-speare intensifying the effect of tragic scenes by light and frivolous songs ; that he did not always use such

an antithesis may be seen by referring to the third
scene of the fourth act of "Othello." This pathetic
portion of the play is as follows; Desdemona has a
presentiment of coming evil and says:

" My mother had a maid call'd — Barbara;
She was in love: and he, she loved, proved mad,
And did forsake her: she had a song of — willow,
An old thing 'twas, but it express'd her fortune,
And she died singing it: That song, to-night,
Will not go from my mind; I have much to do,
But to hang my head all at one side,
And sing it like poor Barbara.   Pr'ythee, despatch.
    Emilia.   Shall I go fetch your night-gown?
    Desdemona.   No, unpin me here.
This Lodovico is a proper man.
    Emilia.   A very handsome man.
    Desdemona.   He speaks well.
    Emilia.   I know a lady in Venice, who would have walked
bare-footed to Palestine, for a touch of his lip.

I.

Desdemona.   [*Sings.*
    ' The poor soul sat sighing by a sycamore tree,
        Sing all a green willow;
      Her hand on her bosom, her head on her knee,
        Sing willow, willow, willow:
      The fresh streams ran by her, and murmur'd her moans;
        Sing willow, etc.
      Her salt tears fell from her, and softened the stones;'
Lay by these:
        ' Sing willow, willow, willow:'
Pr'ythee, hie thee; he'll come anon —
      ' Sing all a green willow, must be my garland.'

II.

' Let nobody blame him, his scorn I approve,' —

Nay that's not next. — Hark ! who is it that knocks ?
  Emilia.   It is the wind.
  Desdemona.
    ' I call'd my love, false love ; but what said he then ?
      Sing willow, etc.
    If I court mo women, you'll couch with mo men.' "

Rolfe, in his edition of " Much Ado About Nothing," cites a number of instances of the willow being emblematic of an unhappy love, as, for example, Spenser in " Faerie Queene : "

" The willow, worne of forlorne Paramours ; "

Lyly, in " Sappho and Phao : "

" Enjoy thy care in covert ;
  Weare willow in thy hat, and bayes in thy heart ; "

Swan, " Speculum Mundi," 1635 :

" It is yet a custom that he which is deprived of his love must wear a willow garland ; "

and Fuller, in his " Worthies," describes the willow as —

" A sad tree, whereof such who have lost their love, make their mourning garlands, and we know what exiles hung up their harps upon such dolefull supporters. The twigs hereof are physick to drive out the folly of children," etc.[1]

[1] Rolfe Notes to " Much Ado About Nothing," p. 131.

Both Rossini and Verdi have set " Othello " as an opera, and both composed plaintive, folk-song-like melody to " O, Salce, Salce," — " O, Willow, Willow." It would have been a charming touch of antiquarian beauty, had the two composers introduced the tune, which Shakespeare himself intended to illustrate his scene, into their scores.

The melody which he employed is given herewith, a charming old English tune. It is taken from a manuscript in the British Museum.

The original words are given by Bishop Percy in his " Reliques of Ancient English Poetry." In the old black-letter copy the forsaken one is a youth and not a maiden ; Shakespeare evidently altered the words slightly to suit his dramatic purpose. The following version (Percy states) is taken from a copy in the Pepys collection, entitled, " A Lover's Complaint, being forsaken of his Love."

> A poore soule sat sighing under a sicamore tree ;
> O willow, willow, willow !
> With his hand on his bosom, his head on his knee :
> O willow, willow, willow !
> O willow, willow, willow !
> Sing, O the greene willow shall be my garland.
>
> He sigh'd in his singing, and after each grone,
> Come willow, etc.
> " I am dead to all pleasure, my true-love is gone.
> O willow, etc.
> Sing, O the greene willow shall be my garland.

OH! WILLOW, WILLOW, WILLOW!*

Words and Music from a Manuscript of Shakespeare's time.

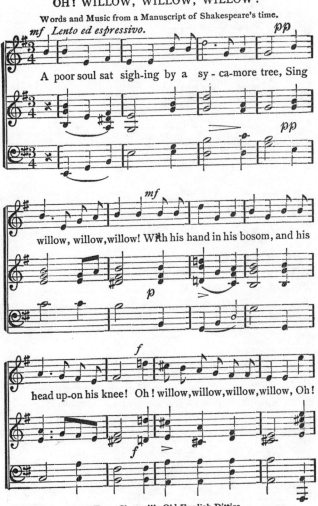

A poor soul sat sigh-ing by a sy-ca-more tree, Sing

willow, willow, willow! With his hand in his bosom, and his

head up-on his knee! Oh! willow, willow, willow, willow, Oh!

* From Chappell's Old English Ditties.

willow, willow, willow, willow,   My gar-land shall be, Sing,

all   a green wil-low,   wil-low, wil-low, wil-low, Ah!

me, the green wil-low my   gar-land must be.

" My love she is turned ; untrue she doth prove ;
    O willow, etc.
She renders me nothing but hate for my love.
    O willow, etc.
Sing, O the greene willow, etc.

" O pitty me " (cried he), " ye lovers, each one ;
    O willow, etc.
Her heart's hard as marble ; she rues not my mone.
    O willow, etc.
Sing, O the greene willow, etc."

The cold streams ran by him, his eyes wept apace ;
    O willow, etc.
The salt tears fell from him, which drowned his face.
    O willow, etc.
Sing, O the greene willow, etc.

The mute birds sate by him, made tame by his mones ;
    O willow, etc.
The salt tears fell from him, which softened the stones.
    O willow, etc.
Sing, O the greene willow shall be my garland !

" Let nobody blame me, her scornes I do prove ;
    O willow, etc.
She was borne to be faire ; I, to die for her love.
    O willow, etc.
Sing, O the greene willow, etc.

" O that beauty should harbour a heart that's so hard !
    Sing willow, etc.
My true love rejecting without all regard.
    O willow, etc.
Sing, O the greene willow, etc.

" Let love no more boast him in palace, or bower;
　　　O willow, etc.
For women are trothles, and flote in an houre.
　　　O willow, etc.
Sing, O the greene willow, etc.

" But what helps complaining? In vaine I complaine:
　　　O willow, etc.
I must patiently suffer her scorne and disdaine.
　　　O willow, etc.
Sing, O the greene willow, etc.

" Come, all you forsaken, and sit down by me,
　　　O willow, etc.
He that 'plaines of his false love, mine's falser than she.
　　　O willow, etc.
Sing, O the greene willow, etc.

" The willow wreath weare I, since my love did fleet;
　　　O willow, etc.
A garland for lovers forsaken most meete.
　　　O willow, etc.
Sing, O the greene willow shall be my garland ! "

PART THE SECOND.

" Lowe lay'd by my sorrow, begot by disdaine,
　　　O willow, willow, willow !
Against her too cruell, still, still I complaine.
　　　O willow, willow, willow !
　　　O willow, willow, willow !
Sing, O the greene willow shall be my garland !

" O love too injurious, to wound my poore heart,
　　　O willow, etc.

To suffer the triumph, and joy in my smart!
     O willow, etc.
Sing, O the greene willow, etc.

"O willow, willow, willow! the willow garland,
     O willow, etc.
A sign of her falsenesse before me doth stand.
     O willow, etc.
Sing, O the greene willow shall be my garland.

"As here it doth bid to despair and to dye,
     O willow, etc.
So hang it, friends, ore me in grave where I lye.
     O willow, etc.
Sing, O the greene willow, etc.

"In grave where I rest mee, hang this to the view,
     O willow, etc.
Of all that doe knowe her, to blaze her untrue.
     O willow, etc.
Sing, O the greene willow, etc.

"With these words engraven, as epitaph meet,
     O willow, etc.
'Here lyes one, drank poyson for potion most sweet.'
     O willow, etc.
Sing, O the greene willow, etc.

"Though she thus unkindly hath scorned my love,
     O willow, etc.
And carelesly smiles at the sorrowes I prove;
     O willow, etc.
Sing, O the greene willow, etc.

"I cannot against her unkindly exclaim,
     O willow, etc.

Cause once well I loved her, and honoured her name.
    O willow, etc.
Sing, O the greene willow shall be my garland.

" The name of her sounded so sweete in mine eare,
    O willow, etc.
It rays'd my heart lightly, the name of my deare;
    O willow, etc.
Sing, O the greene willow, etc.

" As then 'twas my comfort, it now is my griefe;
    O willow, etc.
It now brings me anguish; then brought me reliefe.
    O willow, etc.
Sing, O the greene willow, etc.

" Farewell, faire false-hearted, plaints end with my breath!
    O willow, willow, willow!
Thou dost loath me, I love thee, though cause of my death.
    O willow, willow, willow!
    O willow, willow, willow!
Sing, O the greene willow shall be my garland."

Here then we have a pathetic scene heightened by a tender and melancholy ballad. There is a passing allusion to a very pathetic ballad in " Henry IV. " (Part II. Act ii. Sc. 4), where Pistol says :

" *Pistol.* What! shall we have incision? shall we imbrue? —
                              [*Snatching up his sword.*
Then death rock me asleep, abridge my doleful days!
Why then, let grievous, ghastly, gaping wounds
Untwine the sisters three! Come, Atropos, I say!"

The line in italics is taken from a sorrowful song which is said to have been written by Anne Boleyn, after her downfall, beginning, —

" Oh, Death, rocke me asleep."

The reader will find it in the second volume of Chappell's " Old English Ditties."

It is difficult to decide in which direction Shakespeare has been strongest ; the light songs of Ophelia, the foreboding melancholy of Desdemona, the portrayal of the befuddled Sir Toby by his snatches of refrains of bacchanalian songs, are all different phases of one art. There is still another phase of this art to study, however, and in the next chapter we shall see our poet in the domain of absolute parody.

CHAPTER XII.

THAT Shakespeare should write many lyrics in his plays was a foregone conclusion. He lived in an age when there was the strongest tendency toward the lyric forms. Ritson, in his " Select Collection of English Songs," gives an important historical essay upon this subject, in which he states that not a single composition of the modern lyrical style, containing a spark of literary merit, can be discovered before the Elizabethan era. We are disposed to place "rare Ben Jonson " at the head of the lyrical writers of the era, if it were only on account of that finest of love-songs (as good as any of its length in any language), " Drink to me only with thine eyes. " We may state, *en passant*, that this poem evoked the finest of contemporary music, a melody and harmony so rich and beautiful that many have credited it to Mozart, but as Doctor Burney, contemporary with Mozart, sought in vain to discover its composer, we may dismiss this theory and content ourselves with the fact that one of the best lyrics of the Elizabethan time, both words and music, has come down to us intact.

Shakespeare occasionally made use of the poems of his contemporaries, in his plays, often alluding to them (as we have seen) by some borrowed phrase, frequently giving a title of some poem or song, sometimes interweaving them in the action of his drama, and sometimes even parodying the lyric. A parody of this kind, and a very subtle one, we find in the grave-digging scene in " Hamlet." Fortunately, in this case, both the original poem and the music are left to us, so that we can trace every detail of the poet's humour. The musical part of the scene runs as follows :

"[*First Clown digs and sings.*

' In youth, when I did love, did love,
　　Methought, it was very sweet,
　To contract, O, the time, for, ah, my behove,
　　O, methought, there was nothing meet.'

Hamlet. Has this fellow no feeling of his business ? he sings at grave-making.

Horatio. Custom hath made it in him a property of easiness.

Hamlet. 'Tis e'en so : the hand of little employment hath the daintier sense.

First Clown.   [*Sings.*

   'But age with his stealing steps,
    Hath claw'd me in his clutch,
   And hath shipped me into the land,
    As if I had never been such.'

        [*Throws up a skull.*

 Hamlet. That skull had a tongue in it, and could sing once. How the knave jowls it to the ground, as if it were Cain's jaw-bone, that did the first murder! This might be the pate of a politician, which this ass now o'er-reaches; one that would circumvent God, might it not?

 Horatio. It might, my lord.

 Hamlet. Or of a courtier; which could say, 'Good-morrow, sweet lord! How dost thou, good lord?' This might be my lord such-a-one, that praised my lord such-a-one's horse, when he meant to beg it: might it not?

 Horatio. Ay, my lord.

 Hamlet. Why, e'en so: and now my lady Worm's; chapless and knocked about the mazzard with a sexton's spade. Here's fine revolution, an we had the trick to see 't. Did these bones cost no more the breeding, but to play at loggats with them? mine ache to think on 't.

 First Clown.

   'A pick-axe, and a spade, a spade, [*Sings.*
    For — and a shrouding sheet:
   O, a pit of clay for to be made
    For such a guest is meet.'

        [*Throws up a skull.*"

The words of the song, as they appear above, have little meaning at any time, and occasionally descend to sheer gibberish; yet they had their foundation in a poem which possessed definite meaning. This poem was entitled "The Aged Lover Renounceth

Love," and was written before 1575. It was attributed by Ritson to Nicholas, Lord Vaux ; by Percy to Thomas, his son ; and by Sir Egerton Brydges to William, the grandson of the first-named. The poem, as collated by Percy, runs thus :

> I lothe that I did love,
>   In youth that I thought swete,
> As time requires : for my behove
>   Me thinkes they are not mete.
>
> My lustes they do me leave,
>   My fansies all are fled ;
> And tract of time begins to weave
>   Gray heares upon my hed.
>
> For Age with steling steps
>   Hath clawde me with his crowch,[1]
> And lusty Youthe away he leapes,
>   As there had bene none such.
>
> My muse doth not delight
>   Me, as she did before ;
> My hand and pen are not in plight,
>   As they have bene of yore.
>
> For Reason me denies
>   All youthly idle rime ;
> And day by day to me she cries,
>   " Leave off these toyes in tyme."
>
> The wrinkles in my brow,
>   The furrowes in my face

[1] Probably meaning "clutch."

Say, " Limping Age will lodge him now
  Where Youth must geve him place."

The harbenger of death,
  To me I se him ride :
The cough, the cold, the gasping breath
  Doth bid me to provide

A pikeax and a spade,
  And eke a shrouding shete,
A house of clay for to be made
  For such a guest most mete.

Me thinkes I hear the clarke
  That knoles the careful knell,
And bids me leave my wearye warke,
  Ere Nature me compell.

My kepers knit the knot,
  That Youth doth laugh to scorne,
Of me that shall bee clean forgot,
  As I had ne'er been borne.

Thus must I Youth geve up,
  Whose badge I long did weare;
To them I yelde the wanton cup,
  That better may it beare.

Lo here the bared skull,
  By whose bald signe I know,
That stouping Age away shall pull
  What youthful yeres did sow.

For Beautie with her band
  These croked cares had wrought,
And shipped me into the lande,
  From whence I first was brought.

And ye that bide behinde,
   Have ye none other trust;
As ye of claye were cast by kinde,
   So shall ye turne to dust.

This song was erroneously supposed to have been written by the author upon his death-bed. The Shakespearian scene founded upon it affords a fine example of an illiterate character catching the sound, but not the sense, of a poem. We present the old air as given by Doctor Rimbault in his collection of melodies to Percy's "Reliques."

THE AGED LOVER RENOUNCETH LOVE.

I lothe that I did love, In youth that
For age with ste-ling steps Had clawed me

I thought swete, As time re-quires: for
with his crouch, And lust-y youth a-

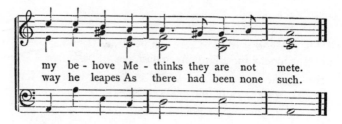

my be-hove Me-thinks they are not mete.
way he leapes As there had been none such.

Many of Shakespeare's own lyrics have been set to
music over and over again; Roffe, in his "Handbook
of Shakespeare Music," and Greenhill, Harrison, and
Furnivall, in their list of Shakespeare songs, give a
computation of the number of musical settings that
becomes almost marvellous. "Take, oh, take those
lips away," has been set more than thirty times;
"Orpheus with His Lute" (which, by the way, was
written by John Fletcher and not by Shakespeare)
has been set twenty-one times; "Who is Sylvia?"
and "It was a lover and his lass," each eighteen
times; Marlowe's "Come live with me and be my
Love," sixteen times.[1]

In connection with the last-named selection it may
be stated that Jaggard printed it in 1599 as Shakespeare's (in "The Passionate Pilgrim"), but it is now
pretty well settled that the verses are Marlowe's, and

[1] Roffe's list is a remarkably full one, and the reader who desires
statistical information in this matter will find it in his well-compiled
index, but recent composers (among them many Americans) have
greatly increased the number of musical settings.

they are credited to that poet in "England's Helicon" (1600); Shakespeare, however, introduces part of the poem in "The Merry Wives of Windsor," in the scene where Sir Hugh Evans is waiting for Doctor Caius (Act iii. Sc. 1).

"*Enter* SIR HUGH EVANS *and* SIMPLE.

Evans. I pray you now, good master Slender's servingman, and friend Simple by your name, which way have you looked for master Caius, that calls himself Doctor of Physic?

Simple. Marry, sir, the city-ward, the park-ward, every way; old Windsor way, and every way but the town way.

Evans. I most fehemently desire you, you will also look that way.

Simple. I will, sir.

Evans. Pless my soul! how full of cholers I am and trempling of mind! — I shall be glad, if he have deceived me; — how melancholies I am! — . . . 'pless my soul!   [*Sings.*

> To shallow rivers, to whose falls
> Melodious birds sing madrigals;
> There will we make our peds of roses,
> And a thousand fragrant posies.
>   To shallow ——

Mercy on me: I have a great dispositions to cry.

> Melodious birds sing madrigals:
> When as I sat in Pabylon, ——
> And a thousand vagram posies.
>   To shallow ——

Simple. Yonder he is coming, this way, Sir Hugh.

Evans. He's welcome ——

To shallow rivers to whose falls ——

Heaven prosper the right ! "

The original passage upon which the above singing
is founded runs :

> " There will we sit upon the Rocks,
>   And see the Shepheards feed their flocks,
>   By shallow Rivers by whose falls
>   Melodious birds sing Madrigals.

> " There will I make thee a bed of Roses
>   With a thousand fragrant Posies," etc.

Furnivall analyses the scene thus :

" In his nervous condition, Evans misquotes the words of
the song, and at last breaks down altogether. The mention
of *Rivers*, however, recalls professional associations ; so that
in his 'trempling of minde,' and with his 'dispositions to
cry,' he unconsciously mingles the sacred and the secular, by
tacking on to Marlowe's verses the first line of the old metrical
version of the 137th psalm (*super flumine*) :

> " When we did sit in Babylon,
>   The Rivers round about,
>   Then in remembrance of Sion,
>   The tears for grief burst out.' "

As there is still some contention regarding the
authorship of " Come live with me," although the
best authorities agree in awarding the authorship to
Kit Marlowe, we reproduce the poem that has caused
so much music, together with what is probably its
earliest setting.

"COME LIVE WITH ME AND BE MY LOVE."

Tune discovered by Sir John Hawkins, in a MS. of Queen Elizabeth's time.

Come live with me   and be my love, And we will all   the pleas-ures prove That val - lies, groves or hills and fields, And all   the stee-py mountain yields.

Come live with me, and be my love,
And we wil all the pleasures prove
That hils and vallies, dale and field,
And all the craggy mountains yield.

There will we sit upon the rocks,
And see the shepherds feed their flocks
By shallow rivers, to whose falls
Melodious birds sing madrigals.

There will I make thee beds of roses,
With a thousand fragrant posies;
A cap of flowers, and a kirtle
Imbrodered all with leaves of mirtle;

A gown made of the finest wool
Which from our pretty lambs we pull;
Fair-linèd slippers for the cold,
With buckles of the purest gold;

A belt of straw and ivie buds,
With coral clasps and amber studs:
And if these pleasures may thee move,
Then live with me, and be my love.

The shepherd swains shall dance and sing
For thy delight each May morning:
If these delights thy mind may move,
Then live with me and be my love.

THE NYMPH'S REPLY.

If that the World and Love were young,
And truth in every shepherd's toung,
These pretty pleasures might me move
To live with thee, and be thy love.

But time drives flocks from field to fold,
When rivers rage, and rocks grow cold,
And Philomel becometh dumb,
And all complain of cares to come.

The flowers do fade, and wanton fields
To wayward winter reckoning yield;
A honey tongue, a heart of gall,
Is fancie's spring, but sorrow's fall.

Thy gowns, thy shoes, thy beds of roses,
Thy cap, thy kirtle, and thy posies,
Soon break, soon wither, soon forgotten,
In folly ripe, in reason rotten.

Thy belt of straw, and ivie buds,
Thy coral clasps, and amber studs;
All these in me no means can move
To come to thee, and be thy love.

But could youth last, and love still breed;
Had joyes no date, nor age no need;
Then these delights my mind might move
To live with thee, and be thy love.

The "Reply" is probably not by Marlowe, since it appears in "England's Helicon" (1600) signed "Ignoto," which has been accepted by many critics as the pseudonym of Sir Walter Raleigh.

It is worthy of note that the early composers were more attached to that very doubtful work, "The Passionate Pilgrim," than to the plays of Shakespeare. The above poem is No. xix. of the set; No. xvii. of the same heterogeneous work — "My flocks feed not" — was set as a madrigal as early as 1597, by Thomas Weelkes, and remains a worthy example of the contrapuntal style of the epoch. But this latter poem was printed in "England's Helicon," in 1600, and also bore the signature, "Ignoto;" there is, therefore, considerable doubt as to whether Shakespeare wrote it. We have seen that to "Take, oh,

take those lips away" belongs the honour of the
most copious setting of any of the lyrics found
in the Shakespearian plays,[1] but even here a question arises and some doubt surrounds the poem. It
reappears in Beaumont and Fletcher's "Bloody
Brother" in 1639 and 1640, and has here two
stanzas, the second running:

> " Hide, oh hide those hills of snow
>   Which thy frozen bosom bears,
>   On whose tops the pinks that grow
>   Are of those that April wears ;
>   But first set my poor heart free,
>   Bound in those icy chains by thee."

The two stanzas are credited to Shakespeare in
the doubtful edition of his poems dated "London,
1640," and many commentators since that time have
attributed both to him. R. G. White believes the
first stanza to be Shakespeare's, and credits the
second to Fletcher, pointing out, also (Vol. III.
p. 126), that the two stanzas do not assimilate well
and could not be sung to the same music if the first
verse be given as presented in "Measure for Measure." Sewel and Gildon added many spurious poems
to the lyrics of Shakespeare, which have since been

---

[1] Yet Shakespeare's lyrics have by no means been set to music as
often as those of certain other poets. Heine's " Du bist wie eine
Blume " has been oftener set to music than any other poem ; more
than *two hundred* settings exist.

rejected from careful editions of his works ; the first stanza of this poem, however, is so charming that one is loath to take the credit of it away from the greatest poet.

Naturally the composers have found their chief material in the Shakespearian comedies, while the histories have yielded the least musical material for musical setting.

The Germans have been eminent in their Shakespearian lyrics, even from the classical period, and have been aided in this by very good and singable translations. For a full presentation of these we refer the reader to the exhaustive "Variorum Edition," by Furness, contenting ourselves here with saying that the great poet Lessing first revealed the glories of Shakespeare to German readers, and since his time Schlegel, Goethe, Wieland, Gervinus, Tieck, Bodenstedt, Mommsen, and a host of others, have given to Germany a Shakespearian literature that is almost as voluminous as the English.[1] The Germans, too, have caught up the spirit of our poet better than any other nation, so much so that there are a few Teutonic writers who boast that the German mind *best appreciates* Shakespeare, and would almost have us believe that Germany led the way

[1] See, also, article on " Shakespeare in Germany " in supplemental volume of Knight's Shakespeare.

toward the full comprehension of the glories of the Englishman !

One German setting of a Shakespearian lyric may be here mentioned with some degree of detail, and for several reasons ; it is a perfect example (both in its words, already quoted, and in its music) of the morning song, the opposite of the serenade; it is one of the poet's most cheery lyrics; and it may illustrate how the poet inspires the musician, — how the spirit of poetry transmutes itself into music.

It was on a pleasant Sunday morning, in the summer of 1826, that Schubert, in accordance with his custom, was taking a stroll (a *Spaziergang*) through the suburbs of Vienna with a party of his boon companions. They had been at Pötzleindorf and were returning to the city through Währing. As they were passing through the latter suburb, Schubert spied his friend Tieze sitting at a table in one of the garden-restaurants which are so numerous in Austria's capital. It was a little establishment bearing the name " Zum Biersack." In his usual light-hearted way Schubert suggested that they all turn in and take breakfast together with Tieze. All assenting, the gay party was soon gathered around the table. Tieze had with him a volume of poetry, and Schubert, ever on the hunt for lyrical subjects, seized the book and began to turn its leaves. Suddenly he became interested in one of the poems, and read and re-read it. The volume was Shakespeare's lyrics translated into German, the poem was " Hark, Hark, the Lark." After a little while (for Schubert's composition was ever spontaneous) he spoke, saying, "What a pity that I have no music-paper! I have just the melody for this poem!" Doppler, one of the party, was equal to the emergency; drawing the lines of the musical staff on the back of the bill of fare, he handed the improvised music-paper to the composer. On the back of that bill of fare, while waiting for his break-fast, amid the hurly-burly of an open-air restaurant, Schubert composed " Hark, Hark, the Lark," a song which has remained a classic ever since. Nor was it changed in any degree from this first improvised sketch, for Schubert was notorious for his careless-ness in the matter of revision; he almost invariably gave his first draught of any composition to his pub-lisher, and it is not stretching the imagination to suppose that he did no more than copy the music in this case. As the words have already been quoted, it is unnecessary to reproduce them here.

It would be unjust to end this chapter without speaking of the great achievements of English com-posers in the Shakespearian field. Even at a time when England did not fully appreciate its greatest poet (the time of Charles II., for example), the com-posers seem to have understood what a mine of poetry was here waiting to be wedded with tones. Dr. John

Wilson [1] was the first to enter the field with worthy music, but an infinitely greater composer soon followed, England's greatest musical genius, — Henry Purcell. This great master's setting of the lyrics and other short poems of Shadwell's version of "The Tempest" was the greatest tribute to Shakespeare up to the time (1690), and the settings of "Come unto these yellow sands" and "Full fathom five" have never been excelled. It is a pity that Shadwell's version departed in a wretched manner from the true Shakespearian lines, and several of Purcell's songs have therefore a spurious text. Of the "Macbeth" music, attributed to Purcell, we shall speak in the final chapter of this work.

We venture to turn aside from our Shakespearian investigation for an instant, to defend the memory of the first musician who adequately transmuted Shakespeare's words into tones. Purcell is accused of dying of a disease brought on by a drunken orgie; this would mean a very acute and feverish malady. A simple statement will set this accusation at rest: Purcell *composed music* during his last illness! The present writer is in possession of a composition (evidently contemporaneous) which is entitled "Rosy Bowers," and claims to be "the last song that was

---

[1] Richard Johnson, contemporaneous with Shakespeare, who set parts of "The Tempest," also deserves mention here, for chronological reasons, chiefly.

HENRY PURCELL.

set by the late celebrated Mr. Henry Purcell, it being in his sickness."

Next to Purcell one must place the famous Doctor Arne, in giving a list of eminent Shakespearian composers. His setting of the musical parts of "As You Like It," in 1740, will probably never be excelled.

Stevens, Linley, Bishop, Haydn, Horn, and numerous others might be mentioned in connection with the lyrical field of Shakespeare, but besides these there was a still wider sphere of composition instigated by the poet, as will be seen in the final chapter of this volume.

CHAPTER XIII.

Children as Singers — Shakespeare's Musical Stage-directions —
The "Chorus" — Musical Interludes — Music after Plays — Fi-
nal Jigs — Trumpet Signals — Drums — Bells — Sennet —
Pageants upon Stage — Historical Music.

In the Shakespearian theatre the performances
generally began at three o'clock in the afternoon,
and the prices of admission varied from twopence to
about sixpence to the pit, and from about a shilling
to half a crown to the boxes. The musicians sat in
a balcony and not in front of the stage as is the present custom. Many of the ultra-fashionables sat or
reclined upon the stage itself, for which privilege
they paid extra. In judging of the vocal music which
Shakespeare introduced in his plays, it may be important to remember that every part was sung by
men or boys, no female appearing upon the English
stage before the civil war. The treble parts were
sustained by boys who were well trained for acting
as well as singing. Regarding these children and
their singing, we can quote Shakespeare himself, for
he gives a criticism of their work in the second scene
of the second act of "Hamlet : "

" *Rosencrantz.* To think, my lord, if you delight not in man, what lenten entertainment the players shall receive from you : we coted them on the way ; and hither are they coming, to offer you service.

Hamlet. He that plays the king, shall be welcome ; his majesty shall have tribute of me : the adventurous knight shall use his foil and target : the lover shall not sigh gratis ; the humourous man shall end his part in peace ; the clown shall make those laugh, whose lungs are tickled o' the sere ; and the lady shall say her mind freely, or the blank verse shall halt for 't. — What players are they ?

Rosencrantz. Even those you were wont to take such delight in, the tragedians of the city.

Hamlet. How chances it, they travel ? their residence, both in reputation and profit, was better both ways.

Rosencrantz. I think their inhibition comes by the means of the late innovation.

Hamlet. Do they hold the same estimation they did when I was in the city ? Are they so followed ?

Rosencrantz. No, indeed they are not.

Hamlet. How comes it ? Do they grow rusty ?

Rosencrantz. Nay, their endeavour keeps in the wonted pace : but there is, sir, an aiery of children, little eyases, that cry out on the top of question, and are most tyrannically clapped for 't : these are now the fashion ; and so berattle the common stages, (so they call them,) that many, wearing rapiers, are afraid of goose quills, and dare scarce come thither.

Hamlet. What, are they children ? who maintains them ? how are they escoted ? Will they pursue the quality no longer than they can sing ? will they not say afterwards, if they should grow themselves to common players, (as it is most like, if their means are no better) their writers do them wrong, to make them exclaim against their own succession.

Rosencrantz. Faith, there has been much to do on both sides ; and the nation holds it no sin, to tarre them on to controversy; there was for awhile, no money bid for argument, unless the poet and the player went to cuffs in the question.

Hamlet.   Is it possible?

Guildenstern.   O, there has been much throwing about of brains?

Hamlet.   Do the boys carry it away?

Rosencrantz.   Ay, that they do, my lord; Hercules and his load too."

It would seem evident from this that Shakespeare scarcely approved of children as actors, and he intimates that the boys are only tolerated because they can sing; the line, " Will they pursue the quality no longer than they can sing ? " would seem to indicate that when their voice changed they might be regarded as useless.   That the children sometimes gave plays by themselves is also indicated in the above scene, but is not to our purpose; we may suppose, since these juvenile performances were given by the choir-boys of St. Paul's, Westminster, the Chapel Royal, etc., that the singing was the important part.

All performances of this epoch were preceded by three flourishes of trumpets, exactly as the Wagnerian performances at Bayreuth have been ushered in during more recent times.   After the third flourish the curtain was drawn to the two sides, from the center, and the prologue was spoken.   The so-called " Chorus," was, of course, not a musical gathering, but a single character who explained the play, after the manner of the ancient Greek choruses, although the Hellenic chorus chanted, while the Elizabethan one merely spoke his lines.

Between the acts dancing and singing, or both combined, were introduced. After the play the clown came to the front and gave a jig, generally to his own accompaniment upon pipe or tabor. Sometimes he had an accompaniment played for him, in which case he generally sang as he danced. A clear instance of this sort can be found in " Twelfth Night," after the play is ended, when the clown enters and sings the following :

" SONG.

Clown.

> When that I was and a tiny little boy,
>   With hey, ho, the wind and the rain,
> A foolish thing was but a toy,
>   For the rain it raineth every day.
>
> But when I came to man's estate,
>   With hey, ho, the wind and the rain,
> 'Gainst knave and thief men shut their gate,
>   For the rain it raineth every day.
>
> But when I came, alas ! to wive,
>   With hey, ho, the wind and the rain,
> By swaggering could I never thrive,
>   For the rain it raineth every day.
>
> But when I came unto my bed,
>   With hey, ho, the wind and the rain,
> With toss-pots still had drunken head,
>   For the rain it raineth every day.

A great while ago the world begun,
   With hey, ho, the wind and the rain,
But that's all one, our play is done,
   And we'll strive to please you every day.

                                        [Exit."

Here we have a song entirely apart from the action. Shakespeare had made this clown especially musical and had probably chosen some capable singer for the part, for he not only gives the character a prominent share in the catch-singing, but adds earnest songs to its repertoire during the play. He possibly, therefore, desired something a little better than the usual jig at the end, in this case, and gave the clown an additional chance to capture public favour with his final song. It is, however, as extraneous to the action as the jig itself would have been.

Some commentators believe the song to be by some other hand than Shakespeare's, and there is inherent probability in the belief; for it may have been allowed to the favoured actor to choose some favourite song of his own repertoire wherewith to capture his audience. Besides this assumption, we find an additional bit of inferential proof in the fact that Shakespeare parodied the song in "King Lear" (written a half-dozen years later) with —

" He that has a little tiny wit, —
   With heigh, ho, the wind and the rain, —
Must make content with his fortune's fit;
   For the rain it raineth every day."

And Shakespeare was not in the habit of parodying himself, however much he delighted in twisting the thoughts of others.

As the traditional tune of this song exists, we present it, together with Chappell's note that it is said to have been the composition of a person named Fielding.

"WHEN THAT I WAS A LITTLE TINY BOY."

In moderate time.

When that I was a lit-tle ti-ny Boy With a heigh ho! the

Wind and the Rain, A foolish thing was but a Toy For the

rain it raineth ev'-ry Day With a heigh ho! The

Wind and the Rain and the rain it raineth ev' - ry Day,

In connection with the above statement of the privileges of the clown, it may be added that this favoured personage was permitted, and even expected, to add "gags" and interpolations to the play, and he sometimes even engaged in improvised repartee with the audience. Steevens gives a quotation from Stowe which speaks of two of the "queen's servants" (*i. e.* actors) as of "extemporall witte." Malone says:

> "The clown often addressed the audience in the middle of the play and entered into a contest of raillery and sarcasm with such of the audience as chose to engage with him."

One can find an allusion to this habit in " Hamlet " (Act iii. Sc. 2).[1]

The stage-directions of Shakespeare, so far as they are connected with music, are quite numerous. "Alarums," rolls of drums, are called for most freely, especially in the historical plays, and very often in connection with "excursions," which were

---

[1] See also the scene at the end of Act iv. of "Romeo and Juliet," which was probably written by Shakespeare to display Will Kempe.

simply sallies or skirmishes. " Flourishes " were simply fanfares, or a series of open tones upon the natural trumpets. In this connection we may state that the only trumpet known in the Shakespearian days was the natural instrument, without keys, the keyed instrument being an invention of the nineteenth century ; there were, however, excellent trumpeters in the Elizabethan epoch, for the instrument was found in all the royal bands, and was the appurtenance of every herald, the ambassador to sovereigns. The art of playing trumpet, therefore, was held to be a " heroic " one, and in Continental Europe, and in some degree in England, it was prized as a "gentlemanly " accomplishment. In Germany, at this time, a guild of trumpeters existed, which claimed many noblemen among its members, and even the Duke of Weimar entered its ranks as late as the middle of the eighteenth century.

Twice does Shakespeare change from the flourish of trumpets to a "flourish of cornets." The " cornet " demanded here is by no means the instrument now known by that name, which was invented less than a century ago, but meant a wooden instrument with a trumpet-like mouthpiece, an instrument which afterward gave way to the oboe. Sometimes the larger cornets were made of metal, but this was rather the exception than the rule. The cornet had holes along its tube, as the common flute has to-day, and Mersennus, writing in 1636, speaks of the wooden serpent as the true bass of the cornet. Artusi, in his work on "The Imperfections of Modern Music" (Venice, 1600), says that the tone of the instrument depends greatly upon the manner of tongueing it, and gives many rules regarding it. He adds:

"To give the best tone, the performer on the cornet should endeavour to imitate the human voice; for no other instrument is so difficult to obtain excellence on as this."

Girolamo da Udine is spoken of as the greatest performer upon this uncouth instrument, which seems to have occupied a position midway between the brass and the wood-wind instruments. The fact that Shakespeare sometimes calls for "hautboys" (oboes) in such flourishes, only emphasises the relationship of the two instruments. Sometimes oboes and trumpets were sounded together in the flourishes.

The "sennet" must have been much the same as a flourish, and probably was originally called "sonnet," taking its rise, as was the case with "sonata," from "*sonare,*" to sound.

Most interesting among the trumpet-signals are those called "tuckets." Shakespeare uses the word but rarely, yet generally with some significance. For example, in the final scene of "The Merchant of Venice," we find the following:

"[*A tucket sounds.*

 Lorenzo. [*To Portia*] Your husband is at hand, I hear his trumpet."

Twice at the entrance of Montjoy, the French herald, in "Henry V.," does the tucket sound. Occasionally, too, we have a trumpet-call which must have been a tucket, as will be seen presently. In "King Lear" (Act ii. Sc. 1), Gloster says, after the stage-direction "*Trumpets within,*" "Hark! the duke's trumpets." In the same play (Act ii. Sc. 4) we find the same stage-direction, and after the trumpet-call Cornwall asks, "What trumpet's that?" whereupon Regan replies, "I know 't; my sister's." And other instances of such recognition of tuckets, whether marked so, or simply called "trumpets," might be cited. The "tucket" was, therefore, a personal trumpet-call, which was as recognisable as the private flourish which a gentleman might use with his signature in the sixteenth century. It was a private trumpet-signal, such as Wagner causes Siegfried to use in the last two operas of the Trilogy ("Siegfried" and "Götterdämmerung"); and the word probably was derived from "*toccare,*" to touch, *i. e.* something requiring skill of touch, or technique. Once we meet with the word in the Shakespearian text, instead of as stage-direction; in "Henry V." (Act iv. Sc. 2) the Constable of France gives the order:

" Sound the tucket-sonance, and the note to mount," —

and here again we have the tucket in the nature of a definite signal ; our cavalry bugle-signals are practically "tuckets" in the sense of having some special and definite meaning.

Possibly the "tucket" was a true historical touch, for it is certain that the old heralds used many a private signal of this kind. There is another historical touch in the play last quoted, connected with music ; it is where the king, after the victory of Agincourt, says, —

" Let there be sung Non Nobis, and Te Deum," —

which is practically what the king *did* say, after his victory, for when all England was pouring adulation upon him he commanded that thanks be given to God instead ; and many sacred musical works followed this behest.

Occasionally bells were used upon the stage, if we may trust the many Shakespearian allusions to them, but these are scarcely to be classed as musical instruments, although Shakespeare sometimes draws delightful musical metaphors from them, as for example in "Hamlet" (Act iii. Sc. 1), where Ophelia speaks of Hamlet thus :

> " *Ophelia.* O, what a noble mind is here o'erthrown !
> The courtier's, soldier's, scholar's, eye, tongue, sword :
> The expectancy and rose of the fair state,

The glass of fashion, and the mould of form,
The observed of all observers! quite, quite down!
And I, of ladies most deject and wretched,
That suck'd the honey of his music vows,
Now see that noble and most sovereign reason,
Like sweet bells jangled, out of tune and harsh;
That unmatch'd form and feature of blown youth,
Blasted with ecstasy: O, wo is me!
To have seen what I have seen, see what I see!"

There is one phrase here in connection with music, which leads to an interesting bit of etymology, the line regarding "the honey of his music vows;" Shakespeare used the word "honey" about twice as often as the word "sugar," yet he was probably one of the first to make copious use of the latter, both as noun and adjective. The introduction of refined sugar into England from Venice, about a century before Shakespeare's time, gave the poets a new adjective, and the people toothache. Hentzner (in his "Itinerary," 1598) speaks of the black teeth of Queen Elizabeth.

"Next came the Queen, in the 65th year of her age, as we were told, very majestic, her face oblong, fair, but wrinkled; her eyes small yet black and pleasant: her nose hooked, her lips narrow, and her teeth black, a defect the English seem subject to from their *too great use of sugar*. She wore false hair, and that *red*."

It is to be noted that Shakespeare occasionally uses funeral music, and that the first part of "King Henry VI." begins with a dead march.

The pageants, which Shakespeare occasionally introduced into his plays, were always very popular with
Elizabethan audiences, who were beginning to culti-
vate a taste for masques, a form of entertainment
still more popular in the Jacobean reign.

We have already fully described the masques and
need only state here that the masques in " Henry
VIII.," in " Timon of Athens," and the procession
in the former play, attracted many of the public who
could not rise to the other and greater glories of the
poet. The allusions to masques, and their actual
introduction, are fairly frequent in the plays, and
the character of such entertainments is suggested
clearly enough by the following excerpt from " Midsummer-Night's Dream " (Act v. Sc. 1) :

" *Theseus.* Say, what abridgement have you for this evening?
What mask? what music? How shall we beguile
The lazy time, if not with some delight?
    Philostrate.   There is a brief, how many sports are ripe;
Make choice of which your highness will see first.

                                        [*Giving a paper.*
    Theseus.   [*Reads*] ' The battle with the Centaurs, to be
        sung,
By an Athenian eunuch, to the harp.'
We'll none of that: that have I told my love,
In glory of my kinsman Hercules.
' The riot of the tipsy Bacchanals,
Tearing the Thracian singer in their rage.'
That is an old device; and it was play'd
When I from Thebes came last a conqueror.

. The thrice three Muses mourning for the death
Of learning, late deceased in beggary.'
That is some satire, keen and critical,
Not sorting with a nuptial ceremony.
' A tedious brief scene of young Pyramus,
And his love Thisbe ; very tragical mirth.'
Merry and tragical ? tedious and brief ?
That, is hot ice, and wonderous strange snow.
How shall we find the concord of this discord ? "

In the above scene there is a mystical line which
is confessedly inaccurate, the allusion to " wonderous
strange snow."   It is barely possible that (to carry
on the contradictions) " wonderous rain-snow " may
have been meant, although the true reading can
probably never be recovered.

CHAPTER XIV.

IT may be regarded as an axiom that great poets, whether musical themselves or not,[1] always lead to great music. If a poet arises, in any age or nation, who is dear to the people, there is certain to follow a tone-poet who will set music to the words that have exerted such power, and thus bring them still closer to the popular heart. Thus Goethe led to Schubert, and Heine found his fullest glory in the works of Schumann and Robert Franz.

In the case of Shakespeare the influence was more far-reaching and was exerted upon composers of three centuries and of all the civilised countries of the earth. It is not too much to say that no man, outside of the art, ever inspired as much, or one-quarter as much, music as Shakespeare has done. Goethe's "Faust" has brought forth very much music, but Shakespeare's musical influence is not confined to a

[1] Tennyson, for example, was not musical, yet his "Break, Break, Break!" has led to many songs, and many other of his poems have inspired much music.

single play, for each of his plays has inspired its own especial music.

Barrett Wendell, in his charming essay on Shakespeare, dwells constantly (in a dozen different places) on the musical quality of Shakespeare's plays, and believes them to be the half-way house on the road to opera. He compares (p. 78 *et seq.*) "Henry VI." to serious opera, "Love's Labour's Lost" to opera comique, and calls (p. 122) the quartette of lamentation over the unconscious Juliet, — "fugue-like;" Mercutio's "Queen Mab" he likens to an interpolated song in a modern comedy, and he gives many other instances of poetry and music coming into closest kinship in the works of Shakespeare.

It may be pardoned us if, in the presentation of this branch of our topic, we become in some degree catalogic. "The Tempest" has been set fourteen times as an opera, the Germans having been especially attracted toward this subject. Since Doctor Arne's first setting (and we do not count Purcell's setting of Shadwell's arrangement of the play in the above list), French, Russians, and Italians, as well as Germans, have turned the subject into opera. John K. Paine, most eminent of American composers, has built a symphonic poem upon the theme, and Ambroise Thomas has turned it into a ballet, in which Ferdinand and Miranda caper, and Caliban crawls, to Terpsichorean rhythms !

The "Merry Wives of Windsor" has been less copiously set, but has led to music of higher character than the preceding. Among the eight operatic settings of the subject one may give precedence to Verdi's "Falstaff," which has admirably caught the Shakespearian spirit and possesses a libretto written in the truest poetic spirit by Arrigo Boïto.   The delightful setting by Nicolai presents most dainty music, and its overture is one of the gems of light opera, but it does not reach the height of the foregoing work.

"Measure for Measure" has received but a single operatic setting of any note, and this setting, although important to the musical historian, is never performed upon the stage.   It was composed by Richard Wagner in his younger days.   The work seems not to have been in the Shakespearian spirit and to have had no very great merit, but it is interesting to know that the greatest operatic composer was in some degree inspired by Shakespeare.   Nor is "Das Liebesverbot" (for so Wagner entitled his second opera) the only case where the great composer was moved by Shakespeare, for we find him studying the works of the English dramatist (thanks to the excellent German translations) assiduously, at the beginning of his career; a good part of Wagner's dramatic instinct may be traced to his early study of Shakespeare.

Sir Henry R. Bishop, who drew many of his texts

from Shakespeare, gave the only tolerable setting of the "Comedy of Errors" to the world; it does not, at present, hold the stage.

"The Taming of the Shrew" has achieved one important operatic setting (not to speak of an almost unknown Spanish setting of the eighteenth century), for it introduced a musical genius to the world, — Hermann Goetz. This German setting (" Die Wider-spenstigen Zahmung ") is not as dramatic as it might be, but is so delightfully melodic and so richly harmonised that it is likely to become a standard work of the modern operatic repertoire.

Max Bruch, also German, gave the only setting of "Winter's Tale," under the title of "Hermione." It contains some excellent music, but has not received sufficiently dramatic treatment to maintain its place in the operatic repertoire of to-day.

"Midsummer-Night's Dream" had its chief musical result in Mendelssohn's incidental music. As a boy of seventeen, Mendelssohn brought forth an overture to this play, that may be called the most dainty bit of musical humour in the entire repertoire. In this bit of programme music one hears Titania and her train and the tricksy Puck, upon the violins, the braying of the "translated" Bottom, in his asinine character, upon the bassoon, and his subsequent snoring most graphically depicted upon the ophicleide. Years afterward, Mendelssohn was commissioned by the King of Prussia to write more music to the Shakespearian text, but the high level of the overture could not be attained to order. Yet one number of the music is imperishable; it has been maliciously stated that the " Marseillaise " and Mendelssohn's " Wedding March " have led more people into combat than any other music in the world, and the latter was inspired by Shakespeare's play. There have been a half-dozen settings of " Midsummer-Night's Dream " as an opera.

" Twelfth Night " has been set by Arne and Bishop, but is not heard as an opera nowadays.

" Richard III." has been set three times as an opera, but has also vanished from the operatic boards. Probably the best musical outcome of this play exists in the shape of an overture by Volkmann. This overture shows a keener appreciation of Shakespeare's hero than of the facts of history, for at the end, where the composer pictures Bosworth field, the tune of " The Campbells are Comin'" accompanies the slaughter; a Scottish tune upon an English battlefield, and in a combat which occurred about a century before the melody was written ! Smetana has written a " Symphonic poem " on " Richard III."

Among the histories, the two parts of " King Henry IV." have possessed the most attraction for librettists and composers. They have melted the two parts into one and have made Prince Hal the hero.

Only Herold's version, in two acts, seems to have remained, of the seven operatic settings of this theme. As the other six composers were Italians (with the exception of Garcia), it is natural to find the title running " La Gioventù di Enrico V."

"Henry VIII." has a single setting, but a very good one. It was St. Saëns who introduced this theme to the operatic stage. It is full of good music, and is finely orchestrated, but swerves somewhat from Shakespearian lines, altering the plot unnecessarily. One would imagine that the composer would make the most of the two pageants introduced by Shakespeare into this play, — the masque and the great procession ; but St. Saëns discards them both and gives instead a ballet, in the " Parc du Richmon " (!) in which Scottish and other un-English caperings are introduced.

"Coriolanus" has had a host of operatic settings by old Italian composers, none of which have held the stage. Beethoven's overture of " Coriolanus " does not deal with the Shakespearian play, but is founded on Collin's tragedy of the same name. When Eleonora von Breuning inducted Beethoven into the delights of poetry, she seems not to have imbued him with that love of Shakespeare which might have resulted in giving to the poet his greatest musical settings.

" Macbeth " has been set many times, and from the

Shakespearian century. The incidental music to Sir William Davenant's amplification of "Macbeth," reputed to be by Matthew Locke, is now more generally believed to be by the great Purcell. Cummings, in his "Life of Purcell," gives all the evidence relative to this subject, and even those who do not agree with the conclusion that the youth Purcell wrote the music, will scarcely be inclined to attribute it to Locke. The Germans took up the tragedy very early, and in 1787 J. F. Reichardt set incidental music to Bürger's translation of the play. The famous Spohr wrote music to the tragedy, all of which is lost with the exception of the overture, and even that is rarely heard at present. Weyse published some excellent incidental music to the play seventy-five years ago. Some extremely modern music to Macbeth was composed by the American, Mr. Edgar S. Kelley, but it has been seldom heard save at the performances of the play in San Francisco in 1885. Very much orchestral music has · been written about "Macbeth," a half-dozen overtures, among them one by Raff and one by Brüll, and a symphonic poem by Richard Strauss, which is probably the greatest musical outcome of the play. As regards operatic settings, one finds only three, not one of them of importance. Auguste Hix wrote a French version, to a libretto by Rouget de l'Isle (composer of the "Marseillaise"), which was afterward translated into German. Mr. Philip Hale (in the *Boston Journal*) writes thus about the setting:

"The music of the first opera, 'Macbeth,' was written by Hippolyte Chélard, text by Rouget de l'Isle and Auguste Hix. It was produced for the first time at the Paris Opéra, June 29, 1827. Derévis was Macbeth; Nourrit, Douglas; Dabadie, Duncan; Mrs. Dabadie, Lady Macbeth, and Miss Cinti, Moïna. The trio of witches and several choruses were remarked, but the opera failed, and was only performed five times.

"It was afterward given in German, and with certain changes, at Munich in 1828; it was then sung in many German towns, and July 4, 1832, it was produced in German at the King's Theatre, London. At Munich Pellegrini was Macbeth and Nanette Schechner was Lady Macbeth. In London the part of Lady Macbeth was sung by Schröder-Devrient. Although Chorley says that her fatal and sinister acting as the lady was hampered, in some measure, by the music, — for this demanded an executive facility which she did not possess, — she nevertheless made a deep impression on him. His criticism is even to-day of interest: 'One could not look at her without at once recollecting the ideal which Mrs. Siddons is reported to have conceived of this "grand, fiendish" character (to use her own epithets). "She had an idea," says Mrs. Jameson, "that Lady Macbeth must, from her Celtic origin, have been a small, fair, blue-eyed woman." Save in stature the great German operatic actress (daughter, by the way, to the great Lady Macbeth of Germany, "die grosse Schröder") gave full justification to this fancy. With an alluring and dignified grace of manner was combined an aspect of evil — a sinister, far-reaching expression in her eyes, all the more terrible for their being at variance with those hues and contours which we have been used to associate with innocence and the tender affections. That which makes the flesh creep, in the name of " the White

Devil," spoke in every line of Madame Schröder-Devrient's face — in her honeyed and humble smile, as she welcomed the doomed king; in the mixture of ferocity and blandishment thrown by her into the scene of the murder; in the ghastly soliloquy of the soul that waked when the body was asleep. When I think of Pasta, as Medea, watching the bridal train pass by her, with her scarlet mantle gathered round her, the figure of Madame Schröder-Devrient's Lady Macbeth, too, rises, as one of those visions concerning which young men are apt to rave and old men to dote.' The libretto departs widely from Shakespeare's tragedy."

Another setting was made by Taubert and performed in Germany, which also departed from the Shakespearian path.

But the strangest alterations that Shakespeare was obliged to submit to, on his journey to the operatic stage, took place in the version composed by Verdi, in 1847, before he decided to follow Wagner into the domain of earnest librettos. "Macbeth," with a ballet introduced, with Lady Macbeth singing a drinking-song, with a chorus of murderers, with Macduff singing a liberty-song, —

> "Our country, forsaken,
> Our tears should awaken;
> 'Gainst Tyrants, unshaken,
> Our courage should rise," —

must have been comical enough for any Shakespearian, but the Italians accepted it cordially, and the "liberty-song" was received with frenzy, as a protest against Austrian tyranny.

Of the three inconsequential settings of " King Lear," Kreutzer's " Cordelia " makes the best opera. The best musical outcome of this subject, however, is an overture, by Berlioz, " Le Roi Lear," which pictures the frenzied monarch in a manner not unworthy of the tragedy. Berlioz was one of the great composers who really studied Shakespeare (as we shall see a little later on), and his Shakespeare settings may be accorded the first rank among the French attempts in this field. His two successes are, however, in the orchestral forms (sometimes with vocal addition), for his opera of " Beatrice and Benedict " (" Much Ado About Nothing ") is not of high rank.

There are but two operatic settings of " Othello," and the first of these, chronologically speaking, was a perversion of Shakespeare, by Rossini. The part of Desdemona was a great favourite with both Pasta and Malibran, for it was very singable music. It was first performed in 1816. The great setting of " Othello," however, is due to Verdi, who, in his later period, discarded the absurdities which marked such librettos as that of " Macbeth " (mentioned above) and treated our poet with becoming respect. This setting of " Othello " may be pronounced one of the very greatest operas of the modern Italian school, and to this result the earnest and poetic Shakespearian, Arrigo Boïto, has contributed in no slight degree.

When he has changed a Shakespearian libretto it has generally been entirely in the spirit of the poet, as witness his introduction of Falstaff's soliloquy on " Honour " (" Henry IV.," First Part, Act v. Sc. 1) into the opera of " Falstaff " (" Merry Wives of Windsor "), or the addition of a diabolical creed, full of " motiveless malignity," to the part of Iago, in this opera of " Othello." But to Verdi, too, all honour is due for his dramatic setting of the text and for the abnegation of all attempts to allow the composer to shine at the expense of the poet.

" Hamlet " has been set as opera, even from the time of Domenico Scarlatti, yet no opera exists that can be called worthy of Shakespeare's greatest topic. Ambroise Thomas's version has held the boards in France chiefly because it is a very tuneful opera. Barbier and Carré (the librettists) have dallied with Shakespeare, in the usual insouciant Gallic fashion ; Ophelia sings the most ornate music, together with a pretty Swedish folk-song, in her mad-scene, instead of the very fitting music which Shakespeare chose for the part, and which could easily have been incorporated into the opera. There is considerable orchestral music founded upon " Hamlet," but this also does not attain the level of the great subject.

" Romeo and Juliet " is the topic toward which musicians have instinctively turned as the one affording them the greatest chances in the display of their art. Mr. William F. Apthorp, in a list of Shake-spearian operatic settings, counts up *seventeen* operas that have been made of Shakespeare's play. They range from Bellini's "I Capuletti ed i Montecchi," with a female Romeo (Madame Pasta loved the part), to a burlesque entitled, with punning ardour, "Rhum et Eau en Juillet," — "Rum and Water in July!" Gounod's sugar-plum, skilfully manufactured out of this subject, is the most popular of all the settings, and will be so as long as a romantic tenor and an attractive soprano can be found for the chief pair of the opera. Its performances in Paris alone are num-bered by many hundreds, and its popularity is by no means confined to France.

"All the world loves a lover," and here the com-posers find two of the most attractive of them made to their hands; therefore it is not astonishing to dis-cover the orchestral settings of the theme as numer-ous and as important as the operatic treatments. It would be well-nigh impossible to collect a list of all the orchestral settings extant; it may suffice to men-tion the two most important. Berlioz has given to the world a "Romeo and Juliet" symphony, which is not a symphony at all, but rather a free cantata, with much orchestral interluding, or a set of orches-tral movements with vocal adjuncts. This is the very best musical outcome of the Shakespearian sub-ject up to the present time. We have already stated

that Berlioz may be ranked as the best French Shakespearian in music; for this preëminence there was a
cause. Berlioz's *grande passion* was his sudden and
vehement affection (not so lasting as intense) for the
young Irish actress, Harriet Smithson. The beautiful actress had carried Paris by storm when she appeared there in Shakespearian rôles. Berlioz saw
her and was one of her willing captives. Moved by
his love, he began to study the poets that Miss
Smithson must have read, and Moore, Byron, and
Shakespeare were studied with some degree of enthusiasm. Each of these poets transmuted himself
into music in Berlioz's hands, but it is pleasant to
notice that only with Shakespeare does he remain
faithful to the poetic model. In addition to the two
Shakespearian works already mentioned, he composed
this third one, the " Romeo and Juliet " symphony.
It is a commendable, at times a glorious, Shakespearian picture. The ball at the Capulets, the picture of
Queen Mab, Romeo brooding alone in the garden,
the combats of the two houses, and, above all, the
balcony scene (purely instrumental, this last) are
beautiful illustrations of the transmutation of our
greatest poet into tones. It was falsely stated that
Berlioz resolved to marry Harriet Smithson, and to
picture in music the scene that won him, when he
first saw her, in the part of Juliet ; he has denied this,
although he accomplished both tasks; yet it is not

too much to say that his fiery passion led him to Shakespeare, and Shakespeare led him to some of his greatest music.

Tschaikowsky, the famous Russian composer, has also won an orchestral triumph through this play. His "Romeo and Juliet" overture must be ranked among his very best works, and as one of the worthy pictures of Shakespeare in orchestral music. It is, however, far less lyrical than Berlioz's romantic scenes, or Gounod's tender amativeness.

In this final chapter we have not endeavoured to give a complete list of Shakespearian orchestral or operatic music. Such a list would be of great dimensions and might even require a volume to itself. We have sought rather to show, by the citation of some of the master-works, what an inspiration Shakespeare has been to the general musician. He has been the same to the painter and to the sculptor. His influence has permeated every art.

Lawyers have been amazed at Shakespeare's legal references; physicians at his medical knowledge; theologians at his evident study of their polemics; we hope that we have shown by this book (and may its faults and shortcomings be pardoned for the sake of its intention) that the musician has more reason than any of these to join in the chorus of homage. Shakespeare loved our art, he understood it, and he most perfectly voiced its beauties to the world. We

can, in common with many another profession, pay
to him the tribute which was written of a lesser
man : [1]

> " Long shall we seek his likeness — long in vain,
>   And turn to all of him which may remain,
>   Sighing that Nature formed but one such man,
>   And broke the die."

[1] Byron's lines on Sheridan.

THE END.

INDEX.

READINGS ON

THE CATCHER
IN THE RYE

OTHER TITLES IN THE GREENHAVEN PRESS LITERARY COMPANION SERIES:

AMERICAN AUTHORS

Maya Angelou
Stephen Crane
Emily Dickinson
William Faulkner
F. Scott Fitzgerald
Nathaniel Hawthorne
Ernest Hemingway
Herman Melville
Arthur Miller
Eugene O'Neill
Edgar Allan Poe
John Steinbeck
Mark Twain
Thornton Wilder

BRITISH AUTHORS

Jane Austen
Joseph Conrad
Charles Dickens

WORLD AUTHORS

Fyodor Dostoyevsky
Homer
Sophocles

AMERICAN LITERATURE

The Adventure of
    Huckleberry Finn
The Glass Menagerie
The Great Gatsby
Of Mice and Men
The Scarlet Letter

BRITISH LITERATURE

Animal Farm
Beowulf
The Canterbury Tales
Lord of the Flies
Romeo and Juliet
Shakespeare: The Comedies
Shakespeare: The Histories
Shakespeare: The Sonnets
Shakespeare: The Tragedies
A Tale of Two Cities

WORLD LITERATURE

The Diary of a Young Girl

THE GREENHAVEN PRESS
Literary Companion
TO AMERICAN LITERATURE

THE CATCHER IN THE RYE

David Bender, *Publisher*
Bruno Leone, *Executive Editor*
Brenda Stalcup, *Managing Editor*
Bonnie Szumski, *Series Editor*
Steven Engel, *Book Editor*

Greenhaven Press, San Diego, CA

Every effort has been made to trace the owners of copy-
righted material. The articles in this volume may have
been edited for content, length, and/or reading level. The
titles have been changed to enhance the editorial purpose.
Those interested in locating the original source will find
the complete citation on the first page of each article.

Library of Congress Cataloging-in-Publication Data

Readings on The catcher in the rye / Steven Engel,
   book editor.
        p.   cm. — (Greenhaven Press literary
   companion to American literature)
      Includes bibliographical references and index.
      ISBN 1-56510-817-5 (lib. : alk. paper). —
   ISBN 1-56510-816-7 (pbk. : alk. paper)
      1. Salinger, J.D. (Jerome David), 1919–   Catcher in
   the rye. 2. Caulfield, Holden (Fictitious character)
   3. Runaway teenagers in literature. 4. Teenage boys in
   literature. I. Engel, Steven, 1968–   . II. Series.
   PS3537.A426C365   1998
   813'.54—dc21   97-43628
                                                       CIP

Cover photo: UPI/Corbis-Bettmann

Copyright ©1998 by Greenhaven Press, Inc.
PO Box 289009
San Diego, CA 92198-9009
Printed in the U.S.A.

66What really knocks me out is a book that, when you're done reading it, you wish the author that wrote it was a terrific friend of yours and you could call him up on the phone whenever you felt like it.99

—Holden Caulfield

CONTENTS

Chapter 4: *The Catcher in the Rye:* A Critical Evaluation

FOREWORD

The story's bare facts are simple: The captain, an old and
scarred seafarer, walks with a peg leg made of whale ivory.
He relentlessly drives his crew to hunt the world's oceans for
the great white whale that crippled him. After a long search,
the ship encounters the whale and a fierce battle ensues.
Finally the captain drives his harpoon into the whale, but
the harpoon line catches the captain about the neck and
drags him to his death.

A simple story, a straightforward plot—yet, since the 1851
publication of Herman Melville's *Moby-Dick*, readers and
critics have found many meanings in the struggle between
Captain Ahab and the whale. To some, the novel is a cau-
tionary tale that depicts how Ahab's obsession with revenge
leads to his insanity and death. Others believe that the whale
represents the unknowable secrets of the universe and that
Ahab is a tragic hero who dares to challenge fate by at-
tempting to discover this knowledge. Perhaps Melville intended Ahab as a criticism of Americans' tendency to become involved in well-intentioned but irrational causes. Or
did Melville model Ahab after himself, letting his fictional
character express his anger at what he perceived as a cruel
and distant god?

Although literary critics disagree over the meaning of
Moby-Dick, readers do not need to choose one particular interpretation in order to gain an understanding of Melville's
novel. Instead, by examining various analyses, they can gain

9

numerous insights into the issues that lie under the surface of the basic plot. Studying the writings of literary critics can also aid readers in making their own assessments of *Moby-Dick* and other literary works and in developing analytical thinking skills.

The Greenhaven Literary Companion Series was created with these goals in mind. Designed for young adults, this unique anthology series provides an engaging and comprehensive introduction to literary analysis and criticism. The essays included in the Literary Companion Series are chosen for their accessibility to a young adult audience and are expertly edited in consideration of both the reading and comprehension levels of this audience. In addition, each essay is introduced by a concise summation that presents the contributing writer's main themes and insights. Every anthology in the Literary Companion Series contains a varied selection of critical essays that cover a wide time span and express diverse views. Wherever possible, primary sources are represented through excerpts from authors' notebooks, letters, and journals and through contemporary criticism.

Each title in the Literary Companion Series pays careful consideration to the historical context of the particular author or literary work. In-depth biographies and detailed chronologies reveal important aspects of authors' lives and emphasize the historical events and social milieu that influenced their writings. To facilitate further research, every anthology includes primary and secondary source bibliographies of articles and/or books selected for their suitability for young adults. These engaging features make the Greenhaven Literary Companion Series ideal for introducing students to literary analysis in the classroom or as a library resource for young adults researching the world's great authors and literature.

Exceptional in its focus on young adults, the Greenhaven Literary Companion Series strives to present literary criticism in a compelling and accessible format. Every title in the series is intended to spark readers' interest in leading American and world authors, to help them broaden their understanding of literature, and to encourage them to formulate their own analyses of the literary works that they read. It is the editors' hope that young adult readers will find these anthologies to be true companions in their study of literature.

INTRODUCTION

A brief biographical blurb in Benet's *Reader's Encyclopedia* includes this description of J.D. Salinger: "Perhaps no other writer of so few works has been the subject of so many scholarly analyses." This comment accurately summarizes the world's continued fascination with Salinger's work *The Catcher in the Rye.*

In spite of the many differences between today's adolescents and the fictional Holden Caulfield, Holden seems to typify the adolescent experience. He is dissatisfied with his parents, hopelessly cynical about life and adults in general, yet intrigued by the adult world. A continued favorite in high schools, the novel is used to launch discussion on the meaning of adolescence and the passage into adulthood.

Catcher's enduring success is testimony to Salinger's ability to draw readers in, engaging them in an almost internal dialogue with his books' characters and their dilemmas. Holden could be speaking of the readers of *Catcher* when he explains: "What really knocks me out is a book that, when you're done reading it, you wish the author that wrote it was a terrific friend of yours and you could call him up on the phone whenever you felt like it." Readers certainly feel this type of intimacy not only with Holden, but with other Salinger characters, including Franny, Zooey, and Buddy Glass.

Paradoxically, Salinger has refused to personally forge any intimacy with his reading public. For the past thirty years, Salinger has remained silent, his voice heard only through legal documents and agents' threats. In so doing, Salinger's mystique has grown in direct proportion to his silence, engaging the reader far more than a more accessible man ever could.

Salinger's written legacy is limited to four books: *The Catcher in the Rye, Nine Stories, Franny and Zooey,* and *Raise High the Roof Beam, Carpenters and Seymour: An Introduc-*

tion. Twenty-two short stories remain uncollected and difficult to find.

This literary companion compiles several essays related to *The Catcher in the Rye* that are chosen to enlighten and engage the first-time reader of literary criticism. The articles cover the most commonly discussed elements of *Catcher*, including Holden Caulfield as narrator, and several of the book's themes. In addition, a biographical sketch presents some less well known facts of Salinger's life. A chronology provides a useful overview of Salinger's works and places them in a historical context. The bibliography identifies valuable resources for students completing further research.

Salinger's life and work continue to generate interest and scholarship. Despite his retreat from the public eye, Salinger has remained one of the more influential writers of the twentieth century.

J.D. SALINGER: A BIOGRAPHY

The story of Jerome David Salinger is incomplete and mysterious at best. Only a handful of articles have been written about his life, and the one unofficial biography contains more information about the lawsuit that followed its original publication than it does about Salinger's life. J.D. Salinger's own account of his life is limited to a few comments prefacing his short stories and a small number of interviews; even these are inaccurate and incomplete. Since Salinger last published in 1965, he has been virtually silent. Unlike most of his contemporaries, the reclusive Salinger has avoided the public eye for over thirty years.

SALINGER'S EARLY YEARS

Jerome David Salinger was born on January 1, 1919, to Solomon S. and Marie (née Jillach) Salinger. The couple had a daughter, Doris, born before Jerome. Not much is known about Salinger's early days, although he has said that his "boyhood was very much the same as that of the boy in the book [Holden]." Salinger went to public schools in Manhattan until 1932, when he transferred to the private McBurney School, where he flunked out a year later. His father, perhaps searching for a firm hand to mold the adolescent Jerry, enrolled his son at the Valley Forge Military Academy, a private military prep school in Pennsylvania. At Valley Forge, Salinger was the literary editor of the yearbook, *Crossed Sabres,* became involved in acting, joining the academy's Mask and Spur Dramatic Club, and was a member of the glee club, aviation club, and French club. School records there indicate that he had an IQ of 115.

After graduation in 1936 and taking classes for less than a year at New York University, Salinger traveled to Austria and Poland to help his father's meat importing business and to improve his German. Salinger wrote in the November/ December 1944 issue of *Story* magazine: "I was supposed to apprentice myself to the Polish ham business. They finally dragged me off to Bydgoszcz for a couple of months, where I slaughtered pigs, wagoned through the snow with the big slaughter-master. Came back to America and tried college for half a semester, but quit like a quitter." Salinger refers to his brief enrollment at Ursinus College in Pennsylvania, after which he tried his hand at acting. In one of his few interviews, Salinger states that he worked on a Caribbean cruise liner, the MS *Kungsholm,* as an entertainer.

The careers of most successful writers seem to take off at some pivotal date or under some key influence. Nineteen thirty-nine proved to be that year for Salinger—he enrolled in a writing course with Whit Burnett at Columbia University. Burnett, who also published the literary magazine *Story,* later wrote that Salinger stared out the window for most of the class but was the "kind who ingests and then comes out with very edited material." That next year, at the age of twenty-one, Salinger published his first short story, "The Young Folks," in *Story,* the first of four stories that Burnett would publish.

Salinger and War

Salinger had published four stories before the December 1941 Japanese attack on Pearl Harbor provoked the U.S. entry into World War II. Within weeks Salinger was drafted, reporting for duty in the Army Signal Corps on April 27, 1942. In October 1943 he was transferred to the army's counterintelligence unit. For some time Salinger was stationed in Devonshire, England; on D day, June 6, 1944, he landed on Utah Beach just five hours after the Allies' first assault. His unit's assignment was to cut off communications and interrogate German prisoners.

While in France, Salinger met American author Ernest Hemingway, who was working as a war correspondent. They apparently discussed the relative merits of the German 9 mm luger and the Colt .45 mm pistol, leading Hemingway to demonstrate the effectiveness of one sidearm by shooting off a chicken's head. Salinger was also reported to have carried his portable typewriter around Europe and continued to submit short stories for publication. He wrote to Burnett that he was "still writing whenever [he] could find the time and an unoccupied foxhole." During the war, Salinger managed to publish another ten stories.

Salinger's military service contained more than literary escapades; he went into combat with the Twelfth Regiment of the Fourth Infantry Division in the Battle of the Bulge, one of the largest and bloodiest battles of World War II. The Fourth Division also played pivotal roles in the battle for the Hurtgen Forest and the battle for Luxembourg at the end of 1944.

Although Salinger is not generally thought of as a war writer, a number of his pieces are related to his wartime experiences. Salinger biographer James E. Miller Jr. writes, "We may readily guess that the war was responsible for, or at least brought to the surface, an alienation from modern existence so profound as to maintain itself at times in an overpowering spiritual nausea." Salinger's stories from this time include "Personal Notes of an Infantryman," "Soft-Boiled Sergeant," and "Last Day of the Last Furlough."

AFTER THE WAR

After the war, Salinger remained in Europe on a six-month "civilian contract with the Defense Department." During this time, he married a French physician named Sylvia (her maiden name is unknown). The couple returned to New York in 1946. Although Salinger claimed a telepathic link with his wife, the marriage was short-lived and ended in divorce the next year. Salinger continued to write; between 1946 and 1950 he published ten short stories. Salinger scholar Warren French characterizes many of Salinger's earlier pieces as "very short, highly colloquial, yet heavily ironic tales in the manner made popular by O. Henry." Very few of these stories were republished, even after Salinger became well known, because Salinger saw them as his apprenticeship in the short-story form. Although Salinger questioned the literary merit of these stories, he became increasingly critical of any editing, refusing to allow his stories to be altered in any way. During this time, Salinger focused on publishing in the competitive first rank of literary markets for short-story writers, the so-called slicks, prestigious magazines such as *Collier's*, the *Saturday Evening Post*, *Harper's*, and the *New Yorker*, known for their polished content and professional pay.

Salinger wrote the following about himself for the contributors' notes section in the April 1949 *Harper's:*

In the first place, if I owned a magazine I would never publish a column full of contributors' biographical notes. I seldom care to know a writer's birthplace, his children's names, his working schedule, the date of his arrest for smuggling guns (the gallant rogue!) during the Irish Rebellion. The writer who tells you these things is also very likely to have his picture taken wearing an open-collared shirt—and he's sure to be looking three-quarter-profile and tragic. He can also be counted on to refer to his wife as a swell gal or a grand person.

I've written biographical notes for a few magazines, and I doubt if I ever said anything honest in them. This time, though, I think I'm a little too far out of my Emily Brontë period to work myself into a Heathcliff. (All writers—no matter how many rebellions they actively support—go to their graves half–Oliver Twist and half–Mary, Mary Quite Contrary.) This time I'm going to make it short and go straight home.

I've been writing seriously for over ten years. Being modest almost to a fault, I won't say I'm a born writer, but I'm certainly a born professional. I don't think I ever *selected* writing as a career. I just started to write when I was eighteen or so and never stopped. (Maybe that isn't quite true. Maybe I *did* select writing as a profession. I don't really remember—I got into it so quickly—and finally.)

I was with the Fourth Division during the war.

I almost always write about very young people.

With these words, Salinger at once both opened the door to speculation and revealed his impatience with people's curiosity about his life.

By the end of the 1940s, Salinger had found an appreciative audience in largely cosmopolitan readers who enjoyed the irony and satire of his stories. Salinger's later work in the *New Yorker* would solidify his position as a writer of literary merit.

SALINGER AND MOVIES

Salinger sought success in Hollywood as well. Former schoolmates remember him hoping to become a screenwriter. In college he wrote film reviews for the school paper, noting in one that he had wanted to throw tomatoes at a Shirley Temple film. His knowledge of film is apparent in *The Catcher in the Rye*, in Holden's comments about a number of contemporary movies. His first Hollywood opportunity came in the late 1940s when producers approached him with an offer to buy the rights to "Uncle Wiggily in Connecticut," a short story originally published in 1948 in the *New Yorker* about a Connecticut housewife whose visit with a high school friend reveals lost love and present indifference. Julius and Philip Epstein, screenwriters of such films as *Casablanca* and *The Brothers Karamazov*, were hired to write the screen adaptation of the story. In 1950, the movie, renamed *My Foolish Heart*, was released starring Dana Andrews and Susan Hayward. The movie received Academy Award nominations for best actress (Hayward) and best song ("My Foolish Heart"). Despite its popular success, the film disappointed Salinger, who has since refused to sell the film rights to any other work. In 1995, however, an Iranian film called *Pari* was released based on Salinger's *Franny and Zooey*.

THE CATCHER IN THE RYE

By 1950 Salinger had established his reputation in the *New Yorker* and his work was already popular among college students. However, it was *The Catcher in the Rye*, the novel he published the next year, that would make him a cultural icon. The publishing company Harcourt Brace originally accepted the book; however, when Salinger was asked to make revisions, he demanded the manuscript's return. Little, Brown then took the book as is, and published it in July 1951.

The Catcher in the Rye was published in the United States with a short biography of Salinger and his photograph on the back cover. His biographical statement reads, in part: "I've been writing since I was fifteen or so. My short stories have appeared in a number of magazines over the past ten years, mostly—and most happily—in *The New Yorker.* I worked on *The Catcher in the Rye*, on and off, for ten years." In fact, six of Salinger's early stories contain references to the Caulfields, including "Slight Rebellion Off Madison" and "I'm Crazy," which were both rewritten into a portion of the novel.

The initial reaction to *Catcher* was somewhat mixed. Critics who were already familiar with Salinger's work responded favorably: Anne L. Goodman wrote in the *New Republic* that the final scene was "as good as anything Salinger has written." However, not all reviewers appreciated the book. Some were put off by the book's language and content. In *Catholic World*, an anonymous reviewer declared that the novel was "monotonous and phony" because of the "excessive use of swearing and coarse language." Ernest Jones wrote that it was the "case history of all of us" and, therefore, boring and predictable. Despite negative reviews, however, *The Catcher in the Rye* continued to sell. By 1961, over 1.5 million copies were sold in the United States. In the decades that followed, the novel remained a favorite of high school and college students. In 1965, *Catcher* sales reached 5 million. By 1975 over 9 million copies of *Catcher* were sold, and in 1986 *Catcher* continued to sell at a rate of twenty to thirty thousand copies a month.

Just as the novel has continued to sell, it continued to gain literary recognition. Arthur Heiserman and James E. Miller Jr., in their article "J.D. Salinger: Some Crazy Cliff," place *Catcher*'s Holden Caulfield in the tradition of literary heroes that includes Ulysses, Aeneas, Jay Gatsby, and Stephen Dedalus. Charles Kaplan, at the same time, published an article comparing *Catcher* and *Huck Finn*, launching a tide of scholarly articles about *The Catcher in the Rye* that would reach its height in the early 1960s. Interestingly, a new—albeit smaller—wave of criticism has recently emerged from non-English-speaking countries, focused on Holden's distinctly American voice and Salinger's use of idioms.

As the critical and popular acclaim for the novel grew, Salinger became more and more reclusive. After the release of the novel, Salinger went to England to avoid publicity. At his insistence, the novel was published in England later in 1951 without the biography and the cover photograph.

On January 1, 1953, Salinger moved to a small rustic cottage in Cornish, New Hampshire. On February 17, 1955, he married Claire Douglas. Surprisingly, Salinger had a large celebration. Later that year a daughter, named Margaret Ann Salinger, was born. Five years later a son, Matthew Salinger, was born.

NINE STORIES

Salinger followed the success of *Catcher* in 1953 with the publication of *Nine Stories*. The book quickly hit number one on the *New York Times* best-seller list.

Nine Stories is a collection of seven short pieces that originally appeared in the *New Yorker*, "Down at the Dinghy," first published in *Harper's*, and "De Daumier-Smith's Blue Period," from *World Review*. The stories appear in the order of their publication. These nine stories are colored by Salinger's growing interest in Eastern thought. In fact, the book contains a Zen koan as an epigraph: "We know the sound of two hands clapping. But what is the sound of one hand clapping?" Warren French has written that *Nine Stories* thus carries us through a series of emblematic tableaux of human spiritual evolution—from an opening portrait of a seer whose spiritual insight has completely outstripped his physical discipline ["A Perfect Day for Bananafish"], through the stages as one loses internal vision to gain external control of his body and emotions and then is projected suddenly into spiritual development that provides momentary insights of timelessness, until one is absorbed altogether into the infinite ["Teddy"]. These stories should not be read, however, as models for behavior, but as what James Joyce called "epiphanies" of manifestations of behavior at typical stages in the human fall from glory and reascension back into it.

LATER WORK

Salinger's later work focuses almost exclusively on the seven children of Les and Bessie Glass: Seymour, Buddy, Boo Boo, the twins Walt and Waker, Zooey, and Franny. Four lengthy short stories were collected into two editions: *Franny and Zooey* in 1961 and *Raise High the Roof Beam, Carpenters and Seymour: An Introduction* in 1963. Both collections were immensely and immediately successful.

Franny and Zooey, subjects of the first book, are the youngest of the Glass children. Their tales lack the humor of *The Catcher in the Rye* but more than make up for it in increased depth of theme and philosophical questioning. In "Raise High the Roof Beam, Carpenters," Buddy Glass tells the story of Seymour's failure to show up at his own wedding and charts the reactions of wedding guests, including his own feelings about his brother. The piece begins with the Taoist tale of a horse judge who is able to look beyond the external attributes of a horse and see its "essential" inner qualities. In much the same way, Buddy perceives Seymour's "spiritual mechanism."

One of Salinger's more ambitious stories is "Seymour: An Introduction," a piece of over one hundred pages. In a nontraditional story without a standard narrative flow, the narrator, Buddy Glass, paints a series of portraits of his deceased brother, Seymour. Buddy Glass is a novelist who at times seems to be Salinger's alter ego. Buddy is a story writer and appears to have some of the same frustrations as Salinger. Here Buddy describes his frustration with critics:

Some people—*not* close friends—have asked me whether a lot of Seymour didn't go into the leading character of the one novel I've published. Actually, most of these people haven't *asked* me; they've *told* me. To protest this at all, I've found, makes me break out in hives, but I will say that no one who knew my brother has asked me or told me anything of the kind—for which I'm grateful, and, in a way, more than impressed, since a good many of my characters speak Manhattanese fluently and idiomatically, have a rather common flair for rushing in where most damned fools fear to tread, and are, by and large, pursued by an Entity that I'd much prefer to identify, very roughly, as the Old Man of the Mountain.

Later in the story, Buddy claims to have written "A Perfect Day for Bananafish," further blurring the distinction between Salinger and his narrator.

AFTER HAPWORTH, SECLUSION AND LEGAL ACTION

The Salinger story after his last published work, the short story "Hapworth 16, 1924," is minimal and sketchy. In 1967, Salinger's marriage to Claire Douglas ended in divorce. In 1970, Salinger repaid, with interest, the advance received from Little, Brown for his next novel.

Salinger and his representatives have been very aggressive in protecting his privacy and copyright. In 1974 an unauthorized, pirated collection of unpublished Salinger short stories titled *The Complete Uncollected Stories of J.D. Salinger* appeared. Salinger's attorneys sued bookstore owners who attempted to sell this typewritten compilation of Salinger's early stories.

In 1986 Salinger blocked the publication of Ian Hamilton's *J.D. Salinger: A Writing Life* due to the inclusion of unpublished letters. After a prolonged court battle, Hamilton was ordered to remove the excerpts of the letters, which Hamilton did, publishing the book in 1988. Ironically, the suit against Hamilton resulted in more publicity than the controversial biography might have caused. Salinger's deposition in the Hamilton case did contain a clue to the author's activities over the last twenty years. He commented that he was at work on a project, "Just a work of fiction. That's all. That's the only description I can really give it. . . . It's almost impossible to define. I work with characters, and as they develop, I just go on from there." There has been no other information on this work since.

Salinger's legal actions have not been limited to print; with the advent of electronic media, it has become easier to publish Salinger's work without permission. In 1996 Salinger's agents forced "The Holden Server," a *Catcher in the Rye* website, to remove quotations from the book that appear randomly as people log on. "The Holden Server" complied with Salinger's wishes; it also posted the correspondence between Salinger's agents and the creator of the website, Luke Seeman.

SALINGER AND POPULAR CULTURE

Although Salinger has conscientiously avoided the public eye for decades, his image (or lack thereof) has infiltrated American society, and the absence of the real Salinger has led to speculation, veiled references, and even impostors. As Ian Hamilton puts it, Salinger is "famous for not wanting to be famous." Kurt Vonnegut's *Blackbeard* includes a curmudgeon ex-writer named "Slazenger." In W.P. Kinsella's *Shoeless Joe* (the literary source of the successful Kevin Costner film *Field of Dreams*), the Salinger mystique becomes pivotal to the plot. The protagonist searches out J.D. Salinger and expects to see "a little man with bifocals sitting in an office that smells of furniture polish and floor wax . . . holed-up like a badger, on an isolated hill-top in New Hampshire" who "guards his privacy as if it were a virgin bride."

In 1982, Salinger sued a man named Stephen Kunes for impersonation. Two contemporary sitcoms have worked the Salinger mystique in two episodes: Both *The Single Guy* and *Frasier* highlight the fact that although millions have read *The Catcher in the Rye* very few know what Salinger looks like or what he is doing.

SALINGER'S LAST WORDS

In 1997 an interesting new chapter was added to the Salinger story. A small literary publisher, Orchises Press, announced it would reprint in book form Salinger's last short story, "Hapworth 16, 1924." With this announcement, the literary world readied itself for the triumphant return of Salinger. However, in typical Salinger fashion, the book has been delayed for over a year, with the final publication date still in question.

Salinger has left behind one novel and thirteen collected short stories. Deep in meaning and importance, all have inspired innumerable readers who see in them a timeless struggle for purity and spiritual harmony.

CHAPTER 1

Themes and Style in *The Catcher in the Rye*

Zen in *The Catcher in the Rye*

Bernice and Sanford Goldstein

After teaching in Japan, Bernice and Sanford Goldstein returned to Purdue University and published
several studies of the influence of Zen on Western
writers. Sanford Goldstein has also edited a number
of collections of Japanese poets. In this excerpt, the
authors first briefly explain some of the tenets of Zen
and then trace these beliefs through *The Catcher in
the Rye*. They also allude to the further development
of Zen ideas in Salinger's later short stories, especially those dealing with the Glass family.

While it is true that Zen has become a glittering catchword
as connotative as existentialism and at times as meaningless, the fact remains that Zen does exist and that Salinger
has shown a definite partiality towards it. Since Zen recog-
nizes that all boundaries are artificial, Salinger's Western experience is not outside the universe Zen encompasses. The
importance of the present moment; the long search and
struggle in which reason, logic, cleverness, and intellect
prove ineffectual; the inadequacy of judgment and criticism
which reinforce and stimulate the artificial boundary between self and other; and some degree of enlightenment
which results from the non-rational and spontaneous blending of dualities, an enlightenment which permits experience
that is complete and unadulterated and makes the moment
and, in effect, life non-phoney—all these aspects of Zen can
be found in Salinger's world.

WHAT IS ZEN?

First, what is Zen and what does the participant in Zen experience? An explanation of the latter may help clarify the
former. The main actor in the typical Zen drama is besieged

Reprinted, by permission, from Bernice Goldstein and Sanford Goldstein, "Zen and
Salinger," *Modern Fiction Studies* 12 (Autumn 1966):313–24; ©1966, The Johns Hopkins University Press.

by doubt and desire. He is not at all certain what enlightenment is, but is convinced it exists, wants it, and is willing to
struggle for it. Believing enlightenment is remote from him
yet intensely desiring it, he pursues it only to find it contin-
ually eludes him. This peculiar dilemma results from the
fact that he believes the search he is making with all his
heart and mind, with all his being and self and ego, is for
something that is *outside* himself. The Zen master, to whom
he has gone for guidance towards the Way, grants him formal interviews with an abundance of ceremony which are
probably intended to make him fully cognizant and thoroughly frightened, so the seeker fails in the exercise of the
spontaneous answer to the irrational question, for example,
"What is the sound of one hand clapping?" When not being
questioned by the Zen master, the disciple spends time in
the traditional method of sitting, ponders over various *koan*
or puzzles like the above, and does various tasks with a
minimum of verbal distraction. He is not permitted any of
the temporary satisfactions which give his ego an illusion of
satisfaction or well-being. These pursuits are not done
merely for the sake of subduing or chastising the ego in an
attempt to make it deny itself, but rather to expose the ego
itself as an artificial entity whose very *searching for enlightenment* is spurious.

A number of Zen poems comment on the state of the universe before the disciple began his search: "The mountains
were mountains and the rivers were rivers." During the disciple's search the appearance of the natural world changes,
but once enlightenment comes, the mountains are again
mountains, the rivers rivers. In the same way in the undif-
ferentiated world of early childhood, the separation between
self and the outside world is at a minimum. As Philip
Kapleau says in his book *The Three Pillars of Zen:*

> But what the student responds to most keenly is the visible
> evidence of the roshi's [Venerable Teacher's] liberated mind:
> his childlike spontaneity and simplicity, his radiance and
> compassion, his complete identification with his (the stu-
> dent's) aspiration. A novice who watches his seventy-eight-
> year-old roshi demonstrate a koan with dazzling swiftness
> and total involvement, and who observes the flowing, effort-
> less grace with which he relates himself to any situation and
> to all individuals, knows that he is seeing one of the finest
> products of a unique system of mind and character develop-
> ment, and he is bound to say to himself in his moments of de-

spair: "If through the practice of Zen I can learn to experience life with the same immediacy and awareness, no price will be too high to pay."

Yet for the uninitiated, with the learning of abstractions (language itself being the foremost), self and other are progressively differentiated. Zen's peculiar problem is to bring the self back into a kind of controlled state of infantile non-separation through which it can recognize the arbitrary nature of all the artificial boundaries set up by abstraction and can see the unity in all experience and the existence of ego within that unity. The student seeking enlightenment, therefore, must proceed through his long search and struggle in which reason, logic, cleverness, and intellect prove useless; he must recognize that judgment and criticism reinforce and stimulate the artificial boundary lines of the ego. Finally in the non-rational blending of spurious dualities, he may acquire some degree of enlightenment which will enable him to fully participate in every moment of his day-to-day life. The Zen Master Yasutani-Roshi recites to one of his students the following lines from a famous master: "'When I heard the temple bell ring, suddenly there was no bell and no I, just sound.' In other words, he no longer was aware of a distinction between himself, the bell, the sound, and the universe."...

CATCHER FORESHADOWS SALINGER'S LATER STORIES

That Salinger has had Zen on his mind for a considerable period of time can be illustrated by *The Catcher in the Rye*, the germ of the enlightened or to-be-partially enlightened Glass children present there. We find Holden wandering through a lost week-end in which he himself belongs with the phonies. He proceeds from experience to experience, searching for something but always ending up with phonies of one kind or another. At the end of the story, however, Holden, who has had a nervous breakdown (as Franny has) and is being treated in a psychiatric institution, comes to some kind of awareness, namely that he misses all of the "phonies." Holden finally identifies in some way with the people he has spent so much time criticizing, but always criticizing with some degree of sympathy. He is not going to wander off to the West as a blind man or hobo, nor is he going to follow any of the other romantic visions he has toyed with during the course of the novel. Ultimately he is headed toward home. That, of course, is where he does go when he meets his sister Phoebe, and it is Phoebe and the very concrete image of her in her blue coat on a carrousel that ultimately brings Holden to the awareness that he has to go home. The final words in the novel seem to portend the major theme of the Glass stories. A psychiatrist mistakenly asks Holden what he is going to do in September. Holden says he does not know. How should he know what he is going to be doing at such a removed time as next September? Holden seems to imply that he knows what he is doing only at the exact moment he is doing it, not at some point in some arbitrarily designated future.

Holden foreshadows in a much less explicit way the highly critical Glasses, for he too is very clever, very judgmental, very witty, always striving for something. As Salinger proceeds and matures in his career as a writer, what he suggests Holden was searching for becomes more explicit in the Glass stories. Not only is Holden the Catcher in the Rye, as he explicitly tells us—the catcher who catches children before they fall from the field of rye—but Holden too is caught. He is caught in a way quite similar to Buddy's being caught, and that is by the image of love for a dead brother. Holden's brother Allie is intended to be the wise, sagacious Seymour-type. When Holden needs help, he turns to his dead brother Allie. Holden is caught by love and an awareness of something better in the universe, and he is similarly caught by his younger sister Phoebe when she tells him there is nothing in the world he likes. The stress once more is that Holden is far too critical, his critical tendencies similar to those of the Glass trio of Franny, Buddy, and Zooey. Holden's recognition that he has separated himself from all the people he has been defining as phonies comes in his awareness that he misses all of them.

It is this overly critical tendency in Salinger's characters that we want to stress as a key point in Salinger's Zen, and that tendency to be overly critical says something profound about our modern American life, this very critical time of our own very critical people.

The Catcher in the Rye as an Antiwar Novel

John Seelye

Although not a single shot is fired in the novel (in fact, the story takes place during the relatively peaceful postwar America), John Seelye writes that *The Catcher in the Rye* echoes many of the images of the thirties and forties and is a precursor to the antiwar novels of the Vietnam War. Seelye argues that Holden's behavior is modeled on Bogart's movies such as *Casablanca* and *To Have and Have Not,* which act as "pretexts," or indicators to World War II. In addition, Holden's antiestablishment attitudes are the same ones voiced in the Vietnam protests which came fifteen years later. Therefore, *The Catcher in the Rye,* without directly dealing with war, both carries some of the undercurrent of World War II and announces the fears of conscription of the 1960s. John Seelye is a professor at the University of Florida. He has written extensively on American literature, including works on Mark Twain, William Faulkner, and Herman Melville.

Though the novel may be identified with the antiestablishmentarian attitude of fifties intellectuals, who contributed to its popularity, as a deposit of cultural stuff it is demonstrably a product of the forties, the period during which *Catcher* was conceived and written. Incubated during the last years of the Second World War, published in the middle of the Korean War, and having had a definable impact on the literary context of the Vietnam War, *The Catcher in the Rye* is itself a war novel once removed, a subliminal war novel in which not a shot is fired but the process of conscription is well under way. . . .

In returning to Salinger's novel after a hiatus of about

twenty years, I was struck by the kinds of things I had forgotten, including some rather remarkable facts, like Holden's
height—six feet, two inches—and his patch of grey hair, a
Hawthornean blazon on one side of his head. We all remember the red hat, but the grey hair had escaped my memory,
and I was, frankly, surprised by Holden's size, having
thought of him as, if anything, shorter than average. Except
for Frankenstein's monster, most of our archetypal outsiders
are not known for superior physical stature, save in moral
matters. But the most significant lapse in my memory had to
do with what was clearly meant by Salinger as a meaningful
characteristic, namely Holden's heavy smoking habit. He
smokes several packs a day, according to his own estimate,
and the story is spelled out by a steady exhalation of those
cigarette-fondling schticks that used to be the standby ges-
ture of every short story, novel, and movie script written in
the good old days when there was a ready market, not a protest line, for stuff with a lot of smoke in it.

THE IMPACT OF BOGART ON HOLDEN

Most important, although Holden frequently dismisses
movies with the same snarl with which he defines all the
phoniness in the world (both identified with his older
brother, D.B.), he has plainly seen a great number of them,
to which references abound, and in several scenes he play-
acts the part of a dying gangster, crediting the inspiration to
"the goddamn movies." Since Holden associates smoking a
cigarette with watching "myself getting tough in the mirror,"
there is a covert, even subliminal suggestion here of
Humphrey Bogart as a role model. Nor is it too difficult to
conceive of Holden as a first-person narrator derived from
those hard-boiled detectives made popular by Chandler and
Hammett, who wrote the books that became the movies that
made Bogart famous. And since *Breathless* was *the* existen-
tial film, Holden stole one on Jean Paul Belmondo also (who
actually *does* die from a bullet in the gut), for if *Catcher* is art,
then it is Bog-art, and like the characters who made Bogart
a famous image, Holden is caught in postures frozen in the
forties. Besides the cigarettes and the world-weary pose
there is the underworld into which Holden descends after he
leaves Pencey Prep, a frozen time frame of 1940s nightclubs,
floozies, and pimps, a world as seen over the back of a cab
driver, starkly. . . .

Again, the Bogart connection reinforces the extent to which Salinger's is a novel deeply imbedded with forties materials and attitudes. Like the Bogart hero, moreover, the forties was a decade without a distinctive milieu, with very little to call its own, except the Second World War and the Willis Jeep. Cars, costumes, dances, furniture, movies, all were aftereffects of the thirties, furnishing out a long wait for the second explosion of popular culture in the fifties. Salinger's book, I think, draws terrific power from the emptiness of the forties, and if as a decade it was an afterimage of the thirties, then *Catcher* can be read as the ultimate thirties after-story, bereft of the usual social consciousness that characterizes so much fiction of the previous period. Rather than being sustained by some W.P.A.–nourished vision of noble but starving farmers or by the proletarian-novel skeleton that sustains the urban context of a James Farrell or Nelson Algren, Salinger's is a story sustained by the movies of the thirties and early forties, most especially the kind of movie that pitted a noble-hearted detective against the filth and corruption of modern city life or transformed a dying gangster into a religious icon of social inequity. Dropping out of prep school, Holden drops through a crack in time into the reality of the world he knows through movies, and what follows is at once a privileging and a painful critique of the movie myth.

For Holden, the urban world is full of signifiers of adulthood, and he is less eager to rub out the Maurices of that world than he is to stop kids before they enter it, to enlist them in the fate of his favorite brother, Allie, whose mystic catcher's mitt is a creative token opposed to the screenplays written by his other brother in Hollywood. A moviegoer who hates movies, Holden mostly hates adulthood, from which he seeks to rescue all children, much as he wants all the girls he knows to remain virgins. There is of course only one way to escape growing up and that is Allie's way, which is why the book can be read as a lengthy suicide note with a blank space at the end to sign your name. The forties finally was our last great age of innocence, and Holden stands at the exit point, trying to hold everybody back from the fifties. Indeed, it is very difficult to imagine any role for him in the world of television and rock 'n' roll. He is intensely a forties kid, a movie kid, a Bogart boy, and the wonder is the extent to which he could nourish the kinds of kids brought up on television and the Beatles.

The original Holden in one of the early Caulfield stories is reported missing in action in the Pacific during the Second World War, but the boy in the novel is much too young to have served in that war. Still, he is seventeen in 1949 (or 1950, depending on your calculations) just the right age to be drafted into the Korean War, which is the only sequel we can project for Salinger's kid, an obit in a movie-screen epilogue, as at the end of *American Graffiti:*

Holden Caulfield was declared missing in action in Korea.

Which is precisely the fate that awaited a number of kids who identified with Holden in the late fifties and early sixties, only (as after *American Graffiti*) it was in Vietnam. "I swear that if there's ever another war," says Holden, "they'd better just take me out and stick me in front of a firing squad," not because he is a war hater, but because he detests regimentation: "It'd drive me crazy if I had to be in the Army and be with a bunch of guys like Ackley and Stradlater and old Maurice all the time, marching with them and all. . . . I'm sort of glad they've got the atomic bomb invented. If there's ever another war, I'm going to sit right the hell on top of it. I'll volunteer for it, I swear to God I will." If *Catcher* as a narrative is an extended death wish, then underlying that fatalism is an apocalyptic fantasy of self- and universal destruction, illuminating Mr. Antolini's intuition that "I can very clearly see you dying nobly, one way or another, for some highly unworthy cause." We tend to forget the extent to which *Catcher* was written in the shadow of the Second World War, if only because there is scant reference to it, limited to an allusion to D.B.'s noncombatant experience in Europe—"All he had to do was drive some cowboy general around all day." Yet D.B., we are told, "hated the war" and gave Holden *A Farewell to Arms* to read, telling him "that if he'd had to shoot anybody he wouldn't've known which direction to shoot in. He said the Army was practically as full of bastards as the Nazis were," an ideological neutrality not much removed from Joseph Heller's in *Catch-22.*

Holden's account of this conversation ends with the declaration by the mystical Allie that Emily Dickinson was a better war poet than Rupert Brooke, which leaves Holden mystified, but should clarify matters for us. Like Salinger, Dickinson is a death-obsessed writer, whose poetry virtually ignores the Civil War while laying out a bone field that is equivalent to a battlefield after the battle is over. If in D.B.'s declaration concerning the lack of difference between the U.S. Army and the Nazis we have a prevision of *Catch-22,* then in the dialogue between Allie and Holden and in Holden's terror of the army as the ultimate conformist zone we have a subliminal flash of *M.A.S.H.* and *Hair* that explodes into an image of gravestones all in a row upon row. That is, *The Catcher in the Rye* is a text derived from the forties whose post-text was the Korean and hence the Vietnam War. For in Holden we have a boy terrified of regimentation but eager for self- and societal destruction, a true anarchist for whom death is not only preferable to social restraints but the ultimate letting go.

A SUBLIMINAL PREPARATION FOR WAR

Bogart's films of the thirties were likewise a subliminal preparation for World War Two, right alongside the C.C.C. camps and other New Deal phenomena of idealistic regimentation, conveying a message concerning the way in which a messy world could be cleaned up, an iconographic cluster centered by the figure of a man holding either a shovel or a gun. It was an idea that gained increasing momentum in *Casablanca* and the movie version of *To Have and Have Not,* featuring cynical American males suddenly motivated to take up arms against a sea full of Nazis. One of Bogart's earliest and lesser-known contributions to the war effort was *Across the Pacific,* set mostly on an ocean liner, with Sidney Greenstreet playing his antagonist, an American university professor so sympathetic to the Japanese people that he is willing to betray his own country. Greenstreet had already figured more famously as the epicene Fat Man in *The Maltese Falcon* (a story virtually without ideology), ironically sharing the name of the bomb that later devastated Hiroshima. *Catcher,* whose pretext is the earlier Bogart films, like those movies lays down the baseline for subsequent conflicts. It provides the rationale not for an anticommunist crusade but for the explosion against the Vietnam War by teenagers unanxious to have their hair cut and their private parts shot off, Procrustean measures associated with the repressiveness of regimentation. At the same time, underlying this anarchistic message there is the essential image of Holden wishing himself on top of the atomic bomb, which evokes that memorable image from *Dr. Strangelove* when Slim Pickens rides down the first shot of World War Three to its Russian target.

This dual nihilistic image is warranted by the pervading gloom of *Catcher*, a Wertherean weltschmerz that provides a threshold for twenty years of death and destruction, much as Goethe's classic of suicide came at the start of the Napoleonic wars. The greatest novel about the Second World War, *The Naked and the Dead*, was built on the thirties-prepared framework of proletarian fiction but with considerable dependence also on a thirties reading of *Moby-Dick* as an antifascist tract. The two most popular antiwar novels that appeared just before or during the Vietnam War, *Catch-22* and *Slaughterhouse-Five*, were set in the Second World War, absurdist fictions that abjured Mailer's doctrinaire third-front framework for surrealistic expeditions into a fatalistic zone. *Catcher* likewise supplied not only the rationale for the antiwar, anti-regimentation movements of the sixties and seventies but provided the anti-ideological basis for many of the actual novels about Vietnam which have been and are still appearing, the early *Catch-22*–inspired fantasies having given way to the dreary, soul-numbing reality of purposeless combat in an empty wasteland of staring eyes.

CATCHER IS A WAR NOVEL

In short, *The Catcher in the Rye* is as much a war novel as is *Moby-Dick*, despite the absence (indeed because of the absence) of an obvious target of bomb-bursting hatred. Appearing in the centennial year of Melville's devastating anatomy of American militaristic/technological culture, which set the whale hunt against the author's personal search for and despair about the meaning and purpose of life, *Catcher* takes place during the same holiday season and provides such an unlikely backdrop to Ishmael's departure. The advent of Christmas is used for ironic effect by both writers, reminding us that the first shots of our entry into World War Two (Salinger's war) also signalled the opening of the Christmas season. *Catcher* is a 'tween-the-wars story without a mad captain or a whale, but American events soon caught up with the book and made good the deficiency, sucking Holden right out of his dark and drizzly December into the maelstrom direct, as the "goddam carrousel" turned into a war machine and Phoebe burst into flame. And now, without a war to give it focus, *Catcher* like *Werther* declines into a tractatus for suicide, which is, as *Moby-Dick* and *M.A.S.H.* both suggest, a reasonable alternative to war, as kids armed with the pistols Holden didn't have hold back saintly rock stars from the corrupting influences of the world by shooting them dead.

The Structure of *The Catcher in the Rye*

Brian Way

Literary critic Brian Way analyzes the tight structure of the novel. Way sees the narrative split into three sections: Holden at Pencey, Holden's escape to New York and his search for sexual adventure, and finally Holden's collapse. Way concludes that the third section is the least successful because Salinger loses the ironic compassion that struck a chord in the first two sections. Way also criticizes Salinger for an unrealistic view of childhood. He finds the novel's strength in the earlier scenes depicting the adolescent's view of the world. Way is the author of *F. Scott Fitzgerald and the Art of Social Fiction.* He has also published pieces on Herman Melville.

The Catcher is not only consistent in tone, but is an extremely well-constructed novel. Beneath its episodic brilliance is a tight three-movement structure. The first movement shows Holden Caulfield at school; the second, his escape to New York and search there for sexual adventure; the third, his collapse, at the conscious level, backward into childhood, at the unconscious forward into madness.

PENCEY AS A MICROCOSM

Holden at Pencey Prep can be taken as the young American in his natural setting, a character and a milieu which are strongly individualized and yet in an important sense representative. He is introduced as a complete misfit in the setting which his society considers appropriate for him. School is the agency by which America more than most countries consciously socializes the immature for entry into the approved adult activities: and so a boy's relation to his school becomes a microcosm of the individual's relation to his so-

Reprinted, with permission, from Brian Way, *"Franny and Zooey* and J.D. Salinger," *New Left Review*, May/June 1962, pp. 72–82.

ciety. In this concentration upon a manageable network of representative relationships, we see at work the only method by which a novel can create with any living force the pressures of a society—as opposed to the cinemascope aspirations of a John dos Passos. Holden is hostile to the spirit of his school—

> Pencey Prep is this school that's in Agerstown, Pennsylvania. You probably heard of it. You've probably seen the ads, anyway.

—but also alienated from it: there is his impending expulsion; his losing the fencing foils; above all his relation to the football game—physically remote ('practically the whole school was there except me') and cynical in spirit ('you were supposed to commit suicide or something if old Pencey didn't win').

His detachment from the game is a key to his rejection of the ethos of his society. What depresses and infuriates him most about his headmaster and Spencer is their insistence that 'life is a game'—

> Game my ass. Some game. If you get on the side where all the hot-shots are, then it's a game, all right—I admit that. But if you get on the *other* side, where there aren't any hot-shots, then what's a game about? Nothing. No game.

Games are a system devised for the benefit of the star-performer; the rules of the game enable him to shine, they are no protection for the weak—for those on the side where there aren't any hot-shots. The pretence of team-spirit is pure hypocrisy, and the cynicism of Holden's attitude the proper reaction to the assertion that the game is played for the common good. The game, as seen by Holden, is an image of the competitive society, in its glorification of success, callousness towards failure, and its most unpardonable assertion—that its hotshots not only have the tangible benefits of success but the moral satisfaction of feeling that they are the finest flower of an incorruptible system. Old Ossenburger is the matured product—enormously rich from his cheap funeral parlours; treated with esteem by his society—his old school names a wing after him; and full of moral self-satisfaction:

> The next morning, in chapel, he made a speech that lasted about ten hours. He started off with about 50 corny jokes, to show what a regular guy he was. Very big deal. Then he started telling us how he was never ashamed, when he was

> in some kind of trouble or something, to get right down on his
> knees to pray to God. He told us we should always pray to
> God—talk to Him and all—wherever we were. He told us we
> ought to think of Jesus as our buddy and all. He said *he* talked
> to Jesus all the time. Even when he was driving his car. That
> killed me. I can just see the big phoney bastard shifting into
> first gear and asking Jesus to send him a few more stiffs.

The only adequate reaction to him is Marsalla's brief pun-
gent wordless comment. The influence of Ring Lardner is
quite evident in this form of broad satiric comedy: Ossenburger is a bloated version of the man from Ogdensburg,
New York State, who 'is a Rotarian and a very convicting
speaker' (*The Golden Honeymoon*).

The other hot-shot at Pencey is Holden's room-mate
Stradlater, an athlete and school hero, 'a very sexy bastard'
who is outstandingly successful in the American form of
adolescent sexuality—the infantile petting with automobile
back-seat as indispensable locale. His fight with Holden over
Jane Gallagher brings in the book's other area of concern,
the agonies of adolescence. Structurally it is the event which
projects Holden into his New York adventures.

HOLDEN'S ATTEMPTS AT SEXUAL SATISFACTION

This second phase is the best part of the book. It describes
Holden's four successive attempts at sexual satisfaction: his
telephone-call to the girl who is 'not quite a whore'; his
evening in the Lavender Room with the three girls from Seattle, Washington; his encounter with the prostitute; and his
proposal to Sally Hayes. Salinger captures with extraordinary power, as well as with comic verve, the euphoria of escape from the formal limits of school, and the excited sense
of being on the town, with which Holden arrives in New
York. Holden's excitement is the excitement of the fantasist:
he is embarking on a dream which is both universally adolescent, and built into contemporary American mass-culture
through Hollywood and television, advertising, pulp fiction
and magazines, and social mores—the offer of unbelievable
possibilities of sexual adventure and satisfaction. This erotic
day-dream is confronted in each of the four incidents with
harsh realities which the day-dream disqualifies the fantasist from handling, in a manner analogous to F. Scott Fitzgerald's Jay Gatsby's experience. Holden is caught in an ironic
and painful dialectic: four times his participation in the com-
munal day-dream propel him into real situations from

which he recoils, even more incapacitated and humiliated, back into fantasy. The profound pessimism which grows steadily beneath the humour of this movement lies in the fact that the reassuring progressive nineteenth century conviction that one learns from experience is reversed. In a tale like *The Shadow-Line,* for instance, Joseph Conrad shows the young inexperienced commander taking his first ship through a series of difficult situations, and emerging at the end of the voyage matured, and accepted by his mentor, Captain Giles. In *The Catcher,* experience incapacitates and destroys, and after the failure of Holden's last attempt at satisfaction, he is moving towards mental collapse. . . .

HOLDEN'S COLLAPSE ON TWO PLANES

After this, the novel's third phase, the account of Holden's collapse, begins. It takes place on two planes: a conscious groping back towards childhood represented most strongly by his clandestine visit to Phoebe. (The element of unconscious sexual symbolism is clear here—his creeping back into the dark room suggests the womb.) Irresistibly at the unconscious level, he is drifting toward mental breakdown. This part of the novel is much less successful than the two earlier, and contains many of the weaknesses of *For Esmé* and *Franny and Zooey,* both of which offer a number of useful clues to the understanding of the last part of *The Catcher.* Potentialities of mental collapse are suggested much more effectively in the fight with Stradlater, the laughter in New York passage, and the Sally Hayes incident, than anywhere in this last section. There is a general loss of narrative impetus and comic verve: Holden's visit to a movie, though funny, is only a repetition of effects already scored against the Lunts. Salinger's ironic compassion is replaced by a self-regarding, and slightly self-pitying whimsicality which recalls Truman Capote rather than any writer of importance.

His nihilism has a pattern as precise as an equation: Conventional society is a nightmare too horrifying to contemplate—the expensive boarding school, the mockery of family-life, the executive's career, and the call-girl system in *The Catcher;* a respectable marriage in *Uncle Wiggily in Connecticut;* a business-man's adultery in *Pretty Mouth and Green my Eyes.* His despairing analysis does not permit even the stoical resistance of Albert Camus, let alone the positive hope of William Faulkner. The alternatives he presents—

life-in-death conformity and mental collapse—eliminate all possibility of creative living.

In the two earlier phases of the novel, the tensions of this dilemma, fused as they are in a classic portrayal of the contradictions of adolescence, are inescapably challenging. In the last section, however, Salinger's moral analysis of the significance of neurosis is unsatisfying. He slips into the current American habit of equating mental disorder with innocence, recalling Benjy in *The Sound and the Fury;* Augie March's brother George; Dove Linkhorn—a commercialised version in Nelson Algren's A *Walk on the Wild Side;* and Dean Moriarty, the holy goof.

SALINGER'S CHILDREN ARE UNREAL

More important still is his failure with children, who are not seen with any of his insight into adolescence, but with all the

---

SALINGER'S DISTINCTIVE STYLE

The language of The Catcher in the Rye *is distinctive.*
Often, reviewers of Catcher *attempt to mimic the vocabulary and rhythms of Holden Caulfield. In this early review of the novel in the July 15, 1951 New York Times Book Review James Stern attempts to capture Salinger's voice as he relates the plot of the novel.*

This girl Helga, she kills me. She reads just about everything I bring into the house, and a lot of crumby stuff besides. She's crazy about kids. I mean stories about kids. But Hel, she says there's hardly a writer alive can write about children. Only these English guys Richard Hughes and Walter de la Mare, she says. The rest is all corny. It depresses her. That's another thing. She can sniff a corny guy or a phony book quick as a dog smells a rat. This phoniness, it gives old Hel a pain if you want to know the truth. That's why she came hollering to me one day, her hair falling over her face and all, and said I had to read some damn story in the *New Yorker.* Who's the author? I said. Salinger, she told me. J. D. Salinger. Who's he? I asked. How should I know, she said, just you read it. . . .

But I was right, if you want to know the truth. You should've seen old Hel hit the ceiling when I told her this Salinger, he has not only written a novel, it's a Book-of-the-Month Club selection, too. For crying out loud, she said, what's it about? About this Holden Caulfield, I told her, about the time he ran away to New York from this Pencey Prep School in Agerstown,

sentimentalizing pre-Freudian unrestraint of a Victorian novelist—the cosiness of Holden's relationship with Phoebe, and his reminiscences of his own childhood visits to the Museum of Natural History. At the same time his children are miniature adults whose opinions gain the factitious piquancy of the pronouncements of Renaissance dwarfs. Esmé is odiously and precociously 'quaint'; Teddy a hateful little Christ disputing with the doctors; all the Glass children were star performers on a radio quiz 'It's a Wise Child'. Salinger's children are as detestable and unreal as Shakespeare's.

His failure here is curiously but closely linked to his success with adolescence: his understanding of adolescent sex is the strength of the earlier passages; his ignorance of the child's relation to sex ruins the close. In the scene where Holden delivers a note to the principal of Phoebe's school and suddenly sees the words '——you' written on the wall, he reflects—

Pa. Why'd he run away, asked old Hel. Because it was a terrible school, I told her, no matter how you looked at it. And there were no girls. What, said old Hel. Well, only this old Selma Thurmer, I said, the headmaster's daughter. But this Holden, he liked her because "she didn't give you a lot of horse-manure about what a great guy her father was.". . .

That's the way it sounds to me, Hel said, and away she went with this crazy book, "The Catcher in the Rye." What did I tell ye, she said next day. This Salinger, he's a short story guy. And he knows how to write about kids. This book though, it's too long. Gets kind of monotonous. And he should've cut out a lot about these jerks and all at that crumby school. They depress me. They really do. Salinger, he's best with real children. I mean young ones like old Phoebe, his kid sister. She's a personality. Holden and little old Phoeb, Hel said, they kill me. This last part about her and Holden and this Mr. Antolini, the only guy Holden ever thought he could trust, who ever took any interest in him, and who turned out queer—that's terrific. I swear it is.

You needn't swear, Hel, I said. Know what? This Holden, he's just like you. He finds the whole world's full of people who say one thing and mean another and he doesn't like it; and he hates movies and phony slobs and snobs and crumby books and war. Boy, how he hates war. Just like you, Hel, I said. But old Hel, she was already reading this crazy "Catcher" book all over again. That's always a good sign with Hel.

> It drove me damn near crazy. I thought how Phoebe and all
> the other little kids would see it, and how they'd wonder what
> the hell it meant, and then some dirty kid would tell them—
> all cockeyed naturally—what it meant, and how they'd all
> *think* about it and maybe even *worry* about it for a couple of
> days. I kept wanting to kill whoever'd written it. I figured it
> was some perverty bum that'd sneaked into the school late at
> night to take a leak or something and then wrote it on the
> wall. I kept picturing myself catching him at it, and how I'd
> smash his head on the stone steps till he was good and god-
> dam dead and bloody.

Salinger is out of touch with the way children actually re-
act to obscenity; they accept it either with complete matter-
of-factness, or with a delighted relish for the forbidden. The
one thing they don't do is worry about it. Salinger is not at all
in control of his material here, and although '——you' is
represented as being a shock to the children, it is the shock
to the rosy, sentimental, backward view of childhood that is
in fact resented. The hysterical violence of 'smash his head
on the stone steps till he was good and goddam dead and
bloody' shows this, and so does the obsessive follow-up,
where Holden finds '——you' written up everywhere he
goes, and is ultimately convinced that it will be inscribed on
his gravestone.

SALINGER'S LOSS OF CONTROL

The fable of the catcher in the rye itself belongs to the same
aberrant tendency. Holden wishes to protect children who
are playing happily in a field of rye from running over the
edge of the cliff that borders the field. Falling over a cliff is a
classic unconscious sexual symbol, and here represents
without any doubt the dividing-line of puberty, separating
the happy innocence of childhood from the dangers and agonies of sexual capability. This perpetuates the conventional
view of the innocence of children, and shows an atavistic belief in the existence of a Fall from grace. It may be objected
here that Holden's sexual failures could convincingly make
him hanker for a return to a pre-sexual state of existence. If
one felt that Salinger were consciously planning this and di-
recting one's responses this way, one would agree, but my
own feeling is that, by this point in the novel, he is completely submerged in Holden Caulfield and no longer pre-
serving that necessary detachment from his main character.
Two features of his writing support this view: first, his

abrupt abandonment of his sense of Holden's comic potentialities, expressed earlier in the novel through Holden's tone
of voice as a note of ironically sympathetic self-mockery. It
is this control of tone that gives the prostitute incident, without curbing the farce or minimising the pain its essential
sanity—a dimension which is obviously lacking in the '——
—you' sequence. Secondly, to understand what is happening, one is forced to drag out unconscious sexual symbols
and atavistic superstitions, evidence that the writer has
failed to order his material, and has left in an unrealised
form what he is really writing about—evidence not of pro-
fundity, but of a collapse of artistic control. Such examina-
tions are always impertinent and usually irrelevant, but here
the indications are so unmistakeable, and the connections
with the artistic failure so clear, that one is forced to follow
this line of analysis. In particular, there is the recurring unconscious symbol of a return to the womb—Phoebe's bed-
room (which I have already mentioned); and the Pharaoh's
tomb in the Museum, a peaceful and quiet place which
Holden is hysterically enraged to find violated once again
with the words '——you'.

At the dénouement, Salinger sees Holden Caulfield's
tragic predicament through the kind of closed system which
nihilistic writers construct with diagrammatic clarity: childhood is the only state of existence which is innocent, un-
spoilt, uncorrupted; escape backwards into it is obviously
impossible; the despair of knowing this inexorable situation
is the tragedy. The effectiveness of the tragedy depends on
our accepting the author's view of childhood—a view which
is manifestly false. And so the novel's greatness is flawed by
the dénouement and rests on those earlier scenes of adolescence where there is no falsity of observation, lapse of consciousness, or failure of control.

Symbolism in *The Catcher in the Rye*

Clinton W. Trowbridge

In this piece, Clinton W. Trowbridge argues that the symbolic value of the final episode in the novel can only be appreciated as the conclusion of the larger structure. He believes that Holden has tested several ideal images of himself only to find each of them phony. In the scene with Phoebe in Central Park, Holden again attempts to save his sister from growing up. Although Holden cannot save his sister, he is able to alter his ideal image of the catcher in the rye. He has learned that the world can be loved in spite of its imperfections. Professor Trowbridge teaches English at the College of Charleston. He has written a number of articles on *The Catcher in the Rye*.

As has been generally recognized, *The Catcher in the Rye* is the story of a quest, a search for truth in a world that has been dominated by falsity, the search for personal integrity by a hero who constantly falls short of his own ideal, who, in fact, participates in the very falsity he is trying to escape. The dramatic power of the novel stems from two things: that the hero's conflict is both internal and external and that it increases in intensity as his vision of inner and outer falsity becomes more and more overwhelming. What Leslie Fiedler calls "the pat Happy Ending" is simply the resolution of this conflict, a superbly appropriate one if we take into account what Salinger's intention is.

Thematically speaking, Salinger's intent is to present us with the plight of the idealist in the modern world. The undergraduate's, particularly the idealist undergraduate's, enthusiasm for *The Catcher* shows a recognition of this basic purpose as well as compliments Salinger's rendering of his theme. A college student writes: "Why do I like *The Catcher*?

Reprinted from Clinton W. Trowbridge, "The Symbolic Structure of *The Catcher in the Rye*," *Sewanee Review* 74 (July–September 1966):681–93, by permission of the *Sewanee Review*.

Because it puts forth in a fairly good argument the problems which boys of my age face, and also perhaps the inadequacy with which some of us cope with them. I have great admiration for Caulfield because he didn't compromise. . . . He likes the only things really worth liking, whereas most of us like all the things that aren't worth liking. Because he is sincere he won't settle for less.". . .

What happens to Holden, and what constitutes, therefore, the structural pattern of the novel, is that, as a result of a frighteningly clear vision of the disparity between what is and what ought to be both in the world and in himself and because of an increasing feeling of incapacity to re-form either, he attempts to escape into a series of ideal worlds, fails, and is finally brought to the realization of a higher and more impersonal ideal, that man and the world, in spite of all their imperfections, are to be loved.

First Ideal Image: Sophisticated Adult

The first of the ideal worlds into which Holden tries to escape is the sophisticated, man-about-town's New York City, the symbol to virtually every New England prep school boy of the glamorous adult life that his school is the monastic and detested antithesis of. Although Holden is hardly in the right frame of mind to enjoy fully the anticipation of the typical prep school boy's dream—a long weekend on the town—and although he has even seen through this dream, his parting words: "Sleep tight, ya morons!" do represent a complete rejection of the adolescent world. The action that immediately follows reveals Holden trying to play the part of an adult. His first encounter, the scene with Mrs. Morrow, is, significantly enough, his most successful one. He is taken, delightfully, on his own terms. He is allowed to play the man-of-the-world, though only, it is evident, because he is so clearly *playing* it. The rest of his experiences as a man-of-the-world, until that image of himself is destroyed by Maurice, are increasingly unsuccessful. It is his lack of sophistication rather than her unwillingness that is the reason for the failure of the Faith Cavendish affair, but he is refused a drink by the waiter and patronized as well as taken advantage of by the three "grools" from Seattle, screamed at by Horowitz the taxi driver, and treated very much as the younger brother by Lillian Simmons at Ernie's. During these scenes we learn more both about Holden's real affections (his love for the childish innocence and simplicity of his sister and Jane Gallagher) and the degree of his detestation for the very part he is playing and the adult world that he believes insists on his playing that part. Then comes the climactic scene with Sunny and its devastating aftermath.

Maurice's question "Innarested in a little tail t'night?" constitutes a challenge to Holden's image of himself as the suave sophisticate and thus must be answered affirmatively. His subsequent failure with Sunny and the brutality of Maurice's treatment of him are forceful ways of destroying Holden's man-of-the-world image of himself. More important to us, however, is our learning at this point of the nature and degree of Holden's sexual and religious idealism. He cannot use people. Like Christ, he finds pity and compassion to be stronger in him than self-will; unlike Christ, he is unable to find anything in himself approximating to the love of God, anything that can make of this pity and compassion a positive force. And so Holden is merely depressed to the point of contemplating suicide. Already we have the suggestion of what is to become so important later in the novel, that since Holden cannot live up to his Christ ideal, he will choose to emulate the only other character in the Bible he likes, the lunatic "that lived in the tombs and kept cutting himself with stones." It is significant that just as Holden rejected the adolescent world in his parting shout to his dormitory mates at Pencey Prep, so Sunny dismisses his pretensions of being an adult with the wonderfully casual, and completely devastating, "So long, crumb-bum.". . .

SECOND IDEAL IMAGE: THE CATCHER IN THE RYE

With Phoebe, Holden is at home in a world of innocence and integrity. He can trust her to take his side, to understand and sympathize. Thus it is doubly depressing when she reacts in just the opposite manner. Without even being told, she knows that he has been kicked out, and her "Oh, why did you *do* it?" affects him so deeply that he confesses far more than he intends to about the extent of his own nihilistic world-weariness. Phoebe's penetrating "You don't like *any*thing that's happening" forces him to make some sort of affirmation, to explain the sort of idealism that would justify so sad-making a picture of the world as it is. Neither his affirmation of his love of goodness (his brother Allie, James Castle) nor what might be called his love of pure being (just being with his sister) satisfies Phoebe, but Holden's memory of James Castle, the only person he has ever known who died for a principle, suggests to him a way in which he can devote his life to the protection of goodness. The significance of the catcher image lies in three things. First of all, it is a saviour image, and shows us the extent of Holden's religious idealism. Secondly, it crystallizes for us Holden's concept of good and evil; childhood is good, the only pure good, but it is surrounded by perils, the cliff of adolescence, over which the children will plunge into the evil of adulthood unless stopped. But finally, the image is based on a misunderstanding. The Burns poem goes "If a body *meet a body*" not "if a body *catch a body*," and the fact that Phoebe is aware of this and Holden is not, plus the manner in which these two words ("catch" and "meet") are reexamined and re-interpreted by Holden at the end of the novel, shows us in a powerful and deeply suggestive way the center of Holden's difficulty. Both Holden's nihilistic view of life as it is and his notion of what life ought to be are based on a misunderstanding of man's place in the universe. In this central metaphor is condensed the essence of the novel, though not until the end does Holden fully understand the significance of the difference between "man catching" and "man meeting."

MR. ANTOLINI

Of course, the catcher image does not represent a workable ideal, and Holden knows that. Its very impossibility means that all Holden is left with is his nihilism. He tells Phoebe that he plans to go out West and work on a ranch, but he shows that his real desire is to be saved from the emptiness of his negativism when he telephones Mr. Antolini and when he admits that he almost hopes that his parents will catch him as he sneaks out of the apartment. The catcher, in fact, wants to be caught, the saviour saved.

Mr. Antolini, a former English teacher of Holden's, is the nearest thing that Holden knows to the non-phony adult, and, as such, he is Holden's last refuge. As the person who protected the body of James Castle, he is also to Holden a kind of catcher figure, an image of his own ideal, therefore. In his understanding concern for Holden, and through his remarkably appropriate advice, Antolini does, in fact, seem to be saving him. Holden's physical relaxation, as well as the fact that he seems to have abandoned his plan to run off to the West (he even tells Antolini that he is planning to call up Jane Gallagher in the morning), augurs well for his spiritual recovery. What Antolini tells him, in essence, is that his present depressed state is a perfectly natural result of an awareness of evil, the imperfectness of man and the world, and what he promises him is that if only he will not give up his quest for truth, he will find a way of incorporating his idealism about man and the world into some sort of action, some constructive way of life. His promise that a formal education will help him discover his potentialities—the ways in which he personally can contribute toward the implementation of the ideal—is what he means by discovering the "size [of one's] mind." The phrase, so close to Carl Luce's "the pattern of your mind," represents a wholly contrary idea. It is not adjustment to the world but adjustment to one's self that Mr. Antolini is advocating. With his quotations from Stekel, he is urging Holden toward maturity and a more practical and less egotistical idealism. But then all is ruined by what is basically Holden's intolerance of human imperfection. He is awakened by Antolini's patting him on the head, and once more he rejects what *is* because of its lack of perfection. Pursued by doubts about his interpretation of Antolini's apparent homosexuality as well as guilt feelings about his rejection of Antolini ("even if he was a flit he certainly'd been very nice to me"), he wanders in a state of terrible depression toward literal as well as figurative death.

The literal and figurative coalesce as Holden seems to be plunging into a void each time he crosses the street; he manages to get to the other side only by praying to his dead brother Allie to save him. So terrible is Holden's depression, so complete his sense of alienation from the world of the living, that in his disturbed imagination only the dead, idealized brother can save him from the nothingness, the hellish state of his own nihilism. Resting on a Fifth Avenue bench he comes to a vision of the only ideal world that now seems left to him. Though he does not believe in the serious possibility of the deaf-mute image of himself any more than he did of the catcher figure, it is equally significant as a metaphor of his state of mind. Just as in the catcher image Holden was showing his devotion to the Christ ideal, so in the deaf-mute figure Holden is revealing his allegiance to the only other character he likes in the Bible, the lunatic who lives in the tombs and cuts himself with stones. They are, of course, obverse images of each other: save the world or completely reject it, cherish and protect the good or wall yourself in from the evil, choose health and happiness or the masochistic lunacy of isolation and self-pity. Holden's disillusionment is complete, his search for truth apparently over. He has only to say good-bye to Phoebe and return to her the money she lent him before he starts West. It is as if he were saying good-bye to life itself, a suggestion that Salinger enforces by having Holden almost killed as he runs across the street.

That Holden has given up his idealism, that his decision to go West represents not an escape into an ideal world, as he had formerly thought of it as being, but rather a rejection of his quest, is made clear to us in the next section of the novel. Throughout the novel Holden has been in search of a world, a way of life, an ideal that does not change. What he has never been able to accept is the mutability of life. The images that he loves are static images: Jane Gallagher as the girl who keeps her kings in the back row; children who, because of their absorption in the present and because of their innocence, seem to be unchanging; and above all (and increasingly as the novel progresses) the world of the dead: the martyred James Castle, the idealized, dead younger brother Allie, the natural history museum where even the smells are the same year after year. Holden's absorption with the idea of death reaches its culmination, appropriately enough, in the Egyptian tombs of the Museum of Art. The marvel of the Egyptians was that they were able to achieve permanence with something as essentially impermanent as the human body. The mummies represent the kind of conquest over time and mutability that Holden has been in search of all along. While to the younger boys that Holden is guiding, the tombs are spooky places from which they soon flee, to Holden they are symbolic of the peace and permanence that he so desperately wants. What he discovers there, in the form of the obscenity written under one of the glass cases, is that the quest for permanence is a hopeless one. "That's the whole trouble. You can't ever find a place that's nice and peaceful, because there isn't any." Even death is no escape. The trip West is embraced, but without the usual Caulfield enthusiasm, as a sort of negative ideal. It is the most pathetic, as well as the most fantastic, image of himself that Holden has yet created; and we see how little he is really interested in it, how sadly he must in fact be contemplating it, in the next scene when Phoebe arrives and insists on going with him.

IRONY OF LAST SECTION

The brilliance of the concluding section of the novel lies almost wholly in its irony. The ironic pattern has already been established that each time one of Holden's ideal images of himself is tested by reality it fails and in so failing shows us the phoniness of that particular image. But the images of himself that have been tested thus far have been phony ones and we have been relieved rather than disappointed that he has failed to act in accordance with them. Consider, for example, his behavior with Sunny. Here, for the first time, however, an apparently genuine image of himself is being tested: Holden the non-phony, the only non-phony left, at least in the adult world, is going to preserve his own integrity by keeping himself unspotted from the world and at the same time provide an oasis in the desert of phoniness for those who are worthy of salvation, mainly Phoebe and his older brother D.B. There are remnants of the catcher image in this picture of himself but more significant is the world-weariness, the alienation of himself from all but a chosen few, his apparent contempt for and hatred of the world.

But this too, when tested, turns out to be a phony image of himself. His refusal to allow Phoebe to accompany him, his anger with her for even wanting to go, provides us, and finally himself, with a climactic insight into his real character. In the first place, he is by no means as alienated from his world as he or we supposed. We have believed the theatre to be the epitome of phoniness to Holden; yet what most infuriated Holden about Phoebe's decision to leave with him is that she will not be acting in her school-play if she does. And consider the ironies involved in the fact that the part she is to play is that of Benedict Arnold. He is concerned over whether or not she has had lunch. He tells her that she *has* to go back to school. In fact, we see quite clearly that she is now behaving like him, has taken on his role. This vision of himself, as well as his sudden realization of the extent to which he has endangered the very goodness and innocence that he most wanted to protect, so horrifies him that he immediately abandons his plan to go West, tells her he is going home instead, and carefully and touchingly tries to lead her back to normalcy. Holden, who has apparently been uninfluenced by the various people who have tried to help him in the course of the novel, acts in this scene like a combination of Mr. Spencer, Antolini, and Phoebe as she had been on the previous night. What he tells her even smacks of his headmaster's statement, so abhorred by Holden at the time, that life's a game and has to be played according to the rules.

Secondly, Holden's behavior with Phoebe proves to us the genuineness of the catcher image. When tested, his love for Phoebe and his desire to save her innocence is far greater than his hatred for the world and his determination to abandon it. His love of good is stronger than his hatred of evil. And so, paradoxically, he is saved through saving; the catcher is caught by the person he most wants to catch. Of course, Holden is by no means completely saved, merely reclaimed from the death-like state of his world-weariness. He does, after all, suffer a nervous breakdown. He doesn't know if he's going to "apply himself" or not. Though the conclusion of the novel is hardly a "pat Happy Ending," then, it is affirmative; for Holden has caught some glimpse of how he can implement the catcher image of himself in action and as a result embraces a higher and more impersonal ideal: that man and the world are to be loved in spite of their imperfections.

HOLDEN'S REALIZATION

The experience that leads Holden to this final affirmation occurs while he is watching Phoebe ride the carousel in the zoo.

> All the kids kept trying to grab for the gold ring, and so was old Phoebe, and I was sort of afraid she'd fall off the goddam horse, but I didn't say anything or do anything. The thing with kids is, if they want to grab for the gold ring, you have to let them do it, and not say anything. If they fall off, they fall off, but it's bad if you say anything to them.

Understood in terms of its connection with the original catcher metaphor, what Holden is saying is something like this: innocence and goodness, epitomized in the condition of the child, are not static conditions; just as the child must grow up through adolescence into adulthood, so must innocence and goodness risk this passage through experience and evil. One cannot push the metaphor too far, but the gold ring suggests the promise of life, the beatific end that is the prize as well as the goal. Some are defeated by experience and evil—fall off the horse; others never get the gold ring— fail to attain the promise of life. The important thing to realize is that these are the conditions of life and that (to put it back in terms of the catcher metaphor), rather than attempt the impossible (catch and hold something that by its very nature cannot be caught and held—childhood, innocence), man should meet man, form a relationship of love and understanding with him, and in so doing help him toward his goal just as Holden is doing here with Phoebe. Man cannot save the world; he should not despise it; he may, however, love it. The effects on Holden are immediate.

> I was damn near bawling, I felt so damn happy, if you want to know the truth. I don't know why. It was just that she looked so damn *nice,* the way she kept going around and around, in her blue coat and all. God, I wish you could've been there.

This final sentence sets the tone for the concluding chapter and shows the effect on Holden of his altered catcher ideal. He misses everybody, even Maurice. The concern to communicate, to establish a relationship with man, has led to the love of man. Holden, whose actions and ideas had been prompted largely by his supersensitivity to evil, is now so sensitive to good that he can even love Maurice.

The Catcher in the Rye Is a Cult Novel

Thomas Reed Whissen

Thomas Reed Whissen attempts to identify the sources of *The Catcher in the Rye*'s immense popularity. He notes that the appeal of the book comes from four of Holden's attributes: Holden's way of classifying phonies, his myopic description, his alienation, and his narcissism. These allow the uncritical reader to identify with Holden. Whissen writes that early cult followers of the book believed they were given permission to act as Holden does because they saw themselves in the same "phony" situations as were depicted in the novel. Whissen is professor emeritus at Wright University. He is the author of *Devil's Advocates: Decadence in Modern Literature.*

Ask anyone to name a cult novel and the answer you are most likely to get is *The Catcher in the Rye*. Just as Johann Wolfgang von Goethe's *The Sorrows of Young Werther* is the prototypical cult novel of all time, J.D. Salinger's book is the prototypical cult novel of modern times. The book continues to cast a spell over young readers, and its popularity shows no signs of waning. It has long been required reading in many high school and college English classes, but it has somehow managed to avoid the fate of other books that have been caught in what has been called "the deadly embrace of the academy."

Ian Hamilton, in his unofficial biography of Salinger, says that when he first read *Catcher*, he felt as if he had stumbled upon a book that spoke not just *to* him but *for* him. No one has described the appeal of cult fiction better than this, for a true cult book is one that seems to address the reader directly and to say things in a way the reader would wish to say them. Not all readers, regardless of their enthusiasm, re-

From *Classic Cult Fiction: A Companion to Popular Cult Literature*, by Thomas Reed Whissen. Copyright ©1992 by Thomas Reed Whissen. Reproduced with permission of Greenwood Publishing Group, Inc, Westport, Conn.

spond to this unique book in the same way. While some find Holden Caulfield a lonely misfit worthy of extreme sympathy, others admire his sardonic wit in the face of insurmountable odds. Still others admire his stoicism, for although he has much to resent about the world he inhabits, he accepts its irritations with grace and humor.

THE APPEAL OF THE BOOK

One of the most immediate appeals of the book is Holden's way of classifying people as phonies. Few in the novel escape the label, although Holden does seem to allow for degrees of phoniness. The nuns he meets are perhaps the least phony (except for his dead brother, Allie, and his kid sister, Phoebe), whereas cute little Sally Hayes is described as the "queen of the phonies."

A phony, apparently, is someone who is only out to impress others, someone whose opinions are secondhand, someone who is unable to just "be himself." Just about everyone Holden has any contact with during this three-day sojourn between leaving prep school and arriving home fits into this category. To him, the most pathetic thing about it is that the phonies do not know they are phonies. Holden's own phoniness—his red hunting cap, his lies, his gut-clutching routine—is at least deliberate. His excuse, of course, is that the *real* phonies leave him no choice. Here, however, even he is self-deceived, and it is this gap between self-deception and self-awareness that accounts for the tone of melancholy smugness in the book, arising from what cult readers see as a sad but honest view of the world. . . .

BLURRED EDGES AND DETAILED INTERIORS

Although *The Catcher in the Rye* seems to take place in an easily recognizable world, Salinger is selective in his details in a way that creates a tension between the sharply etched close-up and the vague, impressionistic long-shot. Things like Ackley's pimples, Stradlater's dirty razor, Mr. Spencer's white chest hairs, and the hats the girls from Seattle wear are well-focused and enlarged. Pencey, though, seems to be seen from the hill from which Holden watches the football game. And New York City is not a bustling metropolis full of cars and people but a wintry, desolate place, a murky backdrop against which Holden is dwarfed and isolated. It is eerily quiet and deserted, as if Holden's cab is the only vehicle on the streets and the few people he encounters are the only people in the city.

Even within the vagueness, however, there is precision. Holden's cab may be the only car on the street, but it has a vomity smell to it. An empty hotel lobby smells of 5,000 dead cigars. And when the snow falls, it is like real snow dropped onto a stage setting. Sometimes Salinger creates the opposite effect. When his mother enters D.B.'s room, where Phoebe is sleeping, her presence in this precisely described room is as evanescent as the smoke from the cigarette that Holden has just hastily put out.

When we put these impressions together, we realize that Salinger has created a world of blurred edges and detailed interiors that conveys the illusion of reality but that is actuary a very clever distortion of it. Central Park, for example, is not the park of muggers and bums and assorted vagrants (as it was even then), but rather an empty stage on which Salinger places ducks or children at play or a lonely Holden Caulfield forlornly watching the children and worrying about the ducks. The scene is described with such precision, however, that we accept it without question. It is the reality of perpetual twilight where untroubled children laugh and skate as the sky grows darker and where grim forces that lurk in the shadows prepare to pounce.

HOLDEN'S ALIENATION

Early in the book we see Holden on a hilltop, looking down at a football game in which he has no real interest, either as player or fan. This scene establishes both the fact of his alienation from others and the reason for it. He alienates himself by choice, sometimes because he cannot stand the company of others, sometimes because he becomes disappointed with their company, and sometimes because his actions seem calculated to drive others away.

In all these situations, however, he is ambivalent. He dislikes Ackley and Stradlater, yet seeks them out, only to find further reason for dislike. He visits Mr. Spencer and Mr. Antolini, only to find their company disagreeable. And after forcing himself on Sally Hayes or Carl Luce, he is at pains to be his most obnoxious. His wanting people close to him yet keeping them at a distance is one of the attractions the book continues to have for readers who share his need for people and, at the same time, his distrust of them.

Holden's alienation, however, goes deeper than his ambiguous relationships with people. His family, for one thing, has come apart at the seams. There is no longer a unit he can rejoin. The various educational institutions he has attended promise one thing and do another. Thus, they become things from which he must disengage himself. He cannot tolerate cheap entertainment, yet that which is not cheap is cheapened by those who praise it without understanding it. And even those who do not need to pander to an audience—people like the Lunts and even the Greenwich Village piano player—show off shamelessly. Holden is heading down a road that has only ruts. Twenty years later, in the late sixties or seventies, Holden might have carved his own rut, followed his dream of dropping out and drifting, and nobody would have stopped him or, for that matter, cared. But in his day such a departure was tantamount to social suicide.

Holden is a fledgling existentialist, learning where he is going by going there. He sees that it is up to him to create values in a world that seems to have lost or abandoned its. This is why his frustrated "escape" spoke to those at the time the book appeared who longed for a new direction but simply did not know which way to turn. All they could do was to follow his example and turn inward and risk being called neurotic—or worse.

CULT READERS IDENTIFY WITH HOLDEN'S ADOLESCENT SIDE

Holden Caulfield is too troubled a young man to honestly enjoy feeling superior to others, but many readers see only the brashness and none of the humility. Granted, he is adolescent enough to patronize others at times, but he is also mature enough to know that he, too, is vulnerable. Cult readers, however, identify with the adolescent side of Holden's character without seeing the mature side in true perspective. This reaction is as much Salinger's fault as it is the reader's, for Salinger succeeds almost too well in supplying us with an irresistible way of observing—and abusing—all those phonies who seem all of a sudden to be coming out of the woodwork. Holden's insight seems uncanny for his age, and perhaps the first thing that intrigues us is his precociousness. It makes us wonder why we never saw things so clearly or expressed things so well.

It is easy to see why a cult reader would be overwhelmed by the accuracy of Holden's cold, appraising eye. Even those

readers who are not cult followers find that the book se-
duces them into seeing people through Holden's eyes and
analyzing them as he might. The uncritical reader, however,
has no problem seeing Holden's fits of depression, even his
ultimate institutionalization, as the result of social injustice
rather than personal psychosis. And if that same reader sees
beyond the black humor to the black despair beneath, then
it is easy to see how that reader can feel smugly sympathetic,
nodding in silent commiseration with a fellow victim of life's
callous ironies.

CULT BOOKS REINFORCE THE
READER'S FEELING OF SUPERIORITY

All cult books reinforce the egos of their readers, otherwise
there would be no cult. Cult books are mirrors in which
committed readers see themselves reflected in only the most
flattering sense, in the way Narcissus felt when he spied his
own image in a pool of water, and it was love at first sight.
Cult followers must feel superior to others, and one of the
best ways to feel superior is to be in possession of knowledge
others are too ignorant or too stupid to share. To be able to
convince Mrs. Morrow that her son is an angel when he
knows him to be an obnoxious little nerd is a pleasurable intellectual game for Holden. It is a game his admirers also enjoy, for they become fascinated with the power to manipulate
someone for whom they have no regard. *The Catcher in the
Rye* has encouraged many to enjoy such power by indulging
in similar manipulation. What greater self-satisfaction than
to feel oneself a genuine among the phonies—or better yet, a
"real" phony among all the second-rate fakes?

Although Holden suffers intense loneliness and alienation, and seems to enjoy every painful pang, he also knows
how to make others squirm. His insults range from the subtle and calculated way in which he annoys Carl Luce during
their conversation at the hotel bar to the direct and deliberate way he concludes the afternoon with Sally Hayes by
telling her that she is a "pain in the ass."

The scene between Holden and Ernest Morrow's mother
on the train to New York is an example of manipulation that
is cruelly dishonest. By building up her son in her eyes,
Holden's lies can only result in worse disillusion for the
mother. His premise is that a mother's blindness is phony
and, therefore, worth exploiting.

PERMISSION TO LIE TO "PHONIES"

Although Holden does not seem to think that the sort of lie he tells is destructive, he is quick to pounce on institutional lies ("This school builds character," "You've got to play the game") as slogans that deceive and thus do harm. Such high-handed double-think give cult readers carte blanche to lie and insult whenever they feel they are in the presence of a phony. In fact, cult readers in the fifties got a kick out of "turning somebody on," a phrase that back then meant to put someone on the defensive.

Catcher Is a Weak Novel That Does Not Explore Its Themes Fully

Maxwell Geismar

Influential critic and essayist Maxwell Geismar has written extensively on modern American literature. Although Geismar finds some passages to be well written, he attacks *Catcher* for its failure to answer the questions it raises: Holden Caulfield certainly rebels against the hypocrisy of society, but in what does he believe? Geismar notes that the novel's tone and ambiguous ending are typical of the stories Salinger published in the *New Yorker*.

He worked on *The Catcher in the Rye* for about ten years, J.D. Salinger told us, and when it appeared in 1951, it evoked both critical and popular acclaim. Here was a fresh voice, said Clifton Fadiman in the Book-of-the-Month Club *News*. "One can actually hear it speaking, and what it has to say is uncannily true, perceptive and compassionate." The novel was brilliant, funny, meaningful, said S.N. Behrman. It was probably the most distinguished first novel of the year, said Charles Poore in *Harper's* magazine. The real catch in *The Catcher*, said *Time*, was novelist Salinger himself, who could understand the adolescent mind without displaying one.

Salinger's short stories in the *New Yorker* had already created a stir. In undergraduate circles, and particularly in the women's colleges, this fresh voice, which plainly showed its debt to Ring Lardner, but had its own idiom and message, began to sound prophetic. Salinger was the spokesman of the Ivy League Rebellion during the early Fifties. He had come to express, apparently, the values and aspirations of college youth in a way that nobody since Scott Fitzgerald (the other major influence in his work) had done as well. He is interesting to read for this reason, and because he is a

Reprinted from Maxwell Geismar, *American Moderns: From Rebellion to Conformity* (New York: Hill & Wang, 1958), by permission of the author's estate.

leading light in the *New Yorker* school of writing. (He is probably their *ultimate* artist.) And besides, Salinger's talent is interesting for its own sake.

CATCHER CAPTURES THE SPIRIT OF THE EARLY FIFTIES

But just what is the time spirit that he expresses? The *Catcher*'s hero has been expelled from Pencey Prep as the climax of a long adolescent protest. The history teacher who tries to get at the causes of Holden Caulfield's discontent emerges as a moralistic pedagogue, who picks his nose. ("He was really getting the old thumb right in there.") During his farewell lecture, Holden is restless, bored—"I moved my ass a little bit on the bed"—and then suddenly uneasy. "I felt sorry as hell for him all of a sudden. But I just couldn't hang around there any longer." This refrain echoes through the narrative; and the rebellious young hero ends up by being "sorry" for all the jerks, morons, and queers who seem to populate the fashionable and rich preparatory school world.

He is also scornful of all the established conventions as "very big deal." (Another standard refrain in the story.) He seems to be the only truly creative personage in this world, and, though he has failed all his courses except English, he has his own high, almost absolute, standards of literature, at least.

"They gave me *Out of Africa* by Isak Dinesen. I thought it was going to stink, but it didn't. It was a very good book. I'm quite illiterate, but I read a lot." By comparison, *A Farewell to Arms* is really a phony book, so we are told. As in Saul Bellow's work, the very human hero of *The Catcher*, who is a physical weakling, who knows that he is at least half "yellow," is also a symbol of protest against the compulsive virility of the Hemingway school of fiction.

The action of the novel is in fact centered around the athlete Stradlater, who is "a very sexy bastard," and who has borrowed Holden Caulfield's jacket and his girl. Stradlater is "unscrupulous" with girls; he has a very *sincere* voice which he uses to snow them with, while he gives them the time, usually in the back seat of the car. Thinking about all this, Holden gets nervous ("I damn near puked"). In his room, he puts on his pajamas, and the old hunting hat which is his talisman of true rebellion and creativity, and starts out to write the English theme (which Stradlater will use as his own) about his dead brother Allie's baseball mitt. Yet when the athlete returns from his date, full of complacency about Holden's girl and of contempt for Holden's essay, this weakling-hero provokes him into a fight. "Get your dirty stinking moron knees off my chest," says Caulfield to Stradlater. "If I letcha up," says Strad, "willya keep your mouth shut?" "You're a dirty stupid sonuvabitch of a moron," says Holden Caulfield.

Later, nursing a bloody nose as the price of his defiant tongue, he wanders in to old Ackley's room for companionship. "You could also hear old Ackley snoring. Right through the goddam shower curtains you could hear him. He had sinus trouble and he couldn't breathe too hot when he was asleep. That guy had just about everything. Sinus trouble, pimples, lousy teeth, halitosis, crumby fingernails. You had to feel a little sorry for the crazy sonuvabitch." But he can find no comfort or solace in the room which stinks of dirty socks. Ackley is even more stupid than Stradlater. "Stradlater was a goddam genius next to Ackley." A familiar mood of loneliness and despair descends upon him. "I felt so lonesome, all of sudden, I almost wished I was dead. . . . Boy, did I feel rotten. I felt so damn lonesome." He counts his dough ("I was pretty loaded. My grandmother'd just sent me a wad about a week before.") and says good-by:

> When I was all set to go, when I had my bags and all, I stood for a while next to the stairs and took a last look down the goddam corridor. I was sort of crying. I don't know why. I put my red hunting hat on, and turned the peak around to the back, the way I liked it, and then I yelled at the top of my goddam voice, *"Sleep tight, ya morons!"* I'll bet I woke up every bastard on the whole floor. Then I got the hell out. Some stupid guy had thrown peanut shells all over the stairs, and I damn near broke my crazy neck.

THE WEAKNESS OF THE NOVEL

These are handsome prose passages, and *The Catcher in the Rye* is eminently readable and quotable in its tragicomic narrative of preadolescent revolt. Compact, taut, and colorful, the first half of the novel presents in brief compass all the petty horrors, the banalities, the final mediocrity of the typical American prep school. Very fine—and not sustained or fulfilled, as fiction. For the later sections of the narrative are simply an episodic account of Holden Caulfield's "lost weekend" in New York City which manages to sustain our interest but hardly deepens our understanding.

There are very ambiguous elements, moreover, in the

portrait of this sad little screwed-up hero. His urban background is curiously shadowy, like the parents who never quite appear in the story, like the one pure adolescent love affair which is now "ruined" in his memory. The locale of the New York sections is obviously that of a comfortable middle-class urban Jewish society where, however, all the leading figures have become beautifully Anglicized. Holden and Phoebe Caulfield: what perfect American social register names which are presented to us in both a social and a psychological void! Just as the hero's interest in the ancient Egyptians extends only to the fact that they created mummies, so Salinger's own view of his hero's environment omits any reference to its real nature and dynamics.

Though the book is dedicated to Salinger's mother, the fictional mother in the narrative appears only as a voice through the wall. The touching note of affection between the brother and sister is partly a substitute for the missing child-parent relationships (which might indeed clarify the nature of the neurotic hero), and perhaps even a sentimental evasion of the true emotions in a sibling love. The only real creation (or half-creation) in this world is Holden Caulfield himself. And that "compassion," so much praised in the story, and always expressed in the key phrase, "You had to feel sorry"—for him, for her, for them—also implies the same sense of superiority. If this hero really represents the nonconformist rebellion of the Fifties, he is a rebel without a past, apparently, and without a cause.

Catcher Fails to Argue for a Belief

The Catcher in the Rye protests, to be sure, against both the academic and social conformity of its period. But what does it argue *for*? When Holden mopes about the New York museum which is almost the true home of his discredited childhood, he remembers the Indian war-canoes "about as long as three goddam Cadillacs in a row." He refuses any longer to participate in the wealthy private boys' schools where "you have to keep making believe you give a damn if the football team loses, and all you do is talk about girls and liquor and sex all day, and everybody sticks together in these dirty little goddam cliques." Fair enough; while he also rejects the notion of a conventional future in which he would work in an office, make a lot of dough, ride in cabs, play bridge, or go to the movies. But in his own private vision of a better life, this little catcher in the rye sees only those "thousands of little children" all playing near the dangerous cliff, "and nobody's around—nobody big, I mean—except me" to rescue them from their morbid fate.

This is surely the differential revolt of the lonesome rich child, the conspicuous display of leisure-class emotions, the wounded affections never quite faced, of the upper-class orphan. This is the *New Yorker* school of ambiguous finality at its best. But Holden Caulfield's real trouble, as he is told by the equally precocious Phoebe is that he doesn't like *any*thing that is happening. "You don't like any schools. You don't like a million things. You *don't.*" This is also the peak of well-to-do and neurotic anarchism—the one world of cultivated negation in which all those thousands of innocent, pure little children are surely as doomed as their would-be and somewhat paranoid savior. "I have a feeling that you're riding for some kind of a terrible, terrible fall," says the last and best teacher in Holden's tormented academic career. But even this prophetic insight is vitiated by the fact that Mr. Antolini, too, is one of those flits and perverty guys from whom the adolescent hero escapes in shame and fear.

He is still, and forever, the innocent child in the evil and hostile universe, the child who can never grow up. And no wonder that he hears, in the final pages of the narrative, only a chorus of obscene sexual epithets which seem to surround the little moment of lyric happiness with his childlike sister. The real achievement of *The Catcher in the Rye* is that it manages so gracefully to evade just those central questions which it raises, and to preserve both its verbal brilliance and the charm of its emotions within the scope of its own dubious literary form. It is still Salinger's best work, if a highly artificial one, and the caesuras, the absences, the ambiguities at the base of this writer's work became more obvious in his subsequent books.

CHAPTER 2

Influences in *The Catcher in the Rye*

Robert Burns's Poem "Comin' Thro' the Rye" and *Catcher*

Luther S. Luedtke

The title *The Catcher in the Rye* alludes to Robert Burns's poem "Comin' Thro' the Rye." In this article, Luther S. Luedtke discusses how the structure, characterization, and imagery of the poem play out in the novel. Luedtke claims the Burns poem is about a sexual encounter in a field and therefore ties into the theme of innocence and experience in the novel. Dr. Luedtke is president of California Lutheran University. He has published extensively on American literature including *Making American: Society and Culture of the United States.*

The central interpretative problem in *The Catcher in the Rye*—the question of the degree and kind of affirmation or rejection the work ends with—has continued to be open to at least two major contradictory arguments. The one claims that Holden does not change in the novel, that his vision remains statically adolescent; and for its support it points to his nostalgia for a timeless and unfallen toy-world of carousels and blue coats. The other claims that Holden is to emerge from the sanitarium a maturing, potential adult, that, unlike [Mark Twain's] Huck, he will return to the urban East from the garden of the West willing to assume the burdens of adult life, and that this transformation occurs not as a result of psychotherapeutic reconditioning but from Holden's quasi-mystic vision that the way down *is* the way up and from his final acceptance of Christ-like responsibility towards the Maurices, Ackleys, and Stradlaters, as well as the Phoebes, of this world. This position finds its support in Holden's decision to let Phoebe grab for the gold ring, never mind the consequences, and in the kiss and all-absolving

Reprinted, by permission, from Luther S. Luedtke, "J.D. Salinger and Robert Burns: *The Catcher in the Rye*," *Modern Fiction Studies* 16 (Summer 1970):198–201; ©1970, The Johns Hopkins University Press.

rain that follow.

I think, however, that we can largely resolve this interpretative deadlock in favor of the latter, affirmative position by returning to the title of the work itself, following the subtle clues Salinger has left us in Holden's various uses of the title in his narration, and reading more attentively the Robert Burns poem from which Salinger took both title and theme for his novel. It is consistent with our growing awareness of Salinger's conscious craftsmanship in *The Catcher in the Rye* to credit him with this near "total relevance" of source, structure, and innuendo.

THE MISRENDERING OF THE TITLE

The first mention of the title of Burns' poem occurs over halfway through the novel when Holden sees "a little kid about six years old" walking in the street oblivious to traffic and singing "If a body catch a body coming through the rye." At the time Holden did not notice the innocent's happy and secure misrendering of the title, and it made him "feel better." It was the title in this form that Holden first excitedly offered to Phoebe in explaining his chosen role in the world. She checked his enthusiasm, however, by pointing out: "It's 'If a body *meet* a body coming through the rye'!" In this latter passage and those that immediately follow it, Salinger makes two important revelations relevant to the meaning of the novel and to Holden's adjustments.

The first is involved with the temporary change in Holden's narrative stance effected by Phoebe's correction. Although Holden tells his entire story about the "madman stuff" that happened "around last Christmas" in retrospect from a Southern California sanitarium, presumably as part of his rehabilitation, throughout the narration itself he remains faithfully within the time frame of the events narrated, with a few significant lapses into the later perspective of the actual writing-down of his story. The passage following Phoebe's retort is one of these. "She was right, though," Holden said. "It *is* 'If a body meet a body coming through the rye.' *I didn't know it then, though.* [latter italics mine] 'I thought it was "If a body catch a body,"' I said." Here for a moment Holden has stepped forward into the balanced perspective of his post-Christmas rest not merely to confess an earlier factual error but to acknowledge that since "last Christmas" he has grown in knowledge and, we are to as-

sume, in wisdom and understanding. Despite Holden's
claim that Mr. Vinson's "Oral Expression" class had not
taught him to order his thoughts or to repress his penchant
for digression, Holden's narration in *The Catcher* is tightly
controlled and progresses with discipline and purpose
through its sequence of events. It is out of the same "healed"
perspective which makes this ordered self-expression finally possible to him that Holden acknowledges in the passage above that Burns wrote of "meeting" (or, confrontation)
rather than "catching" (or, salvation) in the rye.

HOLDEN'S REALIZATION

Holden's final recognition that he cannot be a catcher of children and cannot save them from going off the cliff or from
grabbing for the gold ring has, of course, been often recognized and cited, in support both of Holden's final acceptance
and of his final rejection of the world. But the intrusion here
of the altered perspective of the later Holden, and the internal evidence which this fleeting change in narrative stance
offers for final reconciliation, have not been previously ex-
plicated. The second major revelation these passages have to
make has also escaped notice thus far. It concerns Holden's
relation to Phoebe and the differences, not the compatibili-
ties, in the awareness and maturity of the two.

It should be obvious to us from the first Phoebe is not to be
identified with the unconscious innocence either of the six-
year-old boy or of Holden, for Phoebe already knows, and
tells Holden, that in the rye fields of this world bodies are to
be met, not saved from falling. In addition, moreover, the action of Burns' poem tells us fully as much about Phoebe as
about Holden. Mildred Travis has briefly correlated the kiss-
ing, dampness, and crying of Burns' poem to the imagery of
the climactic park scene in *The Catcher* [in *Explicator*, December 1962], but she did not, as Salinger—and Phoebe—no
doubt had, explore the intention and events of Burns' poem
itself. Burns' poem is not a tale of salvation or frozen innocence, but quite the opposite, a tale of seduction and sexual
dalliance in the rye—which, we might notice, is to the rye itself far less destructive than children's ball-playing. There is
a reason for Jenny's tears and dampness in Burns' poem, for
she "draigl't [bedraggled, dirtied] a' her petticoatie/Comin
thro' the rye." The dirtying, dampness, crying and tears are,
of course, traditional euphemistic symbols of a sexual ad-

venture in the grass, and they place Jenny at the head of a group of "natural" women encompassing, among so many others, not only Thomas Hardy's Tess and William Faulkner's Dewey Dell, Temple Drake, and Caddy Compson (of the soiled underpants), but in due course, we expect, Phoebe as well. It is Phoebe that Holden wants above all others to hold inviolate in the rye field of the children's imaginings, but Phoebe must tell Holden that real rye fields are for private

---

"COMIN' THRO' THE RYE" BY ROBERT BURNS

Scottish poet Robert Burns (1759–1796) wrote both songs and poems in the Scottish dialect. This is the poem Holden incorrectly cites as the source of his idea to be "the catcher in the rye."

> Comin thro' the rye, poor body,
>   Comin thro' the rye,
> She draigl't a' her petticoatie
>   Comin thro' the rye
>
> Oh Jenny's a' weet, poor body,
>   Jenny's seldom dry,
> She draigl't a' her petticoatie
>   Comin thro' the rye,
>
> Gin a body meet a body
>   Comin thro' the rye,
> Gin a body kiss a body
>   Need a body cry.
> Chorus: Oh Jenny's a' weet, &c.
>
> Gin a body meet a body
>   Comin thro' the glen;
> Gin a body kiss a body
>   Need the warld ken!
> Chorus: Oh Jenny's a' weet, &c.

---

meetings, not for universal catchings.

It is through his attitudes towards the various forms of sex that Holden most obviously manifests his nausea of the world. "Sex is something I just don't understand," he tells us early in his narration. "I swear to God I don't." He is repulsed by the touch and wetness of it, yet fascinated by "that girl that was getting water squirted all over her face" in the New York City hotel. Although he is slow to confess it to himself, Holden realizes from the first that even his Phoebe, unlike the young Jane Gallagher, is not meant to "keep her kings in the back row." Holden confesses of Phoebe: "The only trouble is, she's a little too affectionate sometimes." And later he again writes, "She put her arms around my neck and all. She's very affectionate. I mean she's quite affectionate, for a child. Sometimes she's even *too* affectionate. I sort of gave her a kiss."

SIMILAR IMAGERY IN THE POEM AND THE BOOK

But it is Phoebe's genuine love for Holden and her unselfconscious honesty in expressing her affection to him that provide the bridge by which Holden must eventually come to accept love in all its variegations of vision and touch, splendor and squalor. In the final park scene, after Holden has accepted his responsibility for Phoebe and realized his loneliness without her, he can truly accept her kiss, as he had earlier accepted the disembodied grace of her dancing. As if in consequence of this kiss—sad, joyous, prescient and passionate to Holden—it begins to rain, and, like Burns' poem, Salinger's novel ends with ambiguous tears and wet clothes, this time Holden's however, for, although Phoebe's is the instinctual knowledge of woman, in *The Catcher* it is Holden who undergoes Jenny's necessary initiation into the world of the rye. In this moment Holden realizes the beauty of his gain as well as the pathos of his loss, and we can expect that his final response to Burns' rhetorical query, "Gin a body kiss a body/Need the warld ken!", will be a private and appreciative "no.". . .

These elements of narrative structure, source reference, characterization and imagery in *The Catcher in the Rye* suggest that Holden will emerge from his immersion, from his adult baptism, no longer self-consciously innocent and consigned to eternal childhood, like his dead brother Allie, but rather, like Phoebe, free to express and to receive the multitudes of love.

Possible Autobiographical Elements in *Catcher*

Edward R. Ducharme

In this article, Edward R. Ducharme discusses the possible autobiographical elements of Salinger's novel. Because Salinger is reclusive and has been known to provide inaccurate information about his life, the statements that Ducharme makes are, by his admission, assertions that should be read with a critical eye. Nevertheless, Ducharme makes some interesting connections that allow the reader to see *The Catcher in the Rye* as a disguised autobiography. Edward R. Ducharme is the Ellis and Nelle Levit Professor of Education at Drake University. He is also the coeditor of the *Journal of Teacher Education*.

J.D. Salinger is reported to have become very angry when questioned about autobiographical elements in the short story "For Esme: With Love and Squalor." During the conversation that followed he denied that anything he had ever written was autobiographical. On another occasion Salinger authorized the "fact" that he was living in Westport, Connecticut, when he was actually living in Cornish, N.H. Years earlier [in 1945]—writing to *Esquire* in a note accompanying "This Sandwich Has No Mayonaise" (a story in which the death of Holden Caulfield is reported)—Salinger himself asserted that his own Air Corps background had helped in the writing of the story. In the same comment he indicated that he wished to serve in a chorus line after the War was over. W.J. Weatherby, writing in the *Twentieth Century*, quotes Salinger as having said: "It is my subversive opinion that a writer's feelings of anonymity—obscurity, are the second-most valuable property on loan to him during his personal years."

Reprinted, with permission, from Edward R. Ducharme, "J.D., D.B., Sonny, Sunny, and Holden," *English Record* 19 (December 1968):54–58.

LITTLE KNOWN ABOUT SALINGER

The point of all the above is that there is little from Salinger himself on his own life, particularly from 1951 onwards, or, shortly after the publication of *The Catcher in the Rye*. Even those comments given during the earlier years, some of which are referred to above, are a mixture of half-truth and whimsey, difficult sources for the biographer. Yet, in the twentieth century, no man can escape detection altogether; some facts emerge about even the most careful. From those about Salinger can be pieced together a small amount of data relevant to the study of *The Catcher in the Rye* from an autobiographical standpoint. One point must be stressed in reading all of the following: almost every assertion about Salinger's life is from a secondary source and must be regarded as such.

The available facts are as rare and as puzzling as Salinger's stories. There have been several attempts but few successes in the search for facts. Perhaps the most widely used source is William Maxwell's brief biography appearing in the July, 1951, Book-of-the-Month Club *News*. Two of the more ambitious attempts are the *Time* and *Life* articles [Jack Skow's "Sonny: An Introduction" and Ernest Haveman's "The Search for the Mysterious J.D. Salinger"]. These less than complete accounts have received considerable attention. Henry Anatole Grunwald has a lengthy biographical section in his *Salinger: A Critical and Personal Portrait*, the major portion of which is a reprinting of the *Time* and *Life* articles and references to the Maxwell piece. The scarcity of material can be most readily seen when one realizes that even the learned critics have relied upon news magazine articles and a book club notice, sources frequently maligned in literary research. In addition to the above there is a brief passage by Salinger himself in the *First Supplement* to *Twentieth Century Authors*. Finally, one can—if diligent enough—discover a few more things by studying old issues of *Esquire* and *Story* magazines. These are the worthwhile sources.

POSSIBLE AUTOBIOGRAPHICAL ELEMENTS

The attempt to relate the facts to the novel reveals little in the way of extended and extensive material. The simplest facts come first. Salinger and Holden were both born in New York City and spent their early years there. Both attended several secondary schools and left at least one for academic reasons. Salinger attended the McBurney School when he was thirteen, leaving at the end of one year. The McBurney School appears by name in the novel: It is this school that Pencey Prep was scheduled to have a fencing meet with on the day that Holden left the foils on the subway. Related to this point is Grunwald's assertion that Salinger was at one time the manager of the fencing team in one of the schools he attended. Salinger attended the McBurney School because of his parents' concern over his work. Holden was also placed in several schools.

After the McBurney School experience, Salinger went to Valley Forge Military Academy in Wayne, Pennsylvania, the same state in which Pencey Prep is located. The two schools are alike in other respects. Holden speaks of the "crazy cannon" from Revolutionary War days; Jack Skow, in his *Time* story, noted that Valley Forge Military Academy was "heavily fortified with boxwood hedges and Revolutionary War cannon." Holden is wryly amused by the school motto: "Since 1882 we have been molding boys into splendid, clear-thinking young men." The school's pride in its motto is evident in Holden's negative attitude towards it. Both the motto itself and Holden's attitude have probable counterparts. Certainly Valley Forge's motto is similar in intent: "From the embattled fields of Valley Forge went men who built America; from the training fields of Valley Forge go men who preserve America." The 1965 *Handbook of Private Schools* has commercial inserts from over 150 boys schools; only two others in addition to Valley Forge reprint their motto.

There have been some attempts to find the boys who might have served as models for the characters in the novel. Skow states that some like happenings may have occurred at Valley Forge but speculates no further. Grunwald claims that a boy did run away—not Salinger himself, who was too conventional in his revolts for that—and ended up in a West Coast mental institution. He further asserts that another boy committed suicide under circumstances similar to those in James Castle's case. Regardless of the accuracy of such reports, no one has been able to demonstrate that such boys—if they actually did exist—served as models for Salinger.

Both Salinger and Holden had spent some time in Maine during summers. It was in Maine that Holden had played checkers with Jane Gallagher. Skow notes that Salinger had spent several summers at Camp Wigwam in Maine, even being voted the most popular actor.

Other particular places form a common background. Holden speaks of the Museum of Natural History, particularly of the American Indian Room. In a comment to *Story* magazine in 1944, Salinger wrote: " 'I . . . am more inclined to get my New York out of the American Indian Room of the Museum of Natural History, where I used to drop my marbles all over the place.' "

A final note of similarity of Salinger and Holden in young days is revealed by a comment in Skow's piece in *Time.* One of Salinger's schoolboy friends observed that Salinger was always doing slightly unconventional things, the kind of person his own family could not keep track of. Holden's nonconformity is self-evident.

Yet, it is not only as children that relevant likenesses appear. There is the previously mentioned fondness for half-truth and whimsey on Salinger's part. Ernest Haveman, in his article in *Life* tells how Salinger—in his Greenwich Village days during the early fifties—would tell fantastic stories about himself, even convincing one girl that he was the goalie for a professional hockey team. One recalls Holden's fondness for "chucking the old crap around." His entire conversation with Mrs. Morrow while on the train illustrates this point.

The editor's note *Story* magazine in 1944, introducing the story "Once a Week Won't Kill You," tells how Salinger had sent a check for $200 with his story. The check was to be used in some way as a help to young writers. This act of generosity is like Holden's giving money to the two nuns.

The adult Salinger has been much concerned with Buddhism. The two stories "Franny" and "Zooey" contain frequent references; the dedication page of *Nine Stories* contains a quotation from a Buddhist source. Haveman found an ongoing interest in Buddhism at the time of the writing of these works. Towards the end of *The Catcher in the Rye,* Holden speaks of his sister Phoebe as sitting like "one of those Yogi guys."

Phoebe is one of the few whom Holden genuinely likes. She—like Allie and the nuns and James Castle—has a kind of innocence about her that he responds to. Haveman notes that Salinger, in his Village period, had a reputation for dating "the youngest, most innocent kids he could find."

SALINGER, HOLDEN, AND MOVIES

The similarities extend beyond judgment in people. While Holden may have a distaste for some of the things done in films, he nonetheless knows a great deal about them and is quite concerned about certain aspects of filmdom, a side of Holden already well documented. The young and adult Salinger had several relevant experiences with the acting field in general and movies in particular. Young Salinger was so interested in films that he several times expressed the wish of "grabbing the big loot as a Hollywood writer-producer," and "appeared to be intensely interested in getting into the movies or in selling some of his work to Hollywood." The experience at Camp Wigwam has been mentioned; there is, in addition, the evidence that he later specifically mentioned acting as a major interest when being interviewed for the McBurney School. The early Salinger interest is paralleled by Holden's constantly expressing himself in terms of film heroes. The relationship does not stop here, however. Holden is interested in films, but he frequently expresses contempt for them and what they present as well as what they do to the people associated with them. It is in this area that there is a further relationship with the adult Salinger who had some relationship with Hollywood for a brief time.

In 1949 appeared the film *My Foolish Heart* based on Salinger's "Uncle Wiggily in Connecticut," a short story written during the early forties. Salinger's distaste for the film was so great that he has since refused to allow any of his work to be made into films or any plays to be based on his writings. *The Catcher in the Rye* was first published in 1951, two years after the *My Foolish Heart* incident. Thus Holden's distaste for films—despite his considerable knowledge of them—parallels Salinger's. This seems fairly obvious, but there is a more important relationship.

Holden spoke of how his brother D.B. is out working in Hollywood, or as he says, "out in Hollywood . . . being a prostitute." (A further note of parallelism: D.B. wrote a book of short stories in which, according to Holden, the title story called "The Secret Goldfish" is the best. J.D. had, by this time, written and published *Nine Stories;* the most noteworthy in terms of his later preoccupation with the Glass family is "A Perfect Day for Banafish," a title quite like D.B.'s best story. *Nine Stories* also contains "Uncle Wiggily in Connecticut.") The word of importance in Holden's acid description of his brother's activities is *prostitute,* if one is to accept the following.

When Salinger was a teenager and even earlier, his nickname was Sonny. In *The Catcher in the Rye* Holden accepted Maurice's offer to provide a girl for him. While describing his actions while waiting for her and the conversation he has with her, Holden uses the word *prostitute* nine times in reference to the girl. When she arrives, Holden is very reluctant to follow through and engages in what seems like idle conversation. He asks the girl her name and she replies that it is Sunny. Now, it is during these moments that Holden has some of his most discomforting experiences. Salinger—from the evidence available—felt the same way about his film experiences. The real prostitute in the novel, then, has the real name of the real man who had earlier dealt with Hollywood, "being a prostitute," in Holden's words. It is difficult to accept the idea that a writer as perceptive about human beings and as sensitive to language as Salinger is would carelessly give his boyhood nickname to a prostitute, albeit a young one, having already established his adult *alter ego* in the novel as a figurative prostitute.

J.D. Salinger no longer prostitutes himself by having relations with Hollywood. He now lives in near-solitary state in Cornish, N.H. In so doing he is fulfilling one of Holden Caulfield's boyhood dreams: the wish to escape from the world of everydayness to one of undisturbed aloneness. Holden once spoke with Sally Hayes about his wish to live "somewhere with a brook and all." Near the end of the novel, as Holden prepares to run away, he thinks of building a cabin near but not in the woods where he will live by himself with no intrusions from the outside world. Later he says:

> I'd let old Phoebe come out and visit me in the summertime and on Christmas vacation and Easter vacation. And I'd let D.B. come out and visit me for a while if he wanted a nice, quiet place for his writing, but he couldn't write any movies in my cabin, only books and stories.

Comparing *Catcher in the Rye* to *The Adventures of Huckleberry Finn*

Charles Kaplan

Charles Kaplan was one of the first critics to write about the link between Holden Caulfield and Huck Finn. As he notes, both novels share more than the structural similarities of first-person narratives about a boy running away from civilization. In both stories, the young protagonists are on journeys, or quests, to discover themselves, and both attack the hypocrisy of American society. Charles Kaplan taught at San Fernando Valley State College. His other publications include several articles on American fiction, a textbook for composition courses and *The Overwrought Urn*.

Henry Thoreau, himself an interior traveler of some note, says in *A Week on the Concord and Merrimac Rivers:* "The traveller must be born again on the road, and earn a passport from the elements, the principal powers that be for him." In Mark Twain's *Adventures of Huckleberry Finn* (1884) and in J.D. Salinger's *The Catcher in the Rye* (1951) we meet two young travelers—travelers in their native land and also in the geography of their souls. Their narratives are separated in time by almost seventy years, but the psychic connection between them eliminates mere temporal distance: Huck Finn and Holden Caulfield are true blood-brothers, speaking to us in terms that lift their wanderings from the level of the merely picaresque to that of a sensitive and insightful criticism of American life.

Each work, to begin with, is a fine comic novel. Each is rich in incident, varied in characterization, and meaningful

Reprinted from Charles Kaplan, "Holden and Huck: The Odysseys of Youth," *College English* 18 (1956):76–80.

74

in its entirety. In each the story is narrated by the central figure, an adolescent whose remarkable language is both a reflection and a criticism of his education, his environment, and his times. Each is fundamentally a story of a quest—an adventure story in the age-old pattern of a young lad making his way in a not particularly friendly adult world. An outcast, to all intents without family and friends, the protagonist flees the restraints of the civilization which would make him its victim, and journeys through the world in search of what he thinks is freedom—but which we, his adult readers, recognize to be primarily understanding. Society regards him as a rogue, a ne'er-do-well whose career consists of one scrape after another; but the extent to which he is constantly embroiled with authority is exactly the index of his independence, his sometimes pathetic self-reliance, and his freedom of spirit. He is a total realist, with an acute and instinctive register of mind which enables him to penetrate sham and pretense—qualities which, the more he travels through the adult world, the more he sees as most frequently recurring. He has somehow acquired a code of ethics and a standard of value against which he measures mankind—including, mercilessly, himself. There are some people and things—not many, however—that are (in Holden's term) "nice"; there are many more that are "phony." He does not understand the world, but he knows how one should behave in it. The comic irony that gives each novel its characteristic intellectual slant is provided by the judgments of these young realists on the false ideals and romanticized versions of life which they encounter on their travels.

SIMILAR USE OF LANGUAGE

The slangy, idiomatic, frequently vulgar language which Twain and Salinger put in the mouths of their heroes is remarkable for the clarity of the self-portraits that emerge, as well as for the effortless accuracy of the talk itself. F.R. Leavis describes Huck's colloquial language as a literary medium that is "Shakespearian in its range and subtlety." Likewise, Holden's twentieth-century prep-school vernacular, despite its automatic and somehow innocent obscenities and its hackneyed coinages, also manages to communicate ideas and feelings of a quite complex sort within its sharply delimited boundaries. The language, in each case, is personal, distinctive, and descriptive of character. Holden and

Huck are moralists as well as realists: each has a deep concern with ethical valuation, and each responds fully to the
experiences which life offers him. It is the tension between
their apparently inadequate idiom and their instinctively full
and humane ethics that both Twain and Salinger exploit for
comic purposes.

HUCK'S SEARCH FOR IDENTITY

"The traveller must be born again," said Thoreau; and
Huck's voyage down the Mississippi is a series of constant
rebirths, a search for identity. Beginning with the elaborately
staged mock murder which sets him free from the clutches
of Pap, Huck assumes a series of varied roles, playing each
one like the brilliant improviser that he is. Twain counter-
points Huck's hoaxes against the villainous or merely mercenary pretenses of the Duke and the Dauphin; the boy's
sometimes desperate shifts are necessary for his survival
and to both his moral and physical progress. The series
reaches a climax in the sequence at the Phelps farm, when
Huck is forced to assume the identity of Tom Sawyer—when,
for the first time, he cannot choose his own role.

   This, it seems to me, is a significant variation, pointing to
the world which begins to close in upon Huck toward the
end of the novel. Not only is an identity forced upon him, but
with the appearance of the real Tom Sawyer upon the scene,
Huck surrenders the initiative in planning and, in effect,
loses control of his own fate. This is the tragedy of Huckleberry Finn: that he has gone so far only to surrender at the
end to the forces which have been seeking to capture him.
For despite the apparent similarities, there is a vital difference between Huck and Tom: Tom behaves "by the book";
Tom relies on historical precedent; Tom operates within the
conventions of the civilized world, accepting its values and
standards, and merely play-acting at rebellion—Tom, in
short, is no rebel at all, but a romanticizer of reality. Huck's
term to describe Tom's method of doing things is that it has
"style." Style it may have, but it lacks design. Huck's willing-
ness to let Tom take over Jim's rescue indicates Twain's final acquiescence to the world which has been criticized
throughout. True, Huck is going to light out again, he tells us
in the last lines: "Aunt Sally she's going to adopt me and sivilize me, and I can't stand it. I been there before." But, despite the expression of sentiments pointing to another future

escape—and the fact that the limiting article is not part of Twain's title—Huck, by the end of the novel, has been trapped. I should like to add my bit to the perennial debate concerning the artistic validity of the final sequence, and suggest that it is both ironical and true to life. Tom's play-acting before Huck sets off down the river—his ambuscade of the "A-rabs," for example—seems innocent and amusing; but the rescue of Jim seems, as I think it is meant to seem, tedious and irrelevant. After all, something has happened to Huck—and to us—between chapters 3 and 43.

Huck is trapped by a society whose shortcomings he sees, and he says, "I can't stand it." Holden's terminology is "It depresses me" and "It kills me." Ironically, he is revealed as telling us his narrative from an institution of some kind—psychiatric, we are led to suspect—having also been trapped by the people who want to "sivilize" him.

HOLDEN'S DILEMMA

Holden's instinctive nonconformity asserts itself early in the novel. He has been told by one of the masters at Pencey Prep, from which he is about to be dismissed, that life is a game. "Some game," Holden comments. "If you get on the side where all the hot-shots are, then it's a game, all right—I'll admit that. But if you get on the *other* side, where there aren't any hot-shots, then what's a game about it. Nothing. No game." At the age of seventeen he has learned to suspect the glib philosophies of his elders, and to test the coil of experience by determining whether it rings true or false for him, personally.

Like Huck, Holden is also a refugee. He flees the campus of Pencey Prep before he is formally expelled, and returns to New York City to have three days of freedom before rejoining his family. Pencey Prep is merely the most recent in a series of unsatisfactory academic experiences for him. "One of the biggest reasons I left Elkton Hills was because I was surrounded by phonies. That's all. They were coming in the goddam window. I can't stand that stuff. It drives me crazy. It makes me so depressed I go crazy."

Also like Huck, Holden assumes a series of guises during his lone wanderings. "I'm the most terrific liar you ever saw in your life. It's awful. If I'm on the way to the store to buy a magazine, even, and somebody asks me where I'm going. I'm liable to say I'm going to the opera. It's terrible." In a sequence which reminds one forcibly of Huck Finn. Holden finds himself in conversation with the mother of one of his classmates, Ernie Morrow, whom he describes as "doubtless the biggest bastard that ever went to Pencey, in the whole crumby history of the school." But Holden, adopting the name of "Rudolf Schmidt" (the janitor), tells her what she wants to hear about her son, to her wonder and delight. Holden's comment is: "Mothers are all slightly insane. The thing is, though, I liked old Morrow's mother. She was all right." His imagination rampant, Holden tells her a cock-and-bull story which includes an impending brain operation and a trip to South America to visit his grandmother, but he stops just short of revealing himself completely. It is a wonderfully funny scene, showing Holden in several aspects: his instinctive evaluation of the mother's "rightness" overcoming his profound distaste for her son, his adolescent imagination in a frenzy of wild invention, and his own awareness of the limits to which he can act his suddenly-adopted role of Rudolf Schmidt.

TESTS FOR BOTH CHARACTERS

Huck's tortured decision not to "turn in" Jim is made on the basis of his own feelings, which he automatically assumes to be sinful since they have so often put him at odds with society. His personal moral code seems always to run counter to his duty to society, a conflict which serves to confirm him in the belief that wickedness is in his line, "being brung up to it." In the crucial moral act of the novel, Huck must "decide, forever, betwixt two things, and I knowed it. I studied a minute, sort of holding my breath, and then says to myself, 'All right, then I'll *go* to hell.'" Huck's humanity overcomes the so-called duty to society. Holden, also, is "depressed" by the notion that he is somehow a misfit, that he does strange, irrational things, that he is fighting a constant war with society—but his awareness of his own weaknesses (his compulsive lying, for example) is the result of his searching honesty.

The yardstick which Holden applies to the world is a simple one—too simple, perhaps, too rigorous, too uncompromising, for anyone but an adolescent (or, as the popular phrase has it, "a crazy mixed-up kid") to attempt to apply to a complex world: it is the test of truth. The world is full of phonies—so Holden dreams of running away and building his own cabin, where people would come and visit him. "I'd have this rule that nobody could do anything phony when they visited me. If anybody tried to do anything phony, they couldn't stay."

SIMILAR WORLDS

Huck's world, realistically depicted as mid-America in the middle of the nineteenth century, is also the world where the established codes are penetrated as being either hypocritical or superficial; Huck finds peace and reassurance away from the haunts of man, out on the river. After the waste and folly of the Grangerford-Shepherdson sequence, for example, Huck retreats to the river:

> Sometimes we'd have that whole river all to ourselves for the longest time. Yonder was the banks and the islands, across the water; and maybe a spark—which was a candle in a cabin window; and sometimes on the water you could see a spark or two—on a raft or a scow, you know; and maybe you could hear a fiddle or a song coming over from one of them crafts. It's lovely to live on a raft.

But the idyll is interrupted shortly thereafter with "a couple of men tearing up the path as tight as they could foot it"—the Duke and the Dauphin imposing their unsavory world upon Huck's.

HOLDEN'S PHONY WORLD

Holden's world is post-war New York City, from the Metropolitan Museum to Greenwich Village, during Christmas week, where, in successive incidents, he encounters pompous hypocrisy, ignorance, indifference, moral corruption, sexual perversion, and—pervading all—"phoniness." Holden's older brother, a once promising writer, is now a Hollywood scenarist; the corruption of his talent is symptomatic to Holden of the general influence of the movies: "They can ruin you. I'm not kidding." They represent the world at its "phoniest" in their falsification of reality; in addition, they corrupt their audiences, converting them into people like the three pathetic girls from Seattle who spend all evening in a second-rate night club looking for movie stars, or like the woman Holden observes at the Radio City Music Hall. She cries through the entire picture, and "the phonier it got, the more she cried. . . . She had this little kid with her that was bored as hell and had to go to the bathroom, but she wouldn't take him. . . . She was about as kind-hearted as a goddam wolf."

Holden's awareness of sham sensitizes him to its manifestations wherever it appears: in the pseudo-religious
Christmas spectacle at Radio City ("I can't see anything religious or pretty, for God's sake, about a bunch of actors car-
rying crucifixes all over the stage"); in ministers with "Holy
Joe" voices; in magazine fiction, with its "lean-jawed guys
named David" and "phony girls named Linda or Marcia";
and in the performance of a gifted night-club pianist as well
as that of the Lunts. His reaction to the performances of all
three is a comment on the relationship between virtuosity
and integrity: "If you do something *too* good, then, after a
while, if you don't watch it, you start showing off. And then
you're not as good any more." Both mock humility and casual bravura are dangerous to the integrity of the individual:
Holden finds no "naturalness" in the finished and most
artistic performers in his world. His world, he comes to feel,
is full of obscenities, both figurative and actual; even a million years would be inadequate to erase all the obscenities
scribbled on all the walls. His week-end in New York reminds him of the time an alumnus of Pencey visited the
school and inspected the doors in the men's toilet to see if his
initials were still carved there. While he searched for this
memento of his past, he solemnly gave platitudinous advice
to the boys. The glaring disparity between what even "good
guys" say and what they do is enough to make Holden despair of finding anyone, except his sister Phoebe, with whom
he can communicate honestly.

A few things Holden encounters on his voyage through the
metropolis make him "feel better." Like Huck, who has to retreat regularly to the river, to reestablish his contacts with his
sources of value, Holden several times meets perfectly "natural" things which delight him: the kettle-drummer in the
orchestra, who never looks bored, but who bangs his drums
"so nice and sweet, with this nervous expression on his face";
a Dixieland song recorded by a Negro girl who doesn't make
it sound "mushy" or "cute"; and the sight of a family coming
out of church. But these incidents merely serve to reveal in
sharper contrast the phoniness and the tinsel of the adult
world which seeks to victimize Holden, and which, in the
end, finally does. Like Huck, he finds himself at the mercy of
the kindly enemy. The realist's sharp perceptions of the
world about him are treated either as the uncivilized re-
marks of an ignorant waif or—supreme irony!—as lunacy.

In addition to being comic masterpieces and superb portrayals of perplexed, sensitive adolescence, these two novels thus deal obliquely and poetically with a major theme in American life, past and present—the right of the nonconformist to assert his nonconformity, even to the point of being "handled with chain." In them, 1884 and 1951 speak to us in the idiom and accent of two youthful travelers who have earned their passports to literary immortality.

CHAPTER 3

The Character of Holden Caulfield

Holden's Language

Donald P. Costello

Donald P. Costello was one of the first to present a detailed analysis of Holden Caulfield's language. This article focuses on the vocabulary and the grammar of *The Catcher in the Rye.* Unlike many other critical articles, Costello's purpose is not to look at the images or symbols of the novel, but to explore the book as an accurate record of how teenagers in the fifties might have talked. In this excerpt, he writes that Salinger successfully created a character who maintains a distinct personality and speaks the typical prep-school teenager's language. Costello has taught at Roosevelt University and is the author of a book on George Bernard Shaw.

Even though Holden's language is authentic teenage speech, recording it was certainly not the major intention of Salinger. He was faced with the artistic task of creating an individual character, not with the linguistic task of reproducing the exact speech of teenagers in general. Yet Holden had to speak a recognizable teenage language, and at the same time had to be identifiable as an individual. This difficult task Salinger achieved by giving Holden an extremely trite and typical teenage speech, overlaid with strong personal idiosyncrasies. There are two major speech habits which are Holden's own, which are endlessly repeated throughout the book, and which are, nevertheless, typical enough of teenage speech so that Holden can be both typical and individual in his use of them. It is certainly common for teenagers to end thoughts with a loosely dangling 'and all,' just as it is common for them to add an insistent 'I really did,' 'It really was.' But Holden uses these phrases to such an overpowering degree that they become a clear part of the flavor of the book; they become, more, a part of Holden himself, and actually help to characterize him.

Reprinted from Donald P. Costello, "The Language of *The Catcher in the Rye*," *American Speech* 34 (October 1959):172–81, by permission of the author.

HOLDEN'S IDIOSYNCRATIC SPEECH PATTERNS

Holden's 'and all' and its twins, 'or something,' 'or anything,' serve no real, consistent linguistic function. They simply give a sense of looseness of expression and looseness of thought. Often they signify that Holden knows there is more that could be said about the issue at hand, but he is not going to bother going into it:

> . . . how my parents were occupied and all before they had me.
> . . . they're *nice* and all.
> I'm not going to tell you my whole goddam autobiography
> or anything.
> . . . splendid and clear-thinking and all.

But just as often the use of such expressions is purely arbitrary, with no discernible meaning:

> . . . he's my *brother* and all.
> . . . was in the Revolutionary War and all.
> It was December and all.
> . . . no gloves or anything.
> . . . right in the pocket and all.

Donald Barr, writing in the *Commonweal,* finds this habit indicative of Holden's tendency to generalize, to find the all in the one:

> Salinger has an ear not only for idiosyncrasies of diction and syntax, but for mental processes. Holden Caulfield's phrase is 'and all'—'She looked so damn *nice,* the way she kept going around and around in her blue coat and all'—as if each experience wore a halo. His fallacy is *ab uno disce omnes;* he abstracts and generalizes wildly.

Arthur Heiserman and James Miller, in the *Western Humanities Review,* comment specifically upon Holden's second most obvious idiosyncrasy: 'In a phony world Holden feels compelled to reenforce his sincerity and truthfulness constantly with, "It really is" or "It really did."' S.N. Behrman, in the *New Yorker,* finds a double function of these 'perpetual insistences of Holden's.' Behrman thinks they 'reveal his age, even when he is thinking much older,' and, more important, 'he is so aware of the danger of slipping into phoniness himself that he has to repeat over and over "I really mean it," "It really does."' Holden uses this idiosyncrasy of insistence almost every time that he makes an affirmation.

Allied to Holden's habit of insistence is his 'if you want to know the truth.' Heiserman and Miller are able to find characterization in this habit too:

The skepticism inherent in that casual phrase, 'if you want to know the truth,' suggesting that as a matter of fact in the world of Holden Caulfield very few people do, characterizes this sixteen-year-old 'crazy mixed up kid' more sharply and vividly than pages of character 'analysis' possibly could.

Holden uses this phrase only after affirmations, just as he uses 'It really does,' but usually after the personal ones, where he is consciously being frank:

I have no wind, if you want to know the truth.
I don't even think that bastard had a handkerchief, if you want to know the truth.
I'm a pacifist, if you want to know the truth.
She had quite a lot of sex appeal, too, if you really want to know.
I was damn near bawling, I felt so damn happy, if you want to know the truth.

These personal idiosyncrasies of Holden's speech are in keeping with general teenage language. Yet they are so much a part of Holden and of the flavor of the book that they are much of what makes Holden to be Holden. They are the most memorable feature of the book's language. Although always in character, the rest of Holden's speech is more typical than individual. The special quality of this language comes from its triteness, its lack of distinctive qualities.

Holden's Crude Language

Holden's informal, schoolboy vernacular is particularly typical in its 'vulgarity' and 'obscenity.' No one familiar with prep-school speech could seriously contend that Salinger overplayed his hand in this respect. On the contrary, Holden's restraints help to characterize him as a sensitive youth who avoids the most strongly forbidden terms, and who never uses vulgarity in a self-conscious or phony way to help him be 'one of the boys.' *Fuck*, for example, is never used as a part of Holden's speech. The word appears in the novel four times, but only when Holden disapprovingly discusses its wide appearance on walls. The Divine name is used habitually by Holden only in the comparatively weak *for God's sake, God,* and *goddam.* The stronger and usually more offense *for Chrissake* or *Jesus* or *Jesus Christ* are used habitually by Ackely and Stradlater; but Holden uses them only when he feels the need for a strong expression. He almost never uses *for Chrissake* in an unemotional situation. *Goddam* is Holden's favorite adjective. This word is used with no relationship to its original meaning, or to Holden's attitude toward the word to which it is attached. It simply expresses an emotional feeling toward the object: either favorable, as in 'goddam hunting cap'; or unfavorable, as in 'ya goddam moron'; or indifferent, as in 'coming in the goddam windows.' *Damm* is used interchangeably with *goddam;* no differentiation in its meaning is detectable.

Other crude words are also often used in Holden's vocabulary. *Ass* keeps a fairly restricted meaning as a part of the human anatomy, but it is used in a variety of ways. It can refer simply to that specific part of the body ('I moved my ass a little'), or be a part of a trite expression ('freezing my ass off'; 'in a half-assed way'), or be an expletive ('Game, my ass.'). *Hell* is perhaps the most versatile word in Holden's entire vocabulary; it serves most of the meanings and constructions which Mencken lists in his *American Speech* article on 'American Profanity.' So far is Holden's use of *hell* from its original meaning that he can use the sentence 'We had a helluva time' to mean that he and Phoebe had a decidedly pleasant time downtown shopping for shoes. The most common function of *hell* is as the second part of a simile, in which a thing can be either 'hot as hell' or, strangely, 'cold as hell'; 'sad as hell' or 'playful as hell'; 'old as hell' or 'pretty as hell.' Like all of these words, *hell* has no close relationship to its original meaning.

Both *bastard* and *sonuvabitch* have also drastically changed in meaning. They no longer, of course, in Holden's vocabulary, have any connection with the accidents of birth. Unless used in a trite simile, *bastard* is a strong word, reserved for things and people Holden particularly dislikes, especially 'phonies.' *Sonuvabitch* has an even stronger meaning to Holden; he uses it only in the deepest anger. When, for example, Holden is furious with Stradlater over his treatment of Jane Gallagher, Holden repeats again and again that he 'kept calling him a moron sonuvabitch.'

The use of crude language in *The Catcher in the Rye* increases, as we should expect, when Holden is reporting schoolboy dialogue. When he is directly addressing the reader, Holden's use of such language drops off almost entirely. There is also an increase in this language when any of the characters are excited or angry. Thus, when Holden is apprehensive over Stradlater's treatment of Jane, his *goddams* increase suddenly to seven on a single page. . . .

HOLDEN'S ADAPTABLE VOCABULARY

Another aspect in which Holden's language is typical is that it shows the general American characteristic of adaptability—apparently strengthened by his teenage lack of restraint. It is very easy for Holden to turn nouns into adjectives, with the simple addition of a *-y:* 'perverty,' 'Christmasy,' 'vomity-looking,' 'whory-looking,' 'hoodlumy-looking,' 'show-offy,' 'flitty-looking,' 'dumpy-looking,' 'pimpy,' 'snobby,' 'fisty.' Like all of English, Holden's language shows a versatile combining ability: 'They gave Sally this little blue butt-twitcher of a dress to wear' and 'That magazine was some little cheerer upper.' Perhaps the most interesting aspect of the adaptability of Holden's language is his ability to use nouns as adverbs: 'She sings it very Dixieland and whore-house, and it doesn't sound at all mushy.'

As we have seen, Holden shares, in general, the trite repetitive vocabulary which is the typical lot of his age group. But as there are exceptions in his figures of speech, so are there exceptions in his vocabulary itself, in his word stock. An intelligent, well-read ('I'm quite illiterate, but I read a lot'), and educated boy, Holden possesses, and can use when he wants to, many words which are many a cut above Basic English, including 'ostracized,' 'exhibitionist,' 'unscrupulous,' 'conversationalist,' 'psychic,' 'bourgeois.' Often Holden seems to choose his words consciously, in an effort to communicate to his adult reader clearly and properly, as in such terms as 'lose my virginity,' 'relieve himself,' 'an alcoholic'; for upon occasion, he also uses the more vulgar terms 'to give someone the time,' 'to take a leak,' 'booze hound.' Much of the humor arises, in fact, from Holden's habit of writing on more than one level at the same time. Thus, we have such phrases as 'They give guys the ax quite frequently at Pency' and 'It has a very good academic rating, Pency.' Both sentences show a colloquial idiom with an overlay of consciously selected words.

HOLDEN'S SELF-CONSCIOUS DICTION

Such a conscious choice of words seems to indicate that Salinger, in his attempt to create a realistic character in Holden, wanted to make him aware of his speech, as, indeed, a real teenager would be when communicating to the outside world. Another piece of evidence that Holden is conscious of his speech and, more, realizes a difficulty in communication, is found in his habit of direct repetition: 'She likes me a lot. I mean she's quite fond of me,' and 'She can be very snotty sometimes. She can be quite snotty.' Sometimes the repetition is exact: 'He was a very nervous guy—I mean he was a very nervous guy,' and 'I sort of missed them. I mean I sort of missed them.' Sometimes Holden stops specifically to interpret slang terms, as when he wants to communicate the fact that Allie liked Phoebe: 'She killed Allie, too. I mean he liked her, too.'

There is still more direct evidence that Holden was conscious of his speech. Many of his comments to the reader are concerned with language. He was aware, for example, of the 'phony' quality of many words and phrases, such as 'grand,' 'prince,' 'traveling incognito,' 'little girls' room,' 'licorice stick,' and 'angels.' Holden is also conscious, of course, of the existence of 'taboo words.' He makes a point of mentioning that the girl from Seattle repeatedly asked him to 'watch your language, if you don't mind,' and that his mother told Phoebe not to say 'lousy.' When the prostitute says 'Like fun you are,' Holden comments:

> It was a funny thing to say. It sounded like a real kid. You'd think a prostitute and all would say 'Like hell you are' or 'Cut the crap' instead of 'Like fun you are.'

HOLDEN'S GRAMMAR

In grammar, too, as in vocabulary, Holden possesses a certain self-consciousness. (It is, of course, impossible to imagine a student getting through today's schools without a self-consciousness with regard to grammar rules.) Holden is, in fact, not only aware of the existence of 'grammatical errors,' but knows the social taboos that accompany them. He is disturbed by a schoolmate who is ashamed of his parents' grammar, and he reports that his former teacher, Mr. Antolini, warned him about picking up 'just enough education to hate people who say, "It's a secret between he and I."'

Holden is a typical enough teenager to violate the grammar rules, even though he knows of their social importance. His most common rule violation is the misuse of *lie* and *lay*, but he also is careless about relative pronouns ('about a traffic cop that falls in love'), the double negative ('I hardly didn't even know I was doing it'), the perfect tenses ('I'd woke him up'), extra words ('like as if all you ever did at

Pency was play polo all the time'), pronoun number ('it's pretty disgusting to watch somebody picking their nose'), and pronoun position ('I and this friend of mine, Mal Brossard'). More remarkable, however, than the instances of grammar rule violations is Holden's relative 'correctness.' Holden is always intelligible, and is even 'correct' in many usually difficult constructions. Grammatically speaking, Holden's language seems to point up the fact that English was the only subject in which he was not failing. It is interesting to note how much more 'correct' Holden's speech is than that of Huck Finn. But then Holden is educated, and since the time of Huck there had been sixty-seven years of authoritarian schoolmarms working on the likes of Holden. He has, in fact, been overtaught, so that he uses many 'hyper' forms:

> I used to play tennis with he and Mrs. Antolini quite
> frequently.
> She'd give Allie or I a push.
> I and Allie used to take her to the park with us.
> I think I probably woke he and his wife up.

. . . The language of *The Catcher in the Rye* is, as we have seen, an authentic artistic rendering of a type of informal, colloquial, teenage American spoken speech. It is strongly typical and trite, yet often somewhat individual; it is crude and slangy and imprecise, imitative yet occasionally imaginative, and affected toward standardization by the strong efforts of schools. But authentic and interesting as this language may be, it must be remembered that it exists, in *The Catcher in the Rye*, as only one part of an artistic achievement. The language was not written for itself, but as a part of a greater whole. Like the great Twain work with which it is often compared, a study of *The Catcher in the Rye* repays both the linguist and the literary critic; for as one critic has said, 'In them, 1884 and 1951 speak to us in the idiom and accent of two youthful travelers who have earned their passports to literary immortality.'

Holden Caulfield: An Unreliable Narrator

Susan K. Mitchell

The influential critic Roland Barthes made the distinction between viewing the world as a reader or as a writer. Barthes says that whereas readers only encounter a text once, writers encounter a text a number of times. He claims that this writerly way of seeing allows us to explore one story in a deeper, more fulfilling way. Literary critic Susan K. Mitchell adopts this idea and applies it to *The Catcher in the Rye*. She argues that we cannot trust Holden's narration because he refuses to look beyond the surface level of his world (i.e., he sees it "readerly"). Because Holden is not a reliable narrator, the portraits he draws of his family are not entirely accurate. Susan Mitchell teaches at Texas Tech University.

In [*The Catcher in the Rye*], Holden has analyzed his family as a representative slice of society and has concluded that adult society is phony and corrupt. But can we really trust his observations of his family after he has told us that he lies? Is he not, like the Cretan who declared that all Cretans were liars, a person declaring that all people are phony? If everyone is phony, then he is phony, too! Although Holden has claimed that he is a liar, he does not always realize whether he is lying or telling the truth. The distinctions between truth and falsehood become blurred as he often adds the phrase "to tell you the truth" onto whatever he is saying. But does this catchphrase ensure that his words are any more truthful? This unambiguous rhetorical statement is restated in an even more paradoxical way when Holden tells Sally that he loves her and then comments to the reader, "It was a lie, of course, but the thing is, I *meant* it when I said it." Again we are forced to read the work, as Paul de Man sug-

Reprinted from Susan K. Mitchell, "'To Tell You the Truth . . . ,'" *CLA Journal* 36 (1992):145–56, by permission of the College Language Association.

gests, [in "Semiology and Rhetoric," *Contemporary Literary Criticism*, ed. Robert Con Davis (New York: Longman, 1986), p. 474] in "two entirely coherent but entirely incompatible" ways. Is he lying, or does he "mean" it? First we may claim that Holden is telling the truth: he is a liar, people are phony, society is corrupt. Or we may claim that Holden is lying: he is truthful, people are genuine, and society is untainted.

There are obvious problems with both sides of this paradox. Can Holden, people, and society be entirely unchanging—always lying, always corrupt, always phony? Or are there internal forces within each that cause them to change (un)willingly? Holden would argue that each is unchanging, labeled forever. In fact, this is how he presents his information to us. He may go out with Sally, but he does not harbor any hope that she will cast off her phoniness. He may loan Stradlater his coat, but he still believes Stradlater is a phony.

ROLAND BARTHES'S THEORY OF PERCEIVING REALITY

Because we view all of the events in the book through the eyes of one narrator, our observations are necessarily biased. Holden is an unreliable narrator not only because he is a self-proclaimed liar but also because he perceives reality in a simplistic way. In his work *S/Z*, Roland Barthes outlines two ways of perceiving reality: *readerly* and *writerly.* Barthes explains these ideas in terms of reading books. He claims that the only way to read a different story is to reread the same book. By rereading, a person can learn how this book differs from itself rather than how it differs from other books. When a reader rereads a work, he is perceiving writerly. When a reader refuses to reread, Barthes maintains that he is condemned to "read the same story everywhere." Holden refuses to reread as he perceives reality readerly, seeing only the surface differences between people, not the underlying differences within each person. To perceive a person readerly would be to perceive in terms of overt, easily distinguishable differences.

HOLDEN SEES THE SAME STORY EVERYWHERE

Because Holden avoids investigating deeply, he sees the same story everywhere. Everyone is phony, he insists. But can we honestly believe him? Is he telling the truth? Even so, he is not passing on false or limited information since he has not gone to the trouble to read one story well. To approach accuracy, Holden would have to perceive a person writerly, to judge the fragmentation, the differences within the person, the covert, often contradictory intentions that war within and cause overt actions. We can draw conclusions only from the data which Holden perceives and selects to reveal to us (and he does select carefully as when he refuses to discuss his childhood or his parents); hence, we must be astute readers indeed lest we miss the multidimensionality of the characters that he develops. His readerly perception creates blinkers for the reader.

HOLDEN'S VIEW OF HIS PARENTS

Throughout the novel, Holden tries to lull us into accepting his view of surrounding life as he makes statements that seem to make sense, but which, upon closer inspection, do not bear up to a writerly view. This simplistic mode of perception is revealed particularly through his description of his family. First of all, the Caulfield parents are described in such a way as to cause the blinkered reader to view them uncompromisingly as irresponsible, alienated, skittish parents. For example, the parents are off at work away from their children, who are scattered throughout the country: D.B. in Hollywood, Allie dead, Phoebe at home, and Holden at Pencey Prep. Mr. and Mrs. Caulfield seem to be isolated characters. The reader never meets Mr. Caulfield and only hears Mrs. Caulfield when Holden is hiding in Phoebe's room. Holden will not tell much about his parents beyond his veiled opinion that they both are phony hypocrites. The reader is not even told their first names. From the beginning we are led to believe that they are hypersensitive about Holden's revealing their personal life because they want to protect their created image of conformed perfection. Because Mrs. Caulfield is a nervous woman who has smoked compulsively ever since Allie's death, Holden avoids confrontation about his being kicked out of Pencey Prep. He therefore hides from her as he stays in a hotel or in Mr. Antolini's apartment. Each of these examples appears to show that Mrs. Caulfield does not really communicate with her children. On the other hand, Mr. Caulfield is a lawyer. Holden makes no bones about his opinion of lawyers: they "make a lot of dough and play golf and play bridge and buy cars and drink Martinis and look like a hot-shot" and are phony but can't know it.

Holden's warped view of his parents denigrates them without even considering that the Caulfields may be blameless. Can we really trust Holden's view of his parents? Isn't he unethically stacking the deck so that we are prohibited from obtaining an objective view of them? We are given so few facts and scenes to describe them that we have trouble refuting Holden, except that we know he is holding something back from us. No couple could merit such a denunciation from a son. If what he has revealed about the Caulfields is true, carefully selected though the information may be, can we blame them for their anger, hysteria, and desire for privacy? These would be logical reactions if an offspring were so apathetic as to be kicked out of several reputable schools and then became anxious to write a book about his family while recovering from insanity. And what is wrong about working hard to support children, to enable them to have the best education possible? What exactly is phony about being a lawyer? Even though Holden's vagueness works well for him, making his parents appear base, mercenary, isolated, distant, and careless, it denies any redeeming qualities that would upset Holden's persuasive thesis that adult society is corrupt. . . .

HOLDEN PERCEIVES READERLY

Naturally, Holden is the only character shown to be heroically struggling with exactly how to relate to society. He is locked into a self that desires to be genuine but finds no way to return to the pastoral ideal. He believes that he is holed in, trapped by the games of phoniness that society requires its citizens to play. He tries to escape this trap by flunking out of school and by searching for a quiet retreat, only to discover that there is no pure retreat on earth—log cabins are distant and lonely, deserted museum rooms are corrupted with permanent obscenities, private hotel rooms lure prostitutes and pimps. Frustrated by the readerly evidence which he has gathered to support his thesis, Holden is himself fragmented and ravaged by the warring forces within him. For instance, within Holden, the desire to reject others conflicts with the desire to be accepted by others; he doesn't want to lend Stradlater his coat, but his overt actions belie this covert, warring want; he despises Ackely, but he invites him to see a movie; he hates movies, believing them to foster phoniness in society, but during the three days of the book he sees or talks about several; he craves truth, but he tells blatant lies. Despite his own inherent writerliness or differences within, Holden still perceives only readerly. He views himself as a liar, but he refuses to acknowledge that this means that he is phony, too. In fact, Holden views writerliness as a kind of individual fragmentation or disorientation of the individual, a symbol, in his mind, of a corrupt society.

HOLDEN BECOMES AWARE OF HIS WRITERLINESS

When Holden does become aware of his own writerliness, he goes over the brink into insanity. Throughout the work, he has become more and more frustrated in his awkward attempts to establish genuine friendships and to find quiet retreats. He even tries to restore purity in the schools by erasing obscenities so that children can be preserved from corruption for as long as possible. However, he is forced to confront his own writerly corruption when he is in the museum and sees an obscenity written in red beneath a glass plate. He is not the savior of children; he is not called to be the catcher in the rye. He is just a corrupt human being himself, a being who uses obscenities freely in his own casual conversation. Now that he has acknowledged his own writerliness, purged (symbolically through diarrhea) his traditional method of readerly perception, and symbolically fallen to show that he has accepted his writerly nature, he begins to see the world in a writerly manner. He is astonished and delighted to find that the carousel is the same after all these years:

> We kept getting closer and closer to the carousel and you could start to hear that nutty music it always plays. It was playing "Oh, Marie!" It played that same song about fifty years ago when *I* was a little kid. That's one nice thing about carousels, they always play the same songs.

However, now that his eyes are opened, he can see a new richness within the carousel that he has seen many times before. Now it teaches him that children will try to grab the gold ring and he must let them: "If they fall off, they fall off, but it's bad if you say anything to them."

Will Holden slip back into his readerliness? One indication that he will not is that he has decided to write about his own experiences, to analyze himself in terms of the world around him. He is seeking perhaps for the first time to reread his own story and understand it as different from all other stories.

The Catcher in the Rye Should Not Be Reduced to a Novel About Male Adolescence

Mary Suzanne Schriber

In this excerpt, feminist critic Mary Suzanne
Schriber examines how most critical articles about
Catcher tend to generalize the male character
Holden as typical of all adolescents. Schriber argues
that this thinking necessarily excludes women from
the dialogue. Thus, the male critic sees himself in
Holden and assumes the rest of America does as
well. Schriber believes that traditional literary criticism endorses the image of all humanity as strictly
male. This androcentric (or male-centered) point
of view taints the criticism to date on *Catcher* and
therefore *Catcher*'s place in the literary canon is
compromised. Schriber is distinguished professor
of English at Northern Illinois University. She is the
author of *Gender and the Writer's Imagination* and
the editor of *Telling Tales: Selected Writings of
Nineteenth-Century Women Abroad.*

The essential ingredient in the phenomenal success and the
critical reception of *The Catcher in the Rye is* the propensity
of critics to identify with Salinger's protagonist. Holden
Caulfield, c'est moi. Falling in love with him as with their
very selves, they fall in love with the novel as well. The criticism indicates that they see in Holden, and in themselves
through his agency, an incarnation of their youth. Having
identified with Holden, critics then engage in a procedure
that magnifies him. Undeterred by and apparently oblivious
to Holden's gender (and his social and economic class as
well), they first assume maleness as the norm. Next, they

Reprinted from Mary Suzanne Schriber, "Holden Caulfield, C'est Moi," in *Critical Essays on Salinger's "The Catcher in the Rye,"* edited by Joel Salzburg (Boston: G.K. Hall,
1990), by permission of the author.

95

are reinforced in this assumption by male-identified and gender-inflected theories of American literature, regnant for thirty years, within which more than a generation of readers has been taught to situate American novels. Developed by scholars who have themselves conflated the human and the male, these theories guide critics as they construe and construct the meaning of *Catcher* and its place in American literary history. They enable critics to find in Salinger's novel that which has been defined as archetypally American and thus classic, a literary work of timeless and universal significance. . . .

While identifying with Holden in their manhood as well as in their youth, critics have failed "to consider gender a relevant factor in either the configuration of identity or the institution of literature itself."[1] This occurs even when the critic is less than fond of the novel but perceives it nonetheless, like Ernest Jones, as "a case history of all of us," apparently defining "us" as male.[2] Presuming that the male is synonymous with the human, critics absorb the female into the male, particularly in their treatment of Holden and sexuality. Brian Way, for example, writes that in New York Holden embarks "on a dream" that is "universally adolescent": "the offer of unbelievable possibilities of sexual adventure and satisfaction." Way does not perceive this as a male's sense of adventure but, rather, he takes it to be normative; he praises Salinger for going "straight to the fundamental biological situation. [Salinger] sees that all the contradictions, agonies, and exaltations of adolescence stem from the central fact: that the adolescent has newly gained the physical potentialities for sexual experience but has not learnt to integrate them either within himself or in any consistent relation to the demands of society."[3] The notion of a "fundamental biological situation" overlooks the differential development, place, and manifestations of sexuality for males and females in the adolescent years. . . .

A LOOK AT KAPLAN'S ESSAY

The criticism of *The Catcher in the Rye* shows the degree to which literary theory is responsible for the attribution of

---

1. Sidonie Smith, *A Poetics of Women's Autobiography* (Bloomington: Indiana University Press, 1987), 15.   2. Ernest Jones, "Case History of All of Us," *Nation*, 1 September 1951, 176.   3. Brian Way, "'Franny and Zooey' and J.D. Salinger," *New Left Review*, May–June 1962; reprinted as "A Tight Three-Movement Structure" in *Studies*, 194, 196.

global significance to the tale of a WASP preppy male youth. Critics clearly impose on or find in (as the case may be) Holden Caulfield and his adventures the definitions of essential "Americanness" that characterize the work of Lionel Trilling . . . and others. The trend began as early as 1956, in Charles Kaplan's essay entitled "Holden and Huck: The Odysseys of Youth." As the title forewarns us, Huck and Holden are about to become "youth" itself, apparently entirely male, as it sets off, in Kaplan's words, on "an adventure story in the age-old pattern of a young lad making his way in a not particularly friendly adult world." Having immasculated "youth," it is easy to immasculate "adolescence" as well, as Kaplan proceeds to do: "In addition to being comic masterpieces and superb portrayals of perplexed, sensitive adolescence, these two novels thus deal obliquely and poetically with a major theme in American life, past and present—the right of the nonconformist to assert his nonconformity, even to the point of being 'handled with a chain.' In them, 1884 and 1951 speak to us in the idiom and accent of two youthful travelers who have earned their passports to literary immortality."[4] Notice how that which is associated with the male, in Kaplan's rhetoric, has progressively absorbed everything in its path. "Youth" and "adolescence" are first implicitly masculinized. Next, that which has been masculinized is expanded into a theme in the whole of "American life," and even immortalized by being projected into both "past and present." Then this all-consuming male, encompassing "youth" and "adolescence" and "America . . . past and present" draws the "nonconformist" into its system. The coup de grace, however, the most chilling manifestation of the insidious power of this androcentric habit over the perceiving mind—insidious because it remains invisible while selecting that which will become visible—occurs in the quote: "handled with a chain."

Kaplan's relentlessly immasculating rhetoric first does its work on "nonconformist" and then, ironically, on Emily Dickinson's "Much Madness Is Divinest Sense." Having assimilated everything into the male, Kaplan's rhetoric then either contradicts the equation of "nonconformist" with the male or manages to immasculate none other than Emily

4. Charles Kaplan, "Holden and Huck: The Odysseys of Youth," *College English* 18 (November 1956); reprinted in *Studies*, 31, 37–38.

Dickinson. Theories of American literature that implicitly govern Kaplan's reading can be credited with this, theories that conflate American and male experience and proceed to blind the critic even to so strong a female presence as that of Emily Dickinson and to the implicit contradictions in his own critical text. . . .

Thus the popularity and the ascription of broad significance and exceptional literary importance to *The Catcher in the Rye* can be traced to nurturing arrangements, to assumptions that the male is the normative, and to androcentric theories of American literature in which American fiction is routinely framed and taught. Yet a qualification is in order here. The reading experience of many of us, female as well as male (and rural as well as urban, Catholic and Jewish as well as WASP), is articulated in many of the claims made for Salinger's novel. Reader response, and not just the rhetoric of critics, suggests that *Catcher* is a fiction that *does* capture and express recognizable parts of adolescence. Does Salinger's novel more than "seemingly" escape, somehow, the confines of gender to touch broad if not universal human sensibilities? Perhaps the response to this novel should warn us that "concentrating on gender difference can lead us to slight the affinity of women and men . . . the common ground shared by all humans."[5] Moreover, if the criticism of *Catcher* manages by and large to articulate the intuitions of many readers of both genders, how can that criticism fairly be labeled androcentric and accused of a masculinist imperialism that mistakes part of human experience for the whole? Or on the other hand, have we been duped into finding ourselves in Salinger's novel by the androcentric logic in which we are schooled? Is the reading of *Catcher* an instance in which "androcentricity *may* be a sufficient condition for the process of immasculation"?[6]

CATCHER CRITICISM GUILTY OF ANDROCENTRICITY

Catcher criticism is guilty of androcentricity as charged because it fails to be self-reflexive. It remains oblivious to the possibility of a female perspective; it fails to problematize the male (and the urban and the WASP); it remains shackled to "false and damaging 'universals' that saddle the major

---

5. Patrocinio Schweickart and Elizabeth Flynn, *Gender and Reading*, xxix.   6. Patrocinio Schweickart, "Reading Ourselves: Toward a Feminist Theory of Reading," in *Gender and Reading*, 42.

intellectual discourses."[7] It does not declare its assumptions and explain where *Catcher* gets "its power to draw us into its designs," whether from an appeal to authentic desires for liberation and maturity or sheer complicity in our andro-centric conditioning.[8] *Catcher* criticism arrogantly assumes that the male includes, unproblematically and unquestion-ably, the female, the adolescent, and the nation itself, as if this were a given in the natural order of things, requiring no comment and no explanation. Having spoken to and for an exceptionally large audience for four decades, *The Catcher in the Rye* perhaps legitimately deserves its popularity and its designation as a "classic." The critical case for *Catcher*, however, remains to be made. Contrary to the silences and assertions of Salinger criticism to date, an adolescent male WASP is not automatically nature's designated spokesperson for us all.

7. Schweickart and Flynn, *Gender and Reading*, xxix.   8. Schweickart, "Reading Our-selves," in *Gender and Reading*, 42–43.

CHAPTER 4

The Catcher in the Rye: A Critical Evaluation

The Catcher in the Rye Should Not Be Censored

Edward P.J. Corbett

The Catcher in the Rye has been one of the most frequently banned books in America in the past few
decades. High school libraries and classrooms have
removed the book because of objections to its content and language. Ten years after the novel's publication in 1951, Edward P.J. Corbett, a Jesuit priest
and teacher, wrote this defense of the novel, taking
on the specific charges of the critics. He claims that
although the detractors have some justification for
their complaints, the novel as a whole is neither immoral nor corrupting. Corbett has taught at
Creighton University and is a frequent contributor to
America. He also writes on rhetoric and composition.

About six years ago [1955], at a Modern Language Association convention, a group of professors were discussing job
openings, as is their wont at such gatherings. One of the
teachers mentioned an offer he had had from a West Coast
college. A pipe-smoker in the group blurted out: "For
heaven's sake, stay away from *that* place. They recently fired
a man for requiring his freshman students to read *The
Catcher in the Rye.*"

That firing may have been the earliest instance of a
teacher getting into serious trouble over J.D. Salinger's book.
Since that time, reports of irate protests from school boards,
principals, librarians and parents have multiplied. The most
publicized recent stir about the book was the reprimand that
Mrs. Beatrice Levin received from her principal for introducing *The Catcher in the Rye* to her 16-year-old students at
Edison High School in Tulsa, Okla. Scores of subsequent letters to the editor revealed other bans on the book in schools

Reprinted from Edward P.J. Corbett, "Raise High the Barriers, Censors," *America* 104
(January 14, 1961):441–44, by permission of the author.

and libraries. Curiously enough, the same kind of censure was once visited upon the book to which *The Catcher in the Rye* has most often been compared—Mark Twain's *Huckleberry Finn.*

Adult attempts to keep *The Catcher in the Rye* out of the hands of young people will undoubtedly increase, for it is the one novel that young people of postwar generation have been reading and discussing avidly....

To the many people who have come to love the book and its hero, Holden Caulfield, all this controversy is puzzling and disturbing. They regard even the suggestion that the book needs defending as sacrilegious—almost as though they were being asked to vindicate the Constitution. Although their feelings of outrage are understandable, I feel that in view of the vast and continuing popularity of the book the objections should be confronted and appraised. My arguments in defense of *The Catcher in the Rye* are the common ones, quite familiar to those acquainted with other controversies about "forbidden" books.

THE LANGUAGE OF THE BOOK IS CRUDE, PROFANE, OBSCENE

This is the objection most frequently cited when the book has been banned. From one point of view, this objection is the easiest to answer; from another point of view, it is the hardest to answer.

Considered in isolation, the language *is* crude and profane. It would be difficult to argue, however, that such language is unfamiliar to our young people or that it is rougher than the language they are accustomed to hear in the streets among their acquaintances, But there is no question about it, a vulgar expression seen in print is much more shocking than one that is spoken. Lewd scribblings on sidewalks or on the walls of rest-rooms catch our attention and unsettle our sensibilities; and they become most shocking when they are seen in the sanctity of the printed page. Traditionally, novelists have been keenly aware of the shock value of printed profanities. Stephen Leacock has a delightful essay in which he reviews the many circumlocutions and typographical devices that novelists since the 18th century have employed to avoid the use of shocking expressions.

Granting the shock potential of such language, especially to youngsters, must we also grant it a corrupting influence? To deny that words can shape our attitudes and influence our actions would be to deny the rhetorical power of language. But to maintain that four-letter words of themselves are obscene and can corrupt is another matter. Interestingly enough, most reports about the banning of this novel have told that some principal or librarian or parent hastily paged through the book and spotted several four-letter words. That was evidence enough; the book must go. It is natural, although not always prudent, for adults to want to protect the young from shock. And this concern may be sufficient justification for adults wanting to keep the book out of the hands of grade-school children or the more immature high school students. But one of the unfortunate results of banning the book for this reason is that the very action of banning creates the impression that the book is nasty and highly corrosive of morals.

As has happened in many censorship actions in the past, parts are judged in isolation from the whole. The soundest defense that can be advanced for the language of this novel is a defense based on the art of the novel. Such a defense could be stated like this: Given the point of view from which the novel is told, and given the kind of character that figures as the hero, no other language was possible. The integrity of the novel demanded such language.

But even when readers have been willing to concede that the bold language is a necessary part of the novel, they have expressed doubts about the authenticity of Holden's language. Teen-age girls, I find, are especially skeptical about the authenticity of the language. "Prep-school boys just don't talk like that," they say. It is a tribute, perhaps, to the gentlemanliness of adolescent boys that when they are in the company of girls they temper their language. But, whatever the girls may think, prep-school boys do on occasion talk as Holden talks. As a matter of fact, Holden's patois is remarkably restrained in comparison with the blue-streak vernacular of his real-life counterparts. Holden's profanity becomes most pronounced in moments of emotional tension; at other times his language is notably tempered—slangy, ungrammatical, rambling, yes, but almost boyishly pure. Donald P. Costello, who made a study of the language of *The Catcher in the Rye* for the journal *American Speech* (October 1959), concluded that Salinger had given "an accurate rendering of the informal speech of an intelligent, educated, Northeastern American adolescent." "No one familiar with prep school speech," Costello goes on to say, "could seriously contend that Salinger overplayed his hand in this respect."

Holden's swearing is so habitual, so unintentional, so ritualistic that it takes on a quality of innocence. Holden is characterized by a desperate bravado; he is constantly seeking to appear older than he really is. Despite that trait, however, Holden's profanity does not stem from the same motivation that prompts other adolescents to swear—the urge to seem "one of the boys." His profanity is so much ingrained by habit into the fabric of his speech that he is wholly unaware of how rough his language is. Twice his little sister Phoebe reminds him to stop swearing so much. Holden doesn't even pause to apologize for his language; he doesn't even advert to the fact that his sister has reprimanded him. And it is not because he has become callous, for this is the same boy who flew into a rage when he saw the obscenity scribbled on a wall where it might be seen by little children.

SOME OF THE EPISODES IN THE BOOK ARE SCANDALOUS

The episode commonly cited as being unfit for adolescents to read is the one about the prostitute in the hotel room. A case could be made out for the view that young people should not be exposed to such descriptions. It would be much the same case that one makes out in support of the view that children of a certain age should not be allowed to play with matches. But a convincing case cannot be, and never has been, made out for the view that vice should never be portrayed in a novel.

One shouldn't have to remind readers of what Cardinal Newman once said, that we cannot have a sinless literature about a sinful people. That reminder, however, has to be made whenever a censorship controversy comes up. The proper distinction in this matter is that no novel is immoral merely because vice is represented in it. Immorality creeps in as a result of the author's attitude toward the vice he is portraying and his manner of rendering the scene.

Let us consider the scene in question according to this norm in order to test the validity of the charge that it is scandalous. First of all, neither the novelist nor his character regards the assignation with the prostitute as proper or even as morally indifferent. The word *sin* is not part of Holden's vocabulary, but throughout the episode Holden is acutely aware that the situation in which he finds himself is producing an uncomfortable tension, a tormenting conflict, within him. And that vague awareness of disturbance, of something being "wrong," even if the character doesn't assign the label "sin" to it, is enough to preserve the moral tone of the scene in question.

Some readers seem to forget, too, that Holden didn't seek this encounter with the prostitute. He was trapped into it; he was a victim, again, of his own bravado. "It was against my principles and all," he says, "but I was feeling so depressed I didn't even *think*." Nor does he go through with the act. Embarrassment, nervousness, inexperience—all play a part in his rejection of the girl. But what influences his decision most, without his being aware of it, is his pity for the girl. That emotion is triggered by the sight of her green dress. It is that pity which introduces a moral note into Holden's choice. Nor does Salinger render this scene with the kind of explicit, erotic detail that satisfies the pruriency of readers who take a lickerish delight in pornography. All of the scenes about sexual matters are tastefully, even beautifully, treated. Is it any wonder that devotees of the novel are shocked by the suggestion that some of the scenes are scandalous?

HOLDEN, CONSTANTLY PROTESTING AGAINST PHONINESS, IS A PHONY HIMSELF

With this objection we move close to a charge against the novel that is damaging because it is based on sounder premises than the other two objections. No doubt about it, Salinger likes this boy, and he wants his readers to like the boy, too. If it could be shown that Salinger, despite his intentions, failed to create a sympathetic character, all the current fuss about the novel would be rendered superfluous, because the novel would eventually fall of its own dead weight.

Holden uses the word *phony* or some derivative of it at least 44 times. *Phoniness* is the generic term that Holden uses to cover all manifestations of cant, hypocrisy and speciosity. He is genuinely disturbed by such manifestations, so much so that, to use his own forthright term, he wants to "puke." The reason why he finds the nuns, his sister Phoebe and children in general so refreshing is that they are free of this phoniness.

But, as a number of people charge, Holden is himself a phony. He is an inveterate liar; he frequently masquerades as someone he is not; he fulminates against foibles of which he himself is guilty; he frequently vents his spleen about his friends, despite the fact that he seems to be advocating the need for charity. Maxwell Geismar puts this objection most pointedly when he says: "*The Catcher in the Rye* protests, to be sure, against both the academic and social conformity of its period. But what does it argue *for?*" Because of this inconsistency between what Holden wants other people to be and what he is himself, many readers find the boy a far from sympathetic character and declare that he is no model for our young people to emulate.

These readers have accurately described what Holden *does*, but they miss the point about what he *is*. Holden is the classic portrait of "the crazy, mixed-up kid," but with this significant difference: there is about him a solid substratum of goodness, genuineness and sensitivity. It is just this conflict between the surface and the substratum that makes the reading of the novel such a fascinating, pathetic and intensely moral experience. Because Holden is more intelli-

---

A CASE OF CENSORSHIP

In 1989 the Boron, California, school board voted to remove The Catcher in the Rye *from the school's supplemental reading list because they felt it was obscene. The teacher who assigned the book, Mrs. Keller-Gage, likens the small-town censors to the novel's main character, Holden Caulfield: Both are trying unsuccessfully to protect children from losing their innocence.*

BORON, Calif., Aug. 30—If a group of local parents had let her speak to them before "The Catcher in the Rye" was banned from her high school classroom, Shelley Keller-Gage says she would have told them she believes it is a highly moral book that deals with the kinds of difficulties their own children are facing.

But she was asked not to speak, and a group of angry parents, led by a woman who says she has not—and never would—read such a book, persuaded the school board to ban it this month from the Boron High School supplementary reading list.

"Unfortunately, what happened is not at all unusual," said Anne Levinson, assistant director of the Office of Intellectual Freedom in Chicago. "Censorship is still very much with us. As a matter of fact, I think 'The Catcher in the Rye' is a perennial No. 1 on the censorship hit list."

Ms. Levinson said J.D. Salinger's 1951 novel about a troubled

gent and more sensitive than his confreres, he has arrived prematurely at the agonizing transition between adolescence and adulthood. He is precocious but badly seasoned. An affectionate boy, yearning for love and moorings, he has been cut off during most of his teen-age years from the haven of his family. Whatever religious training he has been exposed to has failed to touch him or served to confuse him. Accordingly, he is a young man adrift in an adult world that buffets and bewilders him.

The most salient mark of Holden's immaturity is his inability to discriminate. His values are sound enough, but he views everything out of proportion. Most of the manners and mores that Holden observes and scorns are not as monstrous as Holden makes them out to be. His very style of speech, with its extraordinary propensity for hyperbole, is evidence of this lack of a sense of proportion. Because he will not discriminate, he is moving dangerously close to that most tragic of all states, negation. His sister Phoebe tells him

---

teen-ager named Holden Caulfield seems to have a narrow lead over John Steinbeck's "Of Mice and Men" and "Grapes of Wrath" in arousing the objections of communities or special-interest groups around the country that are increasingly moving to ban books.

On Wednesday, People for the American Way, a group that opposes censorship, issued a report listing 172 incidents in 42 states of attempted or successful censorship in schools in the last year, illustrating what the group's president, Arthur Kropp, called "an unreasonable undercurrent of fear about the so-called 'dangers' of public school instruction."

The report, the group's seventh annual censorship roundup, said efforts to restrict books and curriculums from classrooms and school libraries were on the rise nationwide, with nearly half of them succeeding.

The school board's 4-to-1 vote has aroused this small sun-baked town of 4,000 at the edge of the Mojave Desert, and when Mrs. Keller-Gage, a 35-year-old Boron native, goes out she said she hears a buzzing of, "That's her. There she goes."

Although "The Catcher in the Rye" is now banned from Boron's classrooms, it has gained a new readership among townspeople, and Helen Nelson, the local librarian, has a waiting list of 15 people for the book that she says has been sitting on the shelf all these years pretty much unnoticed.

Seth Mydans, *New York Times*, September 3, 1989.

"You don't like *any*thing that's happening." Holden's reaction to this charge gives the first glimmer of hope that he may seek the self-knowledge which can save him.

Holden must get to know himself. As Mr. Antolini, his former teacher, tells him: "You're going to have to find out where you want to go." But Holden needs most of all to develop a sense of humor. One of the most startling paradoxes about this book is that although it is immensely funny, there is not an ounce of humor in Holden himself. With the development of a sense of humor will come the maturity that can straighten him out. He will begin to see himself as others see him.

The lovely little scene near the end of the book in which Phoebe is going around and around on the carousel can be regarded as an objective correlative of Holden's condition at the end of his ordeal by disillusionment. Up to this point, Holden has pursued his odyssey in a more or less straight line; but in the end, in his confusion and heartsickness, he is swirling around in a dizzying maelstrom. In the final chapter, however, it would appear that Holden has had his salutary epiphany. "I sort of *miss* everybody I told about," he says. Here is the beginning of wisdom. The reader is left with the feeling that Holden, because his values are fundamentally sound, will turn out all right.

I suspect that adults who object to Holden on the grounds of his apparent phoniness are betraying their own uneasiness. Holden is not like the adolescents in the magazine ads—the smiling, crew-cut, loafer-shod teen-agers wrapped up in the cocoon of suburban togetherness. He makes the adults of my generation uncomfortable because he exposes so much of what is meretricious in our way of life.

THE DANGER OF DEFENDING *CATCHER*

In defending *The Catcher in the Rye*, one is liable to the danger of exaggerating J.D. Salinger's achievement and potential. As George Steiner has warned in the *Nation* (Nov. 14, 1959), there is a vigorous "Salinger industry" under way now, which could put Salinger's work badly out of focus. Judged in the company of other post-war fiction, *The Catcher in the Rye* is an extraordinary novel. His earlier short stories, especially "For Esmé—with Love and Squalor," are truly distinguished. But the last two long, diffuse stories to appear in the *New Yorker*, "Zooey" and "Seymour," have been something of a disappointment. They are fascinating as experiments with the short-story form, but they strike me as being an accumulation of finger exercises rather than the finished symphony. If we admirers of Salinger can keep our heads about us, maybe we can make it possible for Salinger to build on the promise of his earlier work.

In the meantime, some concession must be made, I suppose, to the vigilantes who want to keep *The Catcher in the Rye* out of the hands of the very young. Future controversy will probably center on just what age an adolescent must be before he is ready for this book. That may prove to be a futile dispute. But I would hope that any decisions about the book would be influenced by the consideration, not that this is an immoral, corrupting book—for it is certainly not—but that it is a subtle, sophisticated novel that requires an experienced, mature reader. Above all, let the self-appointed censors *read* the novel before they raise the barriers.

An Attack on *Catcher*

Lawrence Jay Dessner

Not all critics like Holden Caulfield. In this attack on
the novel, Lawrence Jay Dessner claims that Salinger
creates a character who is the essence of our most
immature selves and asks readers to admire him.
Dessner does not let his fellow literary critics off the
hook; they too share in some of the blame for praising the book and increasing its popularity. Dessner
writes that some critics' comparisons of *The Catcher
in the Rye* to great works of literature by authors
such as Mark Twain or Fyodor Dostoyevsky is an
embarrassment. Dessner is professor of English at
the University of Toledo. He publishes poetry and is
the author of *How to Write a Poem.*

In the ten years after its publication in July of 1951 *The
Catcher in the Rye* sold over one and one-half million copies.
It was adopted as a text in some 300 American colleges and
universities, and in countless secondary schools. A great
deal of what is called "research" was published on it. In dis-
may, George Steiner did what he could to stem the flood. He
disparaged what he named "The Salinger Industry," called
Holden Caulfield "the young lout," and bemoaned comparisons of him with "Alyosha Karamazov, Aeneas, Ulysses,
Gatsby, Ishmael, Hans Castorp, and Dostoevsky's Idiot."
Steiner added, mischievously but with anger too, that these
comparisons "were always rather to [Caulfield's] own advantage." He spoke of the novel's flattery of the ignorant and
of ignorance itself, and of its "shoddy . . . half-culture," and
he tried to discover why it is that "literary criticism [is] so
determined to get [things] out of proportion." Why, this
"gross devaluation of standards.". . .

The Catcher in the Rye has been most often compared to
Mark Twain's *Adventures of Huckleberry Finn,* compared,
that is, in terms of form, characters, plot, humor and all this

Reprinted from Lawrence Jay Dessner, "The Salinger Story; or, Have It Your Way," in
Seasoned Authors for a New Season: The Search for Standards in Popular Writing,
edited by Louis Filler (Bowling Green, OH: Bowling Green University Popular Press,
1980), by permission of the publisher.

so assiduously that comparison of value, that comparison which would justify making all the others, is ignored, value tacitly assumed. The novels are "akin also in ethical-social import." "Each book," another critic continues, "is a devastating criticism of American society and voices a morality of love and humanity." Steiner grits his teeth; Mark Twain turns over yet again in his grave. And I cannot forbear asking about that "morality of love and humanity." Is there some other kind? Is there a morality of love but not of humanity, or of humanity and not of love? Is this morality "voiced" by Salinger, by Holden? Have we been reading the same book? May one professor turn another one over on his knee and deliver corporal punishment? Is the view of American society which Salinger's novel devastatingly criticizes a fair and accurate view of that society? Is Pencey Prep more than an ill-tempered caricature of some lesser Andover? Is there, in all of *The Catcher in the Rye*, any reference to the historical or political or economic conditions of its moment? Well, I guess there must be, because one of the more eminent commentators on modern literature, after quoting Thoreau and breathlessly wondering "what is the sound of one hand clapping," assures us that "Salinger proves ... to be seriously engaged by a current and a traditional aspect of reality in America." Wow! Both a current *and* a traditional aspect of reality. Once upon a time, Robert Browning sent a copy of his famously obscure long poem, *The Ring and the Book*, to a literary friend who had been seriously ill. "It's my mind," his friend cried out from his sickbed. "My strength is coming back but my mind is going. I can't understand the English language any more."

Since the earlier days of Salinger's prominence, criticism has followed the method of praise by association and implication. Some of the more imaginative professors have found it useful, in considering Salinger, to discuss Beckett and Camus, Saul Bellow, and Martin Buber. And no doubt many other giants have been hitched to Salinger's wagon. Nor should we be surprised to learn that *The Catcher in the Rye* "is a masterpiece of symbolist fiction." There are even signs that the period of evaluation, such as it was, is over, and scholars can turn to source studies. One of our colleagues prints his speculations on the possibility of Sherwood Anderson's influence on Salinger. Confirmation of Salinger's place in the pantheon comes from an energetic German scholar who reviews over one hundred critics and concludes that Salinger has made it into the canon of American literature. Here is a fine chance for us to brush up on our German— what a reward for learning the language for our degrees!

Literary judgments of value are usually made tacitly, as assumptions, not logically argued. Merely to write about Salinger, to mention him in the same breath as Mark Twain or, heaven help us, Dostoevsky, is to make the claim for his place with the immortals. We must assume that these valuations are made in full sincerity. Many critics, like many readers, enjoyed *The Catcher in the Rye*, felt, in the reading, and in the remembering of the reading, the kind of satisfaction they had come to know as aesthetic pleasure. About their pleasure there is no room for dispute. One does not speculate, nowadays, in public, on one's colleagues' taste. But on the morning after, when mind awakes from its binge or its sleep, and pleasures are re-evaluated, criticism has its opportunity. The present critic leaps, no doubt bruising shins and egos, to seize it.

CATCHER FLATTERS THE READER

Beware of the novelists bearing gifts. The more delicious and enthralling the gifts, the more wary we must be. Best of the sweets Salinger has Holden giftwrap and deliver to us is the idea that to the degree that we like Holden Caulfield we were better than anyone who doesn't. The method of Salinger's flamboyant and insidious flattery goes like this: Line up all the people in the world who we, in our weakness, our failures of sympathy, our ignorance, our narrow-mindedness, have ever allowed ourselves to hate. Include in this line-up caricatures of people we know we should not have hated. (Once having hated them, we have a vested interest in seeing them worthy of hatred.) Include persons we hated because we knew they were better than we were. (There is nothing like jealousy to prompt and sustain hate.) Now introduce before that line-up a tortured, bleeding and sublimely "cute" victim of all the insults and injuries all of us have ever imagined ourselves to have suffered. Let this victim be on the edge of insanity, the result, of course, of what others have done to him. Let him ooze the sentimental notion that the doctrine of Original Sin, and all its modern parallels, have been revoked. This is crucial. Not only does it let our victim be perfect, it removes any excuse the evil-doers might otherwise offer on their behalf. Let our victim believe that what the world needs now is not love, not even Coca-Cola, but that fool's gold, Sincerity. He himself has it of course, and some of it rubs off on his admirers, but no one else has it at all. Now the scene is set and the action commences. Blood in his eyes and trickling from his battered little nose, our victim raises a machine-gun and shoots everyone lined up before him. And he cries, weeps, as he does so. You see, utterly guilty as his tormentors are, he forgives them, he likes them! What super-human magnanimity! What delicious revenge, too! Who could resist enjoying this spectacle? Few have. . . .

SALINGER SEEMS TO AGREE WITH HOLDEN

We have no reason to assume that Salinger's attitudes differ from those of Holden Caulfield. It is the author's obligation to unmistakably untangle himself from his hero, or at least to give the reader the means to discover their relationship. But Salinger does neither. It seems absurd that a grown man, and a literate man at that, should hold the jejune opinions of Holden Caulfield. But he does and he lacks the grace or courage to say so outright, in or out of the novel. There isn't a whisper of any other view of life emanating from either quarter. We must take Salinger's silence in the novel to give consent. He is evidently angry that with the exception of himself—and his Holden—sincerity is in very short supply. "Then, after the Rockettes, a guy came out in a tuxedo and roller skates on, and started skating under a bunch of little tables, and telling jokes while he did it. He was a very good skater and all, but I couldn't enjoy it much because I kept picturing him practicing to be a guy that roller-skates on the stage" (ch. 18). Perfect sincerity requires and implies perfect spontaneity. And of course this utterly denies all the arts of life as well as the arts of Art. How does one know, Holden inquires, if the lawyer who has saved his client's life did so because "he really *wanted* to save guys' lives, or because . . . what [he] *really* wanted to do was to be a terrific lawyer, with everybody slapping [him] on the back and congratulating [him] in court when the goddam trial was over" (ch. 22). This is the question Holden asks of everyone. Its force is rhetorical. Holden wants a guarantee of the purity of human motive. He has been given everything else he wanted, but this complete absolution, of himself and his world, he cannot have. He cries "phoney," and takes up his bat and ball and leaves the game. We are to play by his rules or His Holiness will not play with us.

There is little point in using Salinger's text to show that Holden himself behaves with less than perfect kindness, less than Saintly sincerity. And to take that line against this novel is to accept its premise. *The Catcher in the Rye* urges the young to destroy their own, their only world, and to take refuge in their own soft dream-world peopled by themselves and by shadows of their perfected selves. No adolescent has ever entirely avoided this temptation. All of us had what used to be called "growing pains," fell into what used to be called a "brown study." Among the very rich, in our very rich country, all pleasures, no matter how self-deluding and self-defeating, no matter how selfish, are seized upon, and sold, and admired. Holden is a child of wealth, and most children wish they were too. The richer one is, the longer one may prolong one's adolescence. That is what Holden Caulfield is doing, and what Salinger and his admirers, are praising. Joan Didion comes to my aid here: She said that *Franny and Zooey* was "spurious" because of Salinger's "tendency to flatter the essential triviality within each of his readers." Its "appeal is precisely that it is self-help copy: it emerges finally as *Positive Thinking* for the upper middle classes, as *Double Your Energy and Live Without Fatigue* for Sarah Lawrence girls."

Those of us of a "certain age," brought up in the same streets and schools as Holden Caulfield, may be especially susceptible to Salinger's siren song. The present writer, along with a goodly percentage of our country's literati, shared Holden Caulfield's environment. We wondered about the ducks in Central Park lakes. We enjoyed a good cry about the sadness of life, the disappointments, the rain falling on our tennis courts. We too, in Salinger's most un-mean streets, discovered puberty, the painful way. But we managed to grow up, more or less; to see that it was not true, ever, that everybody was out of step but ourselves, to see that the words "compromise," "compassion," "tact," even "hypocrisy," were not obscenities which desecrated God's creation, but marks of the fact that none of us was, himself, God.

SALINGER PREVENTS US FROM SEEING *CATCHER* AS A COMEDY

Holden's youthful idealism, his bitterness toward the world he never made might have, had a Holden himself come before us, made for a successful novel. What could be funnier than the confessions of such a one as he? And while we would laugh at Holden, he would be laughing at us. How young we were, how charmingly silly. We could have had some good laughs, shed a tear for auld lang syne, shaken hands all round, and been on our way. But Salinger's Holden Caulfield is made of soggy cardboard. The death of his younger brother Allie hangs over his story forbidding anyone in it more than a momentary laugh. That death, utterly unrelated to the vapid social criticism which is Holden's prime activity, should have made Holden atypical, a special case whose opinions may be regarded only as pointers to his private distress. But Salinger ignores this; evidently he wants Holden's opinions on the general condition of society to be highly regarded, and he wants no one involved, character, author, reader, critic, to see his story as a comedy. We must, out of courtesy, courtesy that has been uncourteously forced upon us, take it all with high seriousness. Salinger needs the dead Allie in his novel so that we may not laugh. Yet the story itself is the quintessential comedy, the story of maturity looking back, with a wince and a smile and a guffaw at its own immaturity.

No character of Holden Caulfield is the only certifiable "phoney" in the novel. No youth, no matter how emotionally shaken, goes so long, so seriously single-mindedly after his real and imagined enemies. When the real Holden Caulfields encounter the terrors, such as they are, of their gilded ghettoes, they stumble every now and then on those insights which will add up to their definition of being grown-up. Not Holden. His larger considerations are bogus. He meanders about as if he were free to find out about things for himself, free to stumble on the other sides of the "phoney" question, to learn why people behave the way they do. But Salinger has put blinders around the boy. He never learns anything; never considers anything antagonistic to his sustaining faith that everything and everybody is wrong. It is as if Holden grew up at the knee of Abbie Hoffman—but even that is more funny than true. No matter how doctrinaire the upbringing, bright boys have a way of seeing around the blinders their elders set in place. But then Holden is not a real boy at all; he is Salinger's dream-boy, the boy who will not grow up. He is immaturity's best defense, a non-stop assault on maturity.

CATCHER IS AN INSULT TO CHILDHOOD

But after all this we really should petition the court to reduce the charge brought against Mr. Salinger. Boys being what we know them to be, despite the example of Holden, the crime is not impairment of the morals of a minor, but only attempted impairment. No real harm will be done by this book, unless professors succeed in making it a classic. *The Catcher in the Rye* is no more than an insult to all boys, to us who have been boys, and to the girls and ex-girls too. It is an insult to childhood and to adulthood. It is an insult to our ideas of civilization, to our ideal land in which ladies and gentlemen try to grow up, try to find and save their dignity.

Chronology

1919

Jerome David Salinger born January 1 in New York City.

1936

Graduates from Valley Forge Military Academy.

1937–1938

Travels to Austria and Poland; attends Ursinus College and New York University.

1939

Enrolls in writing course at Columbia University with Whit Burnett; World War II begins in Europe.

1940

Publishes first short story, "The Young Folks," in Burnett's literary magazine, *Story*.

1941

Pearl Harbor attack; United States enters World War II.

1942–1945

Drafted, serves in the Army Signal Corps and the Counter-Intelligence Corps.

1944

Lands on Utah Beach on D-day.

1945

World War II ends; Salinger marries Frenchwoman named Sylvia (maiden name unknown).

1946

United Nations holds first session; Salinger divorces.

1948–1949

Berlin blockade and airlift.

1950

Senator Joseph McCarthy launches hunt for communists in the U.S. government; begins what is later called the Red Scare; *My Foolish Heart* (film adaptation of "Uncle Wiggily in Connecticut") released.

1951

Catcher in the Rye published in United States; British edition released without photograph or biography; Rosenbergs sentenced to death for espionage against the United States.

1952

Dwight D. Eisenhower elected president; Salinger retires to house in Cornish, New Hampshire.

1953

Nine Stories published, reaches number one on the *New York Times* best-seller list; Salinger gives one of his last published interviews to high school student Shirley Blaney.

1955

Marries Claire Douglas on February 17; daughter Margaret Ann Salinger born December 10.

1960

Son, Matthew, born; John F. Kennedy elected president.

1961

Catcher tops 1.5 million in sales.

1964–1975

American involvement in Vietnam War.

1965

Salinger's last published work, "Hapworth 16, 1924"; *Catcher* sales hit 5 million.

1967

Divorces Claire Douglas.

1970

Repays, with interest, advance received from Little, Brown.

1974

Unauthorized, pirated collection, *The Complete Uncollected Stories of J.D. Salinger*, published.

1975

Over 9 million copies of *Catcher* sold.

1986

Salinger blocks publication of Ian Hamilton's *J.D. Salinger: A Writing Life* due to the inclusion of unpublished letters; *Catcher* continues to sell at a rate of twenty to thirty thousand copies a month.

1988

Ian Hamilton publishes *In Search of J.D. Salinger*, without the letters in question.

1996

Salinger's literary agents force "The Holden Server," a *Catcher in the Rye* website, to shut down because signing on to the site randomly generates quotes from the book.

1997

Salinger to republish "Hapworth 16, 1924."

FOR FURTHER RESEARCH

ABOUT *THE CATCHER IN THE RYE*

Norbert Blei, "'If You Want to Know the Truth...' *The Catcher in the Rye.*" In *Censored Books: Critical Viewpoints,* Nicholas J. Karolides et al., eds. Metuchen, NJ: Scarecrow, 1993.

Harold Bloom, ed., *Holden Caulfield.* New York: Chelsea House, 1990.

Adam Green, "If Holden Caulfield Spent a Week in Today's Manhattan," *New York Times,* December 23, 1995.

Sanford Pinsker, The Catcher in the Rye: *Innocence Under Pressure.* New York: Twayne, 1993.

William Riggan, "The Naif," *Picaros, Madmen, Naïfs, and Clowns: The Unreliable First-Person Narrator.* Norman: University of Oklahoma Press, 1981.

Gerald Rosen, *Zen in the Art of J.D. Salinger.* Berkeley, CA: Creative Arts, 1977.

Joel Salzberg, ed., *Critical Essays on Salinger's* The Catcher in the Rye. Boston: Hall, 1990.

Jack Salzman, ed., *New Essays on* The Catcher in the Rye. Cambridge: Cambridge University Press, 1991.

Jack R. Sublette, *J.D. Salinger: An Annotated Bibliography: 1938–1981.* New York: Garland, 1984.

ABOUT J.D. SALINGER

Warren French, *J.D. Salinger, Revisited.* Boston: Twayne, 1988.

Henry A. Grunwald, ed., *Salinger: A Critical and Personal Portrait.* New York: Harper, 1962.

Ian Hamilton, *In Search of J.D. Salinger.* New York: Random House, 1988.

Ernest Havemann, "The Search for the Mysterious J.D. Salinger," *Life,* November 3, 1961.

William Maxwell, "J.D. Salinger," *Book of the Month Club News,* midsummer 1951.

James E. Miller Jr., ed., *J.D. Salinger.* Minneapolis: University of Minneapolis Press, 1965.

ABOUT THE 1950s

David Halberstam, *The Fifties.* New York: Random House, 1993.

Karal Ann Marling, *As Seen on TV: The Visual Culture of Everyday Life in the 1950s.* Cambridge, MA: Harvard University Press, 1994.

Douglas T. Miller, *The Fifties: The Way We Really Were.* New York: Doubleday, 1977.

James T. Patterson, ed., *Grand Expectations: The United States 1945–1974.* Oxford: Oxford University Press, 1996.

WORKS BY J.D. SALINGER

"The Young Folks" in *Story;* "Go See Eddie" in *University of Kansas City Review* (1940)

"The Hang of It" in *Collier's;* "The Heart of a Broken Story" in *Esquire* (1941)

"The Long Debut of Lois Taggett" in *Story;* "Personal Notes of an Infantryman" in *Collier's* (1942)

"The Varioni Brothers" in *Saturday Evening Post* (1943)

"Both Parties Concerned" in *Saturday Evening Post;* "Soft-Boiled Sergeant" in *Saturday Evening Post;* "Last Day of the Last Furlough" in *Saturday Evening Post;* "Once a Week Won't Kill You" in *Story* (1944)

"A Boy in France" in *Saturday Evening Post;* "Elaine" in *Story;* "This Sandwich Has No Mayonnaise" in *Esquire;* "The Stranger" in *Collier's;* "I'm Crazy" in *Collier's* (1945)

"Slight Rebellion Off Madison" in *New Yorker* (1946)

"A Young Girl in 1941 with No Waist at All" in *Mademoiselle;* "The Inverted Forest" in *Cosmopolitan* (1947)

"A Girl I Knew" in *Good Housekeeping;* "Blue Melody" in *Cosmopolitan;* "A Perfect Day for Bananafish" in *New Yorker;* "Uncle Wiggily in Connecticut" in *New Yorker;* "Just Before the War with the Eskimos" in *New Yorker* (1948)

"The Laughing Man" in *New Yorker;* "Down at the Dinghy" in *Harper's* (1949)

"For Esmé—with Love and Squalor" in *New Yorker* (1950)

The Catcher in the Rye; "Pretty Mouth and Green My Eyes" in *New Yorker* (1951)

"De Daumier-Smith's Blue Period" in *World Review* (1952)

"Teddy" in *New Yorker; Nine Stories* (1953)

"Franny" in *New Yorker;* "Raise High the Roofbeam, Carpenters" in *New Yorker* (1955)

"Zooey" in *New Yorker* (1957)

"Seymour: An Introduction" in *New Yorker* (1959)

Franny and Zooey (1961)

Raise High the Roofbeam, Carpenters and Seymour: An Introduction (1963)

"Hapworth 16, 1924" in *New Yorker* (1965)

INDEX